Japan's Reluctant Multinationals

Japan's Reluctant Multinationals

Japanese Management at Home and Abroad

Malcolm Trevor

ST. MARTIN'S PRESS · NEW YORK

All rights reserved. For information, write:
St. Martin's Press, Inc., 175 Fifth Avenue, New York, NY 10010
Printed in Great Britain
First published in the United States of America in 1983
ISBN 0-312-44071-5

Library of Congress Cataloging in Publication Data
   Trevor, Malcolm, 1932—
      Japan's reluctant multinationals.
      1. Corporations, Japanese--Great Britain--Management.
   2. Industrial management--Japan.   3. Personnel manage-
ment--Japan.   I. Title.
HD2845.T73   1983   658'.089956   82-25541
ISBN 0-312-44071-5

'Japanese and American management is 95 per cent the same and differs in all important respects.'

(T. Fujisawa, co-founder of Honda Motor Co.)

CONTENTS

TABLES

FOREWORD
by Michael Isherwood

It is currently fashionable to take a passing interest in the phenomenon of 'Japanese-style' management methods and there is a positive glut of newspaper and magazine articles, television documentaries, conferences and seminars exhorting us to learn what we can from the example the Japanese are setting us in the running of factories and the management of industry generally. 'Fashion' is perhaps a dangerous indulgence for Westerners faced with the rapidly growing challenge of Japanese economic penetration because, by definition, 'fashion' is a transitory thing and what we really need is a deeper and longer-term understanding of Japanese methods and motivations.

Much of what is being written and talked about seems, to one who has spent twenty years working inside a Japanese multinational, to be superficial and concerned more with the ideal rather than the reality. One sees the spread of a sort of new mythology—the classless egalitarianism in the workplace, consensus decision making, Quality Control Circles—which is creating images that are almost unrecognizable to locally employed managers in Japanese firms.

The common problem that faces anyone who has to deal with the Japanese in practical terms—the business man conducting negotiations or fulfilling a contract, the diplomat, the scientist or the teacher who is exchanging ideas and information, and those who need to evaluate the Japanese as competitors, customers or partners—is one of cultural translation. It is the dilemma that inevitably arises at an early stage in the understanding of differences in organizational structure and social responses, which are in turn, caused by assumptions that the Japanese have simply followed our ways and have in the process become 'Westernized'.

If there is anything that can be ascribed to the 'secret' of Japanese success, it is perhaps the fact that they have taken

Western science and technology and wedded it to their own
traditional values and social disciplines. It is this unique mixture
that, on the one hand, offers an explanation for Japan's economic
success and, on the other, presents us with perplexing and often
unexpected cultural attitudes. In many ways they appear to
behave and respond to the pattern that is familiar to the Western-
er, but as soon as one begins to scratch the surface, the underlying cultural differences emerge to remind us that they are,
significantly, the only non-Western people to have achieved a
high degree of modern industrialization.

Dr Trevor, in his extremely well-researched study of the
structure and managerial methods of large Japanese enterprises,
presents us with one of the most accurate insights so far of the
inner workings of these giant companies, which are the spear-
head of Japan's phenomenal domestic growth and its recent
expansion into overseas markets all around the world. Based
upon his experience in Japan, where he worked closely with one
of the foremost of these multinationals, and also upon his later
involvement with a long-term university research programme,
which is studying the management of Japanese companies in the
United Kingdom and in Europe, he has evaluated management
techniques and the organizational structure in a most enlightening
and authoritative way.

From the analysis it is clear that Japanese companies are not
following American or European management concepts despite
certain superficial resemblances. Such techniques, for example,
as 'Management by Objectives' do not work in the same way as
they would in an American or British company even though they
bear the same name. In fact, one might conclude that the
Japanese, having studied and considered Western concepts of
management, have now rejected them in favour of systems that
are broadly more compatible with their own social behaviour
patterns.

One supposes that the United States is more receptive to new
approaches to the problems of management and, in particular,
to the ideas of Japanese management, given the long and close
association of the two countries over the past thirty-five years.
But an interesting point is that the experience of local managers in Japanese companies in both the US and in Europe is
remarkably similar not least because all are controlled by a head
office in Japan. The most original and valuable aspect of

Dr Trevor's work is the analysis he has based upon the research carried out in Japanese companies in the United Kingdom and several other countries in Europe. His conclusions must apply with equal significance to the United States. Possibly even more so, since the US is at a more advanced stage in coming to terms with the Japanese.

Michael Isherwood,
Manager, General Affairs and Personnel,
Mitsubishi Corporation,
London.

PREFACE

There is no generally accepted view of Japanese management among writers in Europe and America and yet effective management has been a major factor in the advance of Japanese companies.

The companies successfully adopted Western technology, but there is still a widespread feeling in the West that Japanese management is the exception to the rule of 'modern' organization and that one day it will 'converge' with the Western pattern. Some believe this because they think the nature of management is determined by technology—and we are all using the same type of technology—whereas management promotes the invention of new technology and must decide *how* it is to be employed. In 'the real world' management always faces constraints but work organization in the motor industry, for example, depends on managerial choice. Volvo, Ford, British Leyland, Toyota, and Renault all build the same type of machine, but how they do it is different.

Other people believe that Japanese management should change to a modern or Western pattern, which raises ethical or political problems outside the scope of this book. Others again believe that Japanese management is some sort of survival from history, and that it will inevitably change when Japanese companies catch up as much in management as they have in technology.

The tendency of these views is to think that Japanese companies will evolve into multinationals of the 'modern', particularly American, type. The different approaches to Japanese management and its basic concepts are discussed in Chapter 1, and the problems of multinationalization are set out in Chapter 2.

To gain some insight into Japanese companies' operations in the western hemisphere it is necessary to have a basis of comparison; managerial policies and practices in Japan itself are contrasted with those in a Western environment in Chapters 3 and 4. It should be clear from this analysis that it is fruitless to look for a single 'secret' of success. Control without motivation, technology without investment, research without application of its results, and marketing skill without the benefit of a constructive long-term strategy, are all by themselves inadequate. The secret, if there is one, lies not in any single factor but in the conscious efforts of managers and others to combine as many positive factors as possible, and to push them consistently in the right direction.

Japanese managers have been assisted in their efforts by pragmatic industrial policy, continuously evolving in the process of interaction, and sometimes hard negotiations, between government and industry. These are not the responsibility of managers at the level of daily operations, and are only mentioned in so far as they have a direct bearing on the discussion of managerial practices. Relations between government and industry are more problematical in the United States, not to mention the United Kingdom, where some governments have been less than friendly towards industry.

Key areas of managerial activity, like decision making, which reveal the underlying strategies, are treated in detail in Chapter 4. Japanese companies operating internationally have global strategies which affect whatever location they may be in. The strategies are not restricted to any particular country.

This global approach points to the complexity of management in its social context. Theoretically the two can be separated, but in 'the real world' this is impossible; managers in real companies are always faced with a particular social context and sometimes it is one of their biggest problems. To follow technological or other apparently value free arguments based on an artificial separation between technology and society, or between abstract management principles and society, is of little help in tackling managerial problems.

Japanese management in its British context is discussed in Chapter 5, where it is suggested that the environment has very little Westernizing influence. The questions of whether 'Western' is necessarily the same thing as 'modern' and why Japanese companies may be reluctant to adopt Western management are taken up.

The argument is that Japanese management sees its interests

to lie in the maintenance of its present systems as far as possible and that this will remain the underlying trend in the foreseeable future. This does not exclude pragmatic adjustments to meet changing circumstances and demands, but the changes themselves will be aimed at securing the priorities discussed in the long term.

The standpoint throughout is that management in its American, British, or Japanese, etc., social contexts is a complex process, and that it is simplistic to think that it can be reduced to a single deterministic mechanism by which all its operations are to be explained. I am also writing from the viewpoint that people have things to learn from one another, and that insularity in Britian and Japan, and isolationism in the United States, are intellectually misconceived and therefore harmful. Like many people, I find the recent achievements of Japanese management impressive; and without them large sections of the Japanese population would still be living in poverty. At the same time, one cannot ignore other aspects, and if some observations appear unorthodox to Japanese readers I hope they will bear in mind that a picture that has only light and no shade lacks credibility.

Bearing in mind the differences in employment systems, it might seem contentious to put the same questions to expatriate and local staff, but to ask different questions would obviously make a comparison impossible. That some questions were unusual to most expatriate managers is itself a datum worth exploring. To have prejudged the data by first deciding to leave out some questions would have been unscientific. Not all the answers that were given fitted the well-known stereotypes of Japanese management, as I hope the discussion of decision making, for instance, will make clear.

The problem in interviewing expatriate managers lay in the concept of the interview itself. Conversation in Japanese society generally puts more weight on the quality of the relations between the speakers than on the intellectual content, frequently resulting in a search for agreement (cf. Nakane, 1973, p. 36). This is not conducive to research and the interviewer has to try to avoid giving the impression, perhaps by an inflexion of the voice, that he is after a particular answer.

Japanese firms are very helpful in arranging brief trips around the plant or office, but they are less used to longer, in-depth, studies (cf. Marsh and Mannari, 1976, pp. 15–16). Cole considers that this is due to the closed nature of companies and other organizations in Japanese society, and to the character of Japanese social science (Cole, 1971, p. 42). In addition, a proportion of Japanese social scientists hold pronounced left-wing views, and one can hardly blame the companies for being wary of those who constantly write about 'Japanese monopoly capital' etc.

Outside Japan there may be management anxieties about the local media, trade problems, and other political issues. On the other hand, what might broadly be termed scientific research, education, and scholarship, have stronger positive values for different social strata in Japanese society than they have in the UK or USA (Befu, 1971, p. 145). Once the company had agreed, most expatriates were extremely cooperative during interviews. At one company an outspoken younger manager intimated that I must be either an agent or a dupe of management, but the personnel manager, who was as well aware of his views as anyone else, had put him on the list of interviewees.

I should like to thank all those in Japanese companies and other organizations, whose names are too numerous to mention, for their valuable time and assistance. I am deeply indebted to my wife and family for putting up with everything that has been involved, and this book is dedicated to them. Finally I should like to thank Messrs Simon and Schuster for their kind permission to reproduce the aphorism which appears at the front of this book.

1 JAPANESE MANAGERIAL SYSTEMS

1.1 Basic concepts

The expression 'Japan's Managerial System' was used by Yoshino in 1968 as the title of his book. Here it is used to refer to employment, business, and industrial-relations systems, or established practices, but it is used in the plural. To use it in the singular increases the risk of conceptualizing Japanese management in an over-simplified monocausal way. Empirical evidence shows that there are discrete, if interconnected, systems in such areas as long-term employment, decision making, and industrial relations, and that these vary over time. It is therefore inadequate to characterize them as products of a 'pattern of culture' (Benedict, 1935, 1946).

Japanese managerial systems in areas such as recruitment, induction training, and reward are identifiable as formal organization, but others are abstractions conceptualized by observers, however concrete and effective they may appear to members of Japanese society in daily interaction. An example is *nemawashi* ('binding up the roots'), an informal system, which is generally the most significant part of the *ringi* ('consulting a superior and obtaining his consent') process of decision making. It outweighs the importance of the formal aspects of the system, such as the *ringi* document itself, even if it is harder to grasp analytically.

It is therefore misleading to speak of Japanese management as if it consisted of formal organization alone, and the danger of reification and of forcing informal processes into a deterministic mould of greater uniformity and stability than the data warrant is increased if a single system is referred to. This particularly applies to the case where, as Inohara and others quoted below have argued, the informal systems are frequently the ones followed in practice, whatever the formal system is supposed to be. Some recent writers have pointed out that a concern with structure and strategy at the expense of more intangible data, such as management style, management systems, and 'management's guiding concepts' can lead to inadequate understanding of the sources of organizational effectiveness (Pascale and Athos, 1981, pp. 8–9). 'Informal' need not be a pejorative term, implying for instance deviation from the prescriptions of formal organization, and it will be argued that informal systems are an integral part of Japanese management and frequently represent powerful tools at management's disposal.

In spite of the problems of interpreting the nature and dynamics of Japanese management, or Japanese managerial systems, the identification of the various aspects has generally created less difficulty. Japanese consultants engaged by the UK Department of Industry classified them as: '1. Lifetime employment system; 2. Seniority system; 3. Enterprise unions; 4. Welfare services and benefits provided by companies; 5. Decision making structures.' (Technova, 1980, Vol. 1, p. 98.) Some identify 'three interlocking institutions . . . life long employment, the seniority wage system and the enterprise union' (Kobayashi, 1975, p. 4). A senior manager at the London branch of a trading company asserted that 'the three pillars of Japanese management are the life employment system, the seniority system and the *ringi* decision making system'. This doubtless reflected his activity in this particular large white-collar corporation.

The two last views posit an interlocking connection between different Japanese managerial systems, but it is not always easy to determine the key factors. Analytically, it is necessary to separate out the various aspects of Japanese management which are not found in isolation empirically, but Japanese management itself is a problematical concept and managerial systems in any society exist within a social context. Care is therefore needed in avoiding reification and idealization.

According to Nakase, the Japanese way of management consists of such features as 'the life-long employment system, the promotion system based on seniority, group-oriented loyalty, the collective responsibility system, the consensus obtaining method based on the *ringi* system . . . , the adjustment method of *nemawashi* . . . , the concept of restricting the activities of the labour union to company affairs, management ideology[1] based on the 'sense of community bound together by common fate and the short weekly holiday and annual vacation system' (Nakase, 1980, p. 19). It is significant that Nakase, who is somewhat critical of Japanese companies, gives such a standard list of aspects of Japanese management. His list is more detailed than those quoted above, but it still gives little indication of the relative significance and dynamics of the respective parts, even if it gives more prominence to the informal systems.

In discussing the concept of Japanese management it is useful to draw an analogy with American management. Firms in the United States differ in size, type, state of maturity or development, technology, etc. as in Japan or the UK (Florence, 1972), but it is legitimate to define an ideal type, or 'pure' prototype, of American management (cf. Weber, 1947, pp. 13–14, 92, 110). This would include, for example, the principles taught at the Harvard Business School, a particular type of rationality applied to decision making, profitability, etc. types of organizational behaviour, the social position and prestige of American managers, etc. In decision making the ideal type of the 'New Science of Management Decision' (Simon, 1960) may be contrasted with the Japanese processes of *nemawashi* and *ringi*. The bottom-line type of approach to short-term profitability in decentralized profit centres in Ireland, for example,[2] may be contrasted with the long-term strategy of Japanese companies in Ireland, some of which might otherwise have pulled out. Comparisons with an ideal type of British, German, or French management are equally possible. In the Japanese case the features listed above have continually provided the basis for discussion, from the initial work of Abegglen (1958), through the later work of Dore, Clark, Yoshino, and others to the latest writings of Ouchi, and Pascale and Athos.

In spite of the theory of growth orientation proposed by Galbraith (1972), the importance of profitability in American operations in the UK, evidenced in such cases as Singer, Chrysler, and Ford, has been conspicuous. Ireland provided many examples of interviewees who spontaneously expressed clearly differentiated perceptions of American concepts of profitability and Japanese concepts related to growth and prestige as well as profitability. This was in spite of the slump in the synthetic fibres industry affecting one Japanese firm and problems of quality and productivity affecting another. Figures are also available for some Japanese operations in the UK, listing those reporting 'deficit', 'no dividend', or 'breaking even' (Nakase, 1980, pp. 81–8), but there have been almost no withdrawals. In a rare case, the

Multinational Gas and Petrochemical Co. was forced to withdraw by the bankruptcy of the parent company.

On the analogy of the ideal–typical concept of American management, it is justifiable to use the concept of Japanese management as an analytical tool, provided that it is not permitted to become a stereotype or a deterministic explanation for phenomena that depend on more than one variable. No model can reproduce the variety of individual firms and all models are subject to the limitation of being constructed at a given point in time. These implications must now be discussed.

1.2 Synchronic versus diachronic interpretations[3]

A diachronic analysis of Japanese management (e.g. Hirschmeier and Yui, 1981) shows to what extent it has changed and to what extent its overall strategy and ideological underpinnings have remained the same since the official decision to industrialize in 1868. Following this approach, but remembering that 'social institutions can't be sociologically *explained* in terms of past origins' (Evans-Pritchard, quoted in Cohen, 1974, p. 21), the standpoint is that of the continuity of certain types of strategy at macro level and of the change (or pragmatism or adaptability) at micro level, including daily managerial operations. It is argued that data on Japanese companies, at home and overseas, and on Japanese society itself, support this approach.

In his seminal work Dore expressed 'a general suspicion of all grand theories of social evolution', arguing that the directions of social change cannot be deduced from a few simple premises (Dore, 1973, p. 11). Instead of pinning everything on a single variable, such as Western economic rationality or Japanese values or culture, it is necessary to allow for the complexity of the sociological and economic context and for diachronic processes, e.g. the Black Ships of 1853, the Meiji Restoration of 1868, the Occupation of 1945.

The Japanese economy has been subject to 'long range domestic trends and immediate foreign stimuli' (Reischauer *et al.*, 1962, p. 189). These stimuli, after the Black Ships ultimatum which led to the Meiji Restoration, the opening of Japan, and the decision to industrialize, included war. There was a 'spurt of industrialization under the impact of wars', e.g. the Sino-Japanese

War of 1894, the Russo-Japanese War of 1905, and the First World War (Hirschmeier and Yui, 1975, pp. 146-8).

More recently the Korean War provided the initial boom that enabled the economy to expand (Storry, 1960, p. 255) and the Vietnam War continued the same tendency (Dimock, 1968, pp. 27-9). Korean War procurement accounted for 44 per cent of commercial exports in 1951, 65 per cent in 1952 and 63 per cent in 1953. Vietnam War procurement earned US$1 billion in 1966 and in 1967, out of total export receipts of US$9.7 billion and 11.6 billion respectively (Bieda, 1970, p. 37). The defeat of 1945 forced the modernization of plant and the Occupation gave new life chances to younger managers by purging their superiors and stimulating competition;[4] the *zaibatsu* and their family-controlled holding companies were dissolved (Bisson, 1954; Hadley, 1970), providing an enforced impetus to the managerial revolution of a kind not experienced in the UK, for example.

After 1945 'there was total confusion of value orientation among the Japanese people. To get out of that miserable situation it was as if the nation as a whole had agreed that "from now on we will concentrate our efforts on the rebuilding and expansion of our economy" ' (Funaki, 1981, p. 9). Pragmatic realization of the efforts needed for sheer survival was the foundation of the broad consensus on industrial aims. British society has avoided the shocks to the social system experienced by Japanese society in 1868 and 1945, but arguably at the price of stagnation.

Negative stimuli, such as the 'Nixon shock' of 1970 and the 'oil shock' of 1973, have forced Japanese management to adopt new strategies. After 1973, energy conservation became a major topic of Quality Circles (JETRO, 1981, p. 21), but the reaction to the shocks is significant and can be ascribed to managerial motivation and competence, and to factors in the wider society such as education and meritocratic competition, which foster the will to solve problems. As Dore has argued, Japanese industrial effort has had a patriotic element, which has been missing in the UK and other Western societies, and it can be argued that the general agreement on national economic aims described by Funaki is still not found in Britain in the 1980s (cf. Mant, 1979).[5] Leftist and environmentalist groups have criticized Japanese companies and it would be a travesty of a modern complex society to suggest that consensus has always been uniform. The business strategies adopted have been conscious managerial choices, defended by the constant repetition of strong (managerial) ideology and legitimated by a considerable degree of success. These developments have taken place in a diachronic context, i.e. at particular moments.

Stereotypes of Japanese management or society which portray them synchronically or apparently outside time altogether, have been promoted by non-Japanese, as well as by Japanese anxious to present the society and its normative values in the best light (Kahn, 1970, pp. 40, 43), rather than to analyse the society (or the company).[6] The disadvantage of the deterministic approach, whether culturally or economically based, is that it cannot account for social change. By reducing data to a single variable it becomes tautological and, in the case of economic determinism, fails to explain the differences between, for example, British, American, and Japanese management and society. In practice no firm, managerial system, or process exists apart from a social context over time, i.e. diachronically, and the types of managerial and political elites in Japanese society are major determinants. The interpretation of societal phenomena has been the concern of social theory from Plato and Aristotle to the present (e.g. Abraham, 1977).

Functionalism may be congenial to the British empiricist tradition, rooted in the philosophy of Hume and others, but it can lead to spurious *ex post facto* reasoning in e.g. explaining the necessity for the existence of a given institution, such as Japanese life employment. Some see functionalism as an ideology supporting Parsonian theses and the status quo (Gouldner, 1971, pp. 123-34), while another critic attacks it as 'an oversimplified mechanistic style of sociological theorizing now generally viewed with some contempt' (Leach, 1970, p. 8). While the functionalism of Malinowski and Radcliffe-Brown effectively demystified exotic social institutions, it must be asked how it can cater for change and how it can look to the future rather than to the past.[7]

Determinism based on some synchronic notion of culture similarly fails to account for change, for observed dissensus, and for the detailed workings of e.g. Japanese employment systems. In the case of Japan discussion has been clouded because of the impact of Benedict's pioneering work (1946), written when the war made fieldwork impossible. Earlier empirical, and therefore more political, studies such as Embree's study of a village in 1939, failed to achieve the same impact because they did not aim to explain the whole society. Benedict's 'cultural' approach, for all its insights into the principles of *on* ('obligation') and *giri* ('duty') in Japanese society, is mainly a normative description of values or ideals, which has been quoted by Japanese wishing to represent the ideal as the real and who themselves tend to see other societies in stereotyped cultural terms.[8] Benedict's work is said to have influenced the decision to retain the Emperor after 1945, but it offers little explanation of Japan's industrialization or modernization.

Reischauer's pessimistic forecast of 1950 was based on economic rather than cultural factors, but few saw the Japanese as likely to succeed industrially. In 1881, an observer argued that 'the Japanese are a happy race, and being content with little, are not likely to achieve much' (quoted by B. R. Tomlinson, reviewing 'Human Resources in Japanese Industrial Development', by Levine and Kawada, *Times Higher Education Supplement*, 9 January 1981). Stereotypes of Japan's technological backwardness persisted in the UK as late as 1942 but, as Weber observed, 'the appeal to national character is generally a mere confession of ignorance' (quoted in Bendix, 1966, p. 65).

Stereotypes of national character or 'culture' (cf. Japan Culture Institute, 1977) exist among Japanese managers overseas, and can complicate problems of communication and motivation. Kahn, an admirer of the Japanese 'economic miracle', states that 'they think of themselves as a unique race . . . what is important to them is that the unique Japanese be admired and respected . . . and the more unique and special the techniques used to attain status the better' (Kahn, 1970, p. 44). During Japan's industrialization and emergence from isolation in the nineteenth and twentieth centuries, 'the Japanese [were] determined to preserve their independence. . . . They had early realised [their] smallness compared to the whole cultural unit [China] and . . . began to emphasize their "uniqueness" ' (Reischauer *et al.*, 1962, Vol. 2, pp. 185, 189). The ethnocentric concept of 'uniqueness' affects the perceptions of Japanese managers overseas and of Japanese scholars writing on Japanese management; it is not a negligible factor in their interpretations.

After 1945, Japanese society ingested fresh Western material culture and techniques, including managerial techniques, but not their social context, so that the content or aims were not necessarily identical. Ideological propagation of uniqueness, as a means of motivation and social control as well as a value, has recently led to *Nihonjin ron* ('the theory of being Japanese'). 'The real religion of the Japanese is Nihonism. They believe in their nation first and all other faiths and ideologies are only sects of this one basic religion' (Hirschmeier and Yui, 1975, p. 296). 'Men who are engaged in industry and commerce are regarded very highly in Japanese society; these are the people who bear the banner of the national interest' (Funaki, 1981, p. 9). The expression 'the honour of our race' occurs in the Hitachi company song (Dore, 1973, p. 52). The patriotic aspect of management and economic activity in Japanese society is made explicit in these examples.[9]

Empirically the individual is not 'alone in the group, or any society alone among other societies' (Levi-Strauss, quoted in Leach, 1970, p. 36), and it is frequently not clear that assertions of Japanese uniqueness are valid even on these terms. Korean social institutions appear similar (Crane, 1967). The business philosophy of the Taiwanese Tatung Company, which took over the Decca factory at Bridgnorth in 1981, seems to resemble that of Japanese electronics firms in the UK or Ireland (*Financial Times*, 12 June 1981). Morishima persuasively argues that 'those Asian countries that follow Japan economically, such as Korea, Taiwan, Singapore and Hong Kong, all have more or less similar social philosophies. . . . It is evidently an easy task for any similar country, such as South Korea, to reproduce "Japan" elsewhere' ('Why samurai means business', *Observer*, 6 August 1978).

As Japanese industrial strategy promotes 'clean', high value-added, and knowledge intensive industries, and the economy is moved away from 'pollution-prone and resource-consuming heavy and chemical industries' (Ozawa, 1979, p. 21), countries like Korea and Taiwan purchase e.g. Toyo Royon's Shiga nylon factory, and take over Japan's earlier position in textiles (Halliday and McCormack, 1973, p. 149). But in Japan 'those who run business and those who run the government instinctively attempt to transform the foreign or the universal into something particular that is consistent with their ideas of Japan's inner essence' (Dimock, 1968, p. 14).[10]

This observed social fact, which can be applied to e.g. Quality

Circles in Japan (Trevor, 1983), should be taken into account in the analysis of the instrumental and expressive aspects[11] of Japanese management, but it should be a general principle of social science to treat any actor's model with caution. Popular comparisons, indulged in by Japanese managers as well as by the British or American press, of Japan and the West, ignore differences between Western societies, exaggerate the homogeneity of Japanese society, and make an unreal contrast by leaving out the rest of the world.

In the managerial context, these stereotyped Platonic 'ideas' of uniqueness underpin expatriate solidarity and the exclusion of local staff from decision making. Without ignoring its expressive aspect, this ideology is part of the type of control employed by companies in the pursuit of personnel policies and business strategies abroad; and control cannot be claimed to be culture-bound, even if it reflects the power or social structure and the behavioural norms of a particular society. It is only when a synchronic approach of the cultural type stressing uniqueness, for example, is taken that the instrumental aspect of ideology as a form of control is obscured. When the empirical data are examined in their social and historical context, i.e. diachronically, this aspect immediately becomes clear, permitting a more balanced view of the nature of Japanese management.

1.3 Ideology and values

'Difference' appears a desirable value to many members of Japanese society and the concept is used by Western writers such as Kahn, who sees 'the general energy and dedication of the Japanese and their capacity for purposive communal action' (Kahn, 1970, pp. 85–7 etc.). But some Japanese see pre-industrial practices as discreditable 'survivals' that should be replaced by 'modern' (Western) systems (Odaka, 1975, pp. 1–6). No analysis can be entirely value free (cf. Mannheim, 1936), and for it to have validity the observer must try not to impose personal preconceptions or values on the data observed (Gerth and Mills, 1970, pp. 129–56, Weber's 'Science as a Vocation').

An unusual Japanese disclaimer of uniqueness, from a free market viewpoint, stresses the comparatively low Japanese figures for public employees, public spending, taxation, and social security and concludes that Japan is now more 'American'

than the United States in its market orientation and egalitarianism (Iida, 1981, p. 11). Iida plays down the role of the Ministry
of International Trade and Industry (MITI, popularly known as
'Meetee') in issuing administrative guidance to companies, in contrast to more detailed analysis (Magaziner and Hout, 1981),[12]
but this is not the same as the 'Japan Inc' stereotype popularized
by Time-Life's Tokyo correspondent. Instead it can be argued
that Japan follows neither 'the principle of a free market economy as in the United States, nor the principles of a centrally
planned economy as in the Soviet Union and Eastern Europe'
(Ueno, in Sato, 1980, p. 387). As in the case of the informal
systems employed by Japanese management referred to above,
this is a harder but more refined concept to grasp analytically
than the other two ideal–typical, or abstract, models. Iida's
understatement of MITI's significance and the limitation of his
data detract from what might have been an interesting attempt
to explain Japan's economic success in terms of business rationality. As argued above, no single factor is likely to prove an adequate explanation, even though business rationality is obviously
a component and industries in Japan such as shipbuilding, steel,
automobiles, and electronics are highly rationalized.

Abegglen's 1958 study has been criticized by Cole and others
for excessive reliance on management sources, i.e. precisely
those sources which would encourage a belief in 'loyalty', 'tradition', and other values. Abegglen concluded that 'the Japanese
system is on the whole self-consistent . . . [a] rephasing of
feudal loyalties, commitments, rewards and methods of leadership' (Abegglen, 1958, p. 130). But this 'self-consistency' appears
tautological because social institutions and managerial practices
in Britain, America, and other industrial societies also tend to
be self-consistent (cf. Dore, 1973).

Abegglen posited a single Japanese system and a linear historical progression. This resembles *ex post facto* reasoning and fails
to account for e.g. the revolt of the ambitious lower *samurai*
who formed the Meiji elite in 1868 (T. C. Smith, 1967), the
abolition of the four ascriptive (or hereditary) classes, the promul-
gation of the Imperial Charter Oath to 'learn from the world'
etc., and the changing development of Japanese management
from the Tokugawa period to the present (Hirschmeier and Yui,
1975). Instead of positing a single 'system', the concept here is
of the interlocking of different facets of Japanese management.

Thus it is hard to imagine the seniority system outside the context of long-term employment (cf. Kobayashi, 1975, pp. 4–5), or to deny that large Japanese companies are managed so that they tend to resemble 'total communities' (Dore, 1973, pp. 201–2 etc.).

Nor is it necessary to denigrate the significance of traditional values, such as loyalty, as active fulfilment and not merely passive obedience (Bellah, 1957), found in the analogy of the *samurai* and the 'salaryman' (i.e. salaried employee, or trainee manager) in a large company. Morishima considers that Japan's wartime experience (1931–45) enabled 'Confucian capitalism' to strengthen its collectivist character. 'Workers and staff members are soldiers and officers in the battle of the companies, competing not for themselves but for their companies. . . . In the Confucian world, individualism is suffocated' (Morishima, 1978). This helps to explain the use by management of collectivist ideology, aimed at self-policing control, directed to the concept of 'the enterprise as community'. 'Japan jumped from a feudal form of corporatism to a modern form of enterprise corporatism without ever experiencing . . . a thorough-going *laissez-faire* market economy' (Dore, 1973, p. 420). This is a crucial distinction with the European and American cases.

The interpretation of ideology is therefore a major issue in the interpretation of Japanese management. Those who see ideology (except their own) as 'epiphenomenal' tend to see the emphasis put by Japanese managers in inculcating values in 'spiritual' induction training etc. as frankly instrumental, aimed at management goals. Those who take a philosophically 'idealist' or 'symbolist' view tend to interpret behaviour as arising from the primacy of norms and values. The standpoint here is that 'people often act in terms of the moral values and rules of their society because they truly believe in them', but that 'man is also a manipulator, a self-interested operator, as well as a moral being'. This frequently produces 'pragmatic action dressed up in normative clothes to make it respectable' (Boissevain, 1974, pp. 7, 6, 10). On the other hand, action determined by Weber's 'value rationality', or personal ideals, is frequently observed to hinder actors' instrumental interests.

Comparative sociological research does not support the concept of 'economic man', i.e. the absolute primacy of economic self-interest (e.g. Leclair and Schneider, 1968; Sahlins, 1974), and it is inadequate to discuss normative value systems as 'false consciousness'. The orientation of British, American, and Japanese managers towards profitability cannot be assumed *a priori* to be identical, and it can be argued that all are susceptible to the values and behavioural norms of their respective societies. British and Japanese concepts of the company sphere and the private sphere operate both at the ideological level and at the level of social action, i.e. a Japanese manager is more dependent on his company, which controls his life both more closely and for a greater number of hours per day than is the case for his British counterpart. Ideology of the 'Cycle of Goodness' type (Appendix) may seem unusual in a European context, but it refers, among other things, to compulsory employee investment in the firm out of monthly wages, i.e. to a particular level of managerial control.

A further problem for interpretations of ideology as either purely functional or as part of a pattern of culture is that ideology can be dysfunctional or actively harmful to its own group or society.[13] Different interest groups within the same society can also have competing ideologies. Dysfunction implies that ideology can be semi-autonomous, neither wholly determined by material and other interests, nor wholly free floating, as in the symbolist view. The existence of competing ideologies suggests that the 'consensus model' has been exaggerated and that 'Durkheim begged all the basic questions' (M. G. Smith, personal communication); although Japanese society, with its greater 'mechanical solidarity' (less individualism) and its ubiquitous 'collective effervescence' (group activities, neighbourhood shrine festivals, etc.), is more Durkheimian than British or American society (cf. Lukes, 1975, pp. 139–53).

It is argued here that this is a question of degree and that the concept of 'Japan Inc', i.e. total consensus, is a caricature; failure to consider the difference of degree adequately is also a factor in the failure to reach an agreed definition of Japanese management. There is little problem in listing the formal systems used in large Japanese companies, or the main ideological principles, but it is less easy to determine how far such strikingly 'Japanese' features are sociologically significant (Marsh and Mannari, 1976, p. viii). For many Japanese it is probably the case that 'it is hardly a fish that can discover the existence of water' (Cohen, 1974, p. 8).[14] The standpoint here is that the analytical methods of (Western) social science need to be accompanied by empathy, or the feeling of how the situation appears to the actors in it.[15]

The application of consensus and conflict models to Japanese society and management, reflecting perhaps models in the minds of the writers, may in any case be misleading. Rather than having to choose between two antitheses, it may be possible in the Japanese case to follow Shils in his view of consensus, which affirms a society's basic beliefs and values being able to contain a considerable amount of dissensus. Shils sees coercion as a supplement to and a generator of consensus and holds that coercion does not operate alone for any length of time without a strong consensual reinforcement (Gould, 1981, pp. 69–77). Whether universally valid or not, this approach can be applied to the managerial and societal ideology of consensus in Japan. It is not easy to determine what employees really think about such things; those critical of company management may admit that the methods achieve their aims, and those who complain of long hours etc. may not have an alternative in mind, let alone the intention of leaving the company.

The significance of the observer's standpoint in social science research should be a truism. The approach of Ouchi and of Pascale and Athos (1981) writing for American management, the Marxist approach of Halliday and McCormack (1973), and the financial-structural approach of Clark (1979) result in different conceptions of Japanese management.

The observer's interest in a particular field, such as the macro and industrial policy level (Ozawa, 1979; Magaziner and Hout, 1981), government–industry relations (Dimock, 1968), the financial and organizational relations within industrial groups (Dodwell, 1978), and the relations within 'the dual structure' of major companies and sub-contractors (Broadbridge, 1966)[16] also determines the concept of Japanese management given. These topics can be classified as 'upstream'.

They contrast with the 'downstream' topics of employment systems (Dore, 1973), personnel management (Inohara, 1977), decision making (Kidd and Teramoto, 1981), Quality Circles (JETRO, 1981), Zero Defect movements (Inohara, 1972), and micro level techniques such as the *Kamban* (components supply) system (*Financial Times*, 4 August 1981).

Halliday and McCormack (1973) appear to see little difference between Japanese and American business, or 'capitalism' in their terminology, while Ouchi's 'Theory Z' (1981) is value-laden, with roots in the American human relations school. The more serious intellectual divergence along the lines of Weber's 'expediency', i.e. means to an end, and 'value rationality', i.e. pursuit of ideals, often means in practice that Japanese writers (e.g. Inohara, 1977) give a normative description, while British researchers (e.g. Connors, 1976, 1977) provide an 'instrumental' analysis. The success of the Japanese economy, unforeseen by Reischauer and probably by Japanese managers themselves, compounds the problem by opening the door to further *ex post facto* reasoning and the highlighting of those aspects which with hindsight appear important (Vogel, 1980). It is misleading to look at domestic ideological models while ignoring the importance of the external stimuli that were discussed above in their historical context.

The propagation by Japanese managers and management writers of ideological models on a greater scale than is normal in Europe makes ideology an important factor in the definition of Japanese management, but it needs separating out in all its complexity. As with cultural and other deterministic models, the ideological model by itself cannot cater for the observed untidiness of social reality. What actually happens does not always follow the model.

1.4 Management as control

A model of Japanese managerial systems, referring here to a 'downstream' concept, should include the formal systems of recruitment, employment, etc., and the informal systems in decision making, etc. to be discussed below, and the 'hard' (*katai*) and 'soft' (*yawarakai*) systems, discussed by Pascale and Athos (1981). 'Hard' refers to structural systems in quantitative areas, such as financial and production control. 'Soft' refers to processes, such as motivation, man management, and welfare. Arguably the combination of these apparent antitheses, like the combination of competition and cooperation at different levels, is one of the sources of Japanese managerial success. 'The essence of Japanese personnel management is security and insecurity' (Teramoto, personal communication). 'The Japanese company makes it clear that its substantial benefits to employees are not guaranteed' (Vogel, 1980, p. 149). The benefits depend upon performance and the 'hard' and 'soft' systems are a battery of means at management's disposal, to be pragmatically applied as means of control as and when management sees fit. Pragmatism is expressed in 'the rule of *jojo shakuryo* (taking circumstances into consideration)' (Inohara, 1977, p. 28).

Mant (1979, pp. 15-30, 56-7, etc.) and some others have discussed the meaning of the term 'to manage' and, echoing the title of Bendix's work on managerial ideology and strategy (1974), debated whether industry was a field of power or of authority (ibid., pp. 191-2). Mant takes the meaning, given in the *Concise Oxford Dictionary* of 'management' as 'to take charge of, to subject someone (etc.) to one's control'. For Braverman, 'management is unthinkable except as control' (Braverman, 1974, p. 67), although he subsequently dilutes this to 'management has become administration, which is a labour process conducted for the purpose of control within the corporation' (ibid., p. 267).

Whyte (1960), Galbraith (1972), Florence (1972), and Hill (1981, pp. 71-6) have discussed the separation of 'ownership and control', arising out of Burnham's concept of the 'managerial revolution'. In a discussion of Burnham's book in 1946, Orwell wrote that 'managers [would be] the rulers of this new society . . . the people who effectively control the means of production' (Orwell, 1968, p. 192). Burnham also stressed Pareto's 'circulation of elites' (Aron, 1970, pp. 159-66). These concepts may apply more to Japanese than to British or American society.

Mant, Mintzberg (1973), and others identify managerial roles as 'disturbance handlers', decision makers, possessors of expertise, occupiers of position in the social structure, or in the order of prestige etc. Management cannot empirically be considered only as control, but the term 'manage' is empty if control is absent. Control is universalistic, cutting across cultures and political systems, but how it is expressed may be particularistic, i.e. specific to a particular society, such as the Japanese.

Hill, especially as 'Structures of Control' (Hill, 1981, pp. 16-44) and 'Technology, Control and Orientations' (ibid., pp. 103-23) contrasts the absence of paternalism in the UK with the modern creation of corporate paternalism in Japan. If the assertion of the co-founder of Honda Motors is correct that 'Japanese and American management is 95 per cent the same and differs in all important respects' (quoted in Pascale and Athos, 1981, p. 85), then the type and/or degree of control may also be expected to differ. This would also apply to systems, such as

Quality Circles, that employ the same terminology but whose social dynamics could be expected to vary in different societies.

Cultural analysts might argue that all the techniques of managerial control in Japanese society were particularistic, but it must be asked whether the model of modern corporate paternalism posited by Hill above is 'unique'. The principle that 'every director of the company is an employee of the shareholders just as much as the man who is delivering coal at the boiler' appears 'Japanese', but was stated by Mond in the 1920s. 'The current managerial ideology [is] a set of beliefs which management seeks to propagate in order to inspire acceptance of managerial autonomy by the general public and by specific groups of workers' (McGivering et al., 1960, p. 92). 'Autonomy' here implies control and is perfectly congruent with Japanese managerial ideology. Other points mentioned, such as the implicit assumption that 'the state represents the interests of the community', that it is not respectable to discuss conflict, and that all members of a firm have a common interest in it, again apply to Japan. It cannot therefore be claimed that 'the Japanese system' is either particularly new or 'culture-bound'. The difference would appear to be that whereas Mond's efforts were largely limited to the British chemical industry, in a period of reorganization, the system applies in Japan to companies of all types. In the UK 'real power now resides in the workshop and on the office floor' (Dore, 1973, p. 359). In Japan the balance of power is more in management's favour. To a lesser extent, the latter also applies to American management.

The founding resolution of Nikkeiren, the Japan Federation of Employers' Association, in 1948 was, 'Managers, be fair but strong'. This has proved to be no empty rhetoric and some consider that one reason for Japan's relative industrial peace since the 1950s has been 'the strong yet balanced guidance exercised by Nikkeiren' (Hirschmeier and Yui, 1975, p. 277). Cartels, mentioned by Mond, are more readily available to Japanese management, in spite of anti-monopoly legislation following the pattern of the American Sherman Act (Patrick and Rosovsky, 1976, pp. 483–9).

Given the obfuscation surrounding Japanese management and journalistic treatment of the 'Oriental magic in Welsh valleys' type, it is understandable that some should wish to demythologize the subject. 'Worthy studies are so few that the subject faces the danger of becoming as much a myth as many other things about Japan' (Sato, 1980, p. ix).

The approach advocated here seeks to avoid the extremes of 'culturalism' on the one hand and 'expediency' (Weber's *Zweck-rationalität*), Mayo's 'logic of efficiency' or the economist's model of formal economic rationality on the other. It is argued that control is the *sine qua non* of management, as opposed to routine administration and the exercise of purely technical functions, and that 'among corporate management in the industrialized market economies, there is no doubt that it is the Japanese managers above all, who maintain most of their traditional prerogatives and hold firm to the reins of power' (Cole, 1979, p. 252). It is further argued that Japanese management consciously, and unconsciously, utilizes mechanisms that are already to hand in Japanese social institutions (De Vos, 1973); and that this is the only type of approach that can cater adequately for both universalistic phenomena, found in other industrial societies, and particularistic phenomena, specific to the Japanese case. Failure to deal with both sides and the often complex relations between them can only result in throwing out the baby with the bathwater.

Notes

1. See 'The Cycle of Goodness' (Appendix).
2. Ireland is a good research field for the comparative study of subsidiaries of many nationalities; 656 started production between 1960 and 1978 (Industrial Development Authority, 1979, p. i).
3. Synchronic refers here to an analysis made at one moment, like a snapshot, or apparently outside time altogether. Diachronic analysis locates the present situation in the context of choices and events from previous times. It is not historical determinism but an examination of processes.
4. Few foresaw how effectively the severe postwar economic problems in Japan would be dealt with. E. O. Reischauer, Japanese scholar and subsequently US Ambassador, believed that Japan faced 'slow economic starvation' (Lyons, 1976, p. 57). The difficulties of US steel and automobile firms later facing Japanese competition are partly 'unintended consequences' (Weber) of GHQ assistance with productivity and quality control in Japan after 1945 (cf. Nakaoka, 1981).
5. For a proposed solution see e.g. 'Industry, education and management' (Department of Employment, July 1977, London).
6. 'Loyalty' and the 'individualistic/groupish dimension' discussed by Dore (1973), or the unimportance of the individual in the Western sense (Nakamura, 1971) are relevant. Cf. British tendencies to criticize the group and to (over?)value individual opinions.

7. Social science itself has a context, which appears in interpretations of Japanese society. In its formative period, British *social* anthropology examined existing social structures and political systems (Kuper, 1975). American *cultural* anthropology concentrated on values, beliefs, customs, etc. that survived Indian political systems. De Tocqueville saw Americans as 'new men', requiring a new identity, later assumed by immigrants—hence the significance of values. The approach of e.g. Levi-Strauss reflects the French intellectual tradition. Any of these approaches can be one-sided if taken to extremes. Some anthropologists may have exaggerated differences between societies, while sociologists preoccupied with Western industrial societies may have done the opposite. It is hard for independent inquiry and analysis to develop in societies with strong collectivist pressure, as in Japan (Mannheim, 1936, pp. xiv–xv).

8. For a good example see 'A Culture of Love and Hate' (Germany) in Lebra and Lebra (1974), pp. 27–36.

9. Puritanical British views of business as money grubbing and as a low-status occupation are factors in the low prestige and morale of British managers, unrelieved by a patriotic element (cf. Mant, 1979). Talent is directed away from business into the professions (Nishiguchi, 1981, pp. 18–35).

10. But from a Western point of view, Japanese society is less exotic than those studied in the classic anthropological monographs.

11. 'Instrumental' refers here, for example, to acts with a specific advantage in business etc. 'Expressive' refers to acts that are not strictly necessary to achieve results, but that are felt to be called for in social relations. This is significant in *nemawashi* (see decision making) and in group work. The two aspects are not necessarily easy to separate.

12. See also JETRO (1979), 'An Outline of the New Economic and Social Seven-Year Plan'.

13. Mant (1979) shows the debilitating effect of anti-industrial ideology on British industrial and managerial performance.

14. This applies to all societies; the more so when there is strong pressure to conform.

15. Weber's *Verstehen*, cf. Weber (1947), pp. 9–10, 87–8, 94.

16. See also JETRO (1981–2) on 'medium and small enterprises'. The model of long-term employment discussed below applies primarily to large companies, but it is an ideal to be followed if finance allows.

2 THE PROBLEM OF INTERNATIONALIZATION

2.1 The Basic Problem

Convergence theory [begins] with the assumption that wherever industrialization begins, it sets into motion an unending process of further industrialization. Once a nation[1] goes down this road there is no turning back. Further,
the journey engenders its own 'logic', so that *all* such journeys share certain
universal characteristics or imperatives. A primary example is the elabora-
tion of an industrial 'web of rule' that defines the relationship between the
managers *of* and the managed *in* industrial operations (the very nature of
the production system requires both types of actors, it is assumed).[2] Unless
the 'web' evolves, industrialization would stop dead in its tracks, impeded
by lack of incentives and coordination [Levine, in Dore, 1971, pp. 246-7,
with reference to the theory of Clark Kerr *et al.*, 1962].

Such statements appear to some observers to be sweeping and
deterministic. Dore in his seminal work of 1973, for example,
referred to the theories 'of convergent social evolution—from
Marx in the last century to Galbraith or Clark Kerr among our
contemporaries', and noted that 'the convergence theory assumes
. . . that the same technology is likely to produce the same sort
of institutions' (Dore, 1973, pp. 10-11). He then went on to
challenge the concept of a 'state of modernity which, once
reached, is never likely to be abandoned', again specifically referring to Clark Kerr (ibid., p. 12).

One aspect of the debate concerning both convergence and
modernity involves the spread of multinational enterprises, also
described as 'the internationalisation of business' (Sampson,
1974, p. 279). This multinational spread of Western, particularly
American, firms since 1945 has been accepted as an important
phenomenon by many writers. Vernon, for example, has discussed it in terms of his 'product cycle' explanation and of the
political, economic and industrial relations controversies to which
it continues to give rise (Vernon, 1977). Others have produced
models of the 'multinationalization' of large enterprises. Stopford and Wells (1972), for instance, put forward a three-phase

model of the process. In such terms it can be argued that Japanese firms have not yet reached the third phase, in which 'the relatively independent international divisions are dissolved and integrated into the mainstream of business activities' (Thurley *et al.*, 1980, p. 5). Sampson draws a parallel between the spread of multinationals in the second half of the twentieth century and the spread of railways in the nineteenth century with regard to commercial expansion and the debate on the nature and extent of the increase in international connections that both processes have generated. In Sampson's view, multinationals have become 'less an American than a world phenomenon' (op. cit., pp. 272-3), largely because of the efforts of corporations in other states to compete with multinationals of American origin on equal terms, thus promoting a 'universalistic' and convergent concept.

According to Kindleberger 'the nation-state is just about through as an economic unit' (quoted in Sampson, op. cit., p. 266). The description of ITT given by Sampson is of a transnational corporation, dominated by the business systems introduced by Geneen and with a strong 'corporate culture', in which national differences among managers had become extremely blurred (ibid., pp. 15-19). This seems to imply the convergent development of multinational management structures and practices and their standardized introduction into whatever national context a corporation of this type is operating in, even though the systems are being operated by local managers and employees. While using standardized managerial practices and procedures, the multinationals are at the same time pursuing a policy of 'localization' in personnel terms; if only as a device for gaining local acceptance in some cases.

The models of multinationals given in the literature generally refer to American or other Western examples. Because of the newness of the subject and the paucity of data available, especially on Japanese operations in Europe, it is not clear how far these models are applicable to Japanese companies. At a structural level there is evidence, for example, that many medium-sized Japanese firms that have established operations in South-East Asia are 'immature' in comparison with American multinationals. At the level of managerial practice, there is considerable debate as to whether Japanese companies in Europe, the USA, and elsewhere will be likely to seek to maintain what are often claimed to be their particularistic managerial systems. This issue of the 'internationalization of business', to use Sampson's phrase, has major implications for the theories of convergence, modernity, and multinational development that have been outlined above, and also for the 'internationalization' or otherwise of Japan's economy and society. Given the differences that are asserted to exist between, for example, American multinationals and Japanese companies operating overseas in terms of managerial structures, policies, and practices, can it be claimed that there is a universalistic 'logic' of convergence or multinationalization? In order to shed more light on this problem, the empirical part of the book sets out, in Chapter 4, to investigate what types of managerial practices are being used in Japanese firms in the UK, in comparison with those in use in Japan itself.

Different interpretations of Japanese management were discussed in Chapter 1 above, particularly those that rested upon some synchronic notion such as 'culture' and those, on the other hand, that catered more for a number of different factors, including managerial power and historical developments. Particularistic interpretations are the antithesis of the universalistic theories discussed above and, if they are correct, they lead to the conclusion that differences in social structure and beliefs lead to differences in managerial practices. When the latter are validated in many people's eyes by economic success at home and abroad, they are likely to be used overseas. But only empirical evidence can show how far this may be the case.

Differences in interpretation are to some extent explained by the approach used. The spread of Japanese firms overseas since the 1960s has been discussed in terms of managerial systems by Yoshino (1976); in terms of business strategy and economic rationality by Ozawa (1979); and in terms of financial investment by Sekiguchi (1979)—to name but three writers who will be referred to below and who have studied different aspects of their development. While Yoshino and Ozawa are sympathetic towards the companies and discuss methods of overcoming the managerial problems that arise, others are hostile. This is particularly the case with Marxist writers, such as Nakase (1980) and Halliday and McCormack (1973), who criticize the companies as 'exploiters', 'tools of American capitalism', etc. The argument to some extent parallels the debate between those in the West who see multinational spread as a provider of investment, employment, and technology transfer (e.g. in Ireland, where in 1980 there were six Japanese production firms) and those who see it as a threat to local labour and to national sovereignty and economic interests. These issues have been discussed by Vernon (1977) in his book with the self-explanatory title, *Storm over the Multinationals* and in Bergsten *et al.* (1978). In the Japanese case the resentment that surfaced in Malaysia, Thailand, and Indonesia in the 1970s, particularly during the visit of the Japanese prime minister, Tanaka, took Japanese companies by surprise (Ozawa, 1979, pp. 220–3).

A factor in this resentment was that Japanese firms were alleged not to have localized their operations to the same extent as Western firms that had a longer experience in the region. The alleged policy of centralization was said to account for the restricted opportunities available to local staff, especially in regard to the key issue of promotion. Similar allegations have been made in the United States and elsewhere. How far they apply in the UK will be discussed below. If there is indeed a policy opposed to localization, does this mean that the universalistic logic of the convergence-theory type breaks down? If so, what are the reasons? Are Japanese companies operating overseas likely to evolve a rationalized international division of labour, as proponents of the internationalization of the Japanese economy imply; or is there, as the British media are prone to assert, a policy aimed at one-sided economic domination, whereby Japanese firms spread overseas, while foreign participation in the Japanese economy is effectively prevented by constraints such as non-tariff barriers? Part of any answer to this question must necessarily be a prediction, but an attempt is made in the concluding chapter to suggest in which direction observable trends are moving.

Ozawa and others have elaborated upon the economic reasons for the spread of Japanese overseas operations. These include the need to secure raw materials from Australia, Indonesia, and the Middle East; the removal of textile and other older industries to South-East Asia;[3] the defence and promotion of export markets in the USA and Europe; the need for large companies to fight off competition from Japanese rivals and to attain the economies of scale and other advantages produced by growth, and the need for smaller firms to secure growth by expanding overseas in the absence of room domestically. These are significant data because they provide an economic rationale for Japanese operations in the UK and elsewhere, but they can only be included here to the extent that they are relevant to the basic problem. This central issue concerns the universality of managerial practices and can be expressed in the following question: How far are managerial practices empirically found in Japanese firms in the UK similar to those used in Japan and, if they differ in degree or kind, what are the reasons?

The answer to this question has implications for the convergence theory and for the 'logic' it posits, including the 'universal characteristics and imperatives' that are asserted to affect 'the web of rule' between managers and the managed. This aspect is predominantly dealt with below in terms of control. Regarding the 'logic' of the development of international firms, data on, for example, the extent to which British staff are recruited for or promoted to positions of substantive responsibility might be expected to show whether major Japanese corporations of the Mitsubishi, Sony, or NSK type are following, or are likely to follow, a similar type of multinational path to that followed by IBM, Shell, or Philips.

The overseas expansion of Japanese firms has been and still is a dynamic process, similar to the postwar development of the firms in Japan itself, and it would be erroneous to regard their situation as static. The prognosis in the concluding chapter is intended to avoid *ex post facto* reasoning. Whatever path the companies do in fact take, it will have significant implications for the internationalization of Japan's economy and society as a whole, as well as for the debate over the universalistic or particularistic nature of managerial practices in Japanese companies.

The basic question also arises in current discussions of the policies and practices of Japanese firms and their intentions in the UK economy. This has considerable topical and political, as well as theoretical, significance. Respected journals, such as the *Financial Times*, include reports on Japanese business activity on an almost daily basis, and in 1981 its management page featured a series entitled 'Learning from the Japanese' on Japanese managerial practices and their relevance for British managers.

In many cases media accounts of the efficient and socially egalitarian aspects of managerial practices, whether actual or supposed, employed in Japanese firms in the UK have helped to create highly positive local images of Japanese management.

Indeed they may have helped to generate expectations of Japanese management almost as a panacea; these expectations apply to some employees of Japanese firms in the UK as well as to the public in general.

Media accounts may suggest that Japanese firms are introducing a considerable degree of Japanese managerial practice into the UK. They even imply that there may be little difference between how a company is managed in Japan and how it is run in the UK. An article entitled 'Oriental Magic in Welsh Valleys' asserted that 'Japanese businessmen have been quietly importing their own special brand of industrial management into the UK during the last few years and their results so far have been markedly successful' (*Financial Times*, 21 January 1977). Under the heading of 'The Japanese Way to Industrial Harmony' a writer described how 'National Panasonic has found a successful formula in a management style which breaks down the barriers between "them" and "us"' (*The Director*, Vol. 30, January 1978): referring to the gap that often exists between management and workforce in British firms.

A glowing account of how 'the Japanese way to work wins Geordie loyalty' explained that NSK had 'imported a tiny segment of their country's industrial efficiency into the wilds of England's industrial north' (*Daily Telegraph*, 13 February 1981). Another article reported the same company as having brought 'Togetherness to County Durham' and concluded that 'whatever view one might take of the Japanese penchant for uniformity and togetherness, it appears to work—on three shifts' (*The Times*, 30 July 1980). Subsequently in 'Japanese Culture in County Durham', the company training officer outlined 'the highly successful working atmosphere [that] has been created and sustained' (*Personnel Management*, March 1982). It is noteworthy that the above examples come from professional journals and 'serious', not 'popular', newspapers.

One Japanese factory, the Sony television manufacturing plant at Bridgend, has been given a Queen's Award to Industry for its export performance. In 'The Rising Sun shines in the Valleys' an *Observer* correspondent described how the company had 'introduced the concept of the company as family'—a key feature of Japanese companies according to many stereotyped accounts. The reaction of the workforce to 'paternalistic Japanese management' was then discussed, accompanied by photographs of the plant manager on the shop floor, eating in the single-status canteen, etc. (*Observer* magazine, 26 April 1981). The award of an official decoration, the OBE,[4] to the plant manager was commented on in the *Financial Times* of 26 November 1980 and, four days later, in the *Observer*.

The 'excellent relationship' between Mitsubishi Electric and its workforce at its television plant in Scotland was commented on by the *Financial Times* of 6 April 1981. Three days earlier it had reported 'Toshiba takes on a salvage mission', after the dissolution of the joint venture with Rank at Plymouth, and gave details of Toshiba's new single-status employment system, representative constitution, and plans for an increase in productivity. These developments were reported as if they had been an expatriate initiative; in fact, as will be discussed below, local management was heavily involved. An official of the Electrical, Electronic and Plumbing Trade Union (EEPTU), who had been to Japan, was quoted as saying 'working conditions were far superior to those in this country, with higher wage rates in real terms—at any rate in the main (T.V.) assembly factories. That breeds a good relationship between workers and management' (*The Times*, 24 November 1978).

'The sun is really rising for Japanese companies operating in the UK', reported *Training Times* No. 63 (October 1980) in its account of 'How a Japanese firm solved its consultation problem'; although it did point out that 'the paper which John Hancox subsequently delivered may have disappointed some listeners in that it contained no magic Japanese formula for instant success in industrial relations'.

A great deal of media coverage is concerned precisely with the expectation of a 'magic Japanese formula'. 'The secret of Japan Steel's success' and 'Nippon Steel's high-strength survival kit', for example, was said to be not only the rationalization of production, research, and development, but also its extensive use of Quality Circles, known in-house as *jishu kanri* ('self-management'). The advice of the company's chief corporate and economic researcher to Western industrialists was quoted (*Financial Times*, 14 October 1980). Following a leading article of 12 June 1980 entitled 'Learning from Japan', the same newspaper printed a letter from a Senior Lecturer in Management Studies urging British managers to take the advice given: 'to emulate the Japanese in involving everyone in the decision-making process' (23 June 1980).

The magic formula is frequently implied to be some type of participative or egalitarian management style. Quality Circles and participation, for instance, were discussed in 'Ford brings home some Eastern philosophy' (*Financial Times*, 9 May 1980), in the context of Ford's plans for its 'After Japan' (AJ) movement in Europe. An article on the management page (i.e. again not popular journalism), with the title 'Confucius still holds sway in Japanese industry', showed a photograph of Japanese shipyard workers with the caption 'No clear distinction between management and workers' (*Financial Times*, 23 April 1979).

The many television programmes broadcast about Japanese industry have fostered perceptions similar to those of a shop-floor employee of one of the manufacturers in this study who stated that 'I've seen films about the Japanese on TV . . how they have meetings with all the workers and participation. You don't get any of that here—[British] management isn't like that; it wants to keep itself apart.' The example gives an idea of the diffusion of positive images of Japanese managerial practices —and of correspondingly unfavourable ones of British management. 'Lessons in learning from the Japanese' dealt with the training of engineers in Japan and how they were employed in industry (*Times Higher Education Supplement*, 30 October 1981). The question of participation was raised again in a report on the *kamban* components supply and stock control system, by asking 'Is your workforce engaged in decision making?' (*Financial Times*, 4 August 1981).

Whereas in the early postwar years productivity missions from Britain visited plants in the United States, there is currently greater popular interest in management in Japan. A team from the Industrial Participation Association, led by its Director, for example, spent a fortnight in Japan 'studying the experience of Japanese companies in industrial relations and employee participation, and how they have involved their workforce in the introduction of new technology' (Bell, 1981).

From the above examples it is clear that there is widespread interest in Japanese management, frequently accompanied by extremely high expectations, and that the positive images are, in many cases, the obverse of the negative images of what is perceived to be 'wrong' with managerial practices in British firms. Comparisons are made, for instance, between the educational levels of Japanese and British managers; and attention is drawn to the increase in the numbers of patents granted to Japanese (*Times Higher Education Supplement*, 1 May 1981).

Many of the above points, with emphasis on what are represented as the basic principles of Japanese management, such as a participative management style, good employee relations, total quality control, and close attention to production organization, as well as the advantages to the UK of the presence of Japanese firms, were alluded to in a series of advertisements entitled 'Insight into Japanese Management' in the *Financial Times* in May 1981. The series featured Toshiba, National Panasonic and Mitsubishi Electric in the production sector; the Sumitomo Bank and the Bank of Tokyo, and Marubeni and C. Itoh in trading. The concluding 'Review of the Series' drew attention to cardinal principles of Japanese managerial practice such as 'total involvement of the individual with his company', 'innovation' and 'consensus', in very positive terms.

Journalistic accounts do not always define their basic assumptions, but many reports of the type quoted above appear to be based on three presuppositions. The first, explicitly stated in many cases, is that there is some sort of Japanese managerial formula which leads to success. The second assumption is that there is something which British managers and employees can profitably learn from Japanese examples, whether in Japanese firms in the UK or in Japan itself. The third assumption, which generally receives less overt attention, is that Japanese managerial practices are being 'imported' into the UK.

The last of these three assumptions would appear to be the most contentious. It would be otiose to quote all the books that have appeared since the 1970s on Japanese success in the business and economic field, some of them promising a revelation of the 'formula'. On the second presupposition, reports such as that of the Industrial Participation Association (Bell, 1981), and that of Gibbs (1980), for the National Economic Development Office (NEDO) are predicated on the assumption that there is something that British managers and others can learn from the Japanese experience, whatever other differences of custom and practice there may be. The whole question of 'transferability' is discussed by de Bettignies (1980). From a purely economic point of view, the fierce competition among regional development corporations for the proposed Nissan investment has received wide publicity, for example

'The fight for Japan's golden egg' (*Financial Times*, 25 February 1981).

The validity or otherwise of the third assumption, that Japanese managerial practices are being introduced on a significant scale into Japanese operations in the UK, has been discussed by Thurley (1981) and is involved in his more recent discussion (*Personnel Management*, February 1982) of the relevance of Japanese models to the UK. Reports such as 'So British—a Japanese company in the stockbroker belt' (*The Times*, 31 July 1980), by the same reporter who had described the 'Japaneseness' of NSK, contradict popular images of an implantation of Japanese managerial practices. In this case (Nittan) it was stated that 'there is little sign of Japanese influence and the Japanese management style—on the surface at least'. This contentious problem will be dealt with, both empirically and in its implications for the main problem, in Chapters 4 and 5 below.

The volume of negative comment on Japanese economic activity may not always be directly relevant to managerial practices in the UK, but Japanese managers are sensitive to the climate that it creates. It is likely to impel them to adopt a lower profile and to be more hesitant to draw attention to themselves by introducing home-country practices on a more radical scale.

The suspicion and hostility of many headlines are explicit: 'Jostled by Japan' (*Economist*, 5 July 1980); 'Japan's unstoppable motor industry' (*Financial Times*, 12 July 1980); 'Fears over Japan's march into Britain' (*Now!*, 12 September 1980); 'Electronics firms fear Japanese chip competition' (*Daily Telegraph*, 19 September 1980); 'Japan's next assault' (*Observer*, 5 October 1980); 'How to cope with Japan' (*Financial Times*, 27 November 1980); 'Success in one country only' (*Financial Times*, 28 November 1980); 'The Japanese Challenge' (*Daily Telegraph*, 18 December 1980); 'Toyota takes Spain' (*Observer*, 8 February 1981); 'How the Japanese trapped half a car market' (*Financial Times*, 13 February 1981); 'Japan blamed for British jobs loss' (*Financial Times*, 16 March 1981); 'Joining battle with Japan' (*Management Today*, October 1981).

Such criticisms have led some, such as the chairman of the development corporation that was successful in attracting NSK to its area, to engage in 'debunking the many myths about Japanese foreign investment' (*Financial Times*, 6 December 1977). The reference in this case was to the Hitachi affair, when

management and union opposition forced Hitachi to drop its
plans for a wholly-owned television tube factory in the North
East, after it had received an understanding from the government
of the day that its investment would be welcome. In 1980 a
public clash between British and Japanese union officials from
the motor industry took place at a meeting of the International
Metalworkers Federation World Auto Council, and was reported
in *The Times* on 19 November 1980.

Some of the problems of adaptation and communication
faced by Japanese companies in the UK have been discussed
under such headings as 'Japan's management style suffers trans-
plant trials' (*Financial Times*, 16 May 1980), and 'Learning to
live in harmony' (*Financial Times*, 1 June 1981): the latter
referring specifically to the GEC–Hitachi joint venture that was
set up after Hitachi's original bid had failed.

One popular newspaper asserted that 'the top people, from
the Prime Minister down, are frightfully keen that the British
working man should learn the secrets of success from the awe-
some example of his counterpart in Japan' (*Daily Mail*, 'Comparative serfdom', 26 September 1981). It went on to the
ambivalent conclusion that although 'puerile' notices hung up in
plants ('presumably exhortations to work harder') and the wearing of uniform were disliked ('because East is East and West is
West'), British workers were in fact more heavily taxed than
their Japanese counterparts.

At a more general level, questions about the costs as well as
the benefits of Japanese group organization and what this means
in human terms have been raised: e.g. 'Which should come first
—the individual or the group?' (*The Times*, 16 August 1978).
This problem will be dealt with below in terms of the 'indivi-
dual/groupishness dimension' identified by Dore (1973), and in
the context of the reactions of British managers, white-collar
and blue-collar employees respectively, to Japanese practices.

The above references suggest considerable gaps in public
knowledge of Japanese managerial practices in general and of
the extent to which they are being applied in the UK in particular. It is the latter problem with which this book is principally
concerned, since it refers to the question of how far managerial
practices used in Japanese firms in the UK resemble those used in
Japan, and to the reasons for the differences that there may be
between them.

2.2 Research design

In order to establish a basis for comparison, an analysis of the managerial systems typically found in established companies in Japan is given in Chapter 3. This is followed by an empirical examination in Chapter 4 of the processes of adaptation of Japanese companies in the UK, based on fieldwork. The aim is to investigate practices actually being used in the UK and to test the reality of 'localization'. The situation in Japan is compared with that in the UK, showing for example to what extent home country or host country practices are used, and to what extent local staff are being promoted to positions of substantive responsibility. The data can be expected to give an indication of how far localization or internationalization has proceeded: a point that will be taken up again in Chapter 5.

The conceptual and theoretical problems in building models of Japanese management, discussed in Chapter 1, show that a number of models are possible, based on: economic rationality, 'culture', values, control, social organization, historical develop- ment, competence, etc. The analysis of managerial practices in Japan in Chapter 3 begins with 'life employment' because it is argued here that this is the main premise to which the other systems refer and because it is a prime indicator of the high degree of control enjoyed by management in Japan. From the standpoint of British or American personnel management the different systems may appear to be discrete technical functions, but in the Japanese context they belong together conceptually (cf. Inohara's 1977 description of the basis and essentials of Japanese personnel management). It is contended that the various practices together constitute 'Japanese managerial systems' and this concept provides the theoretical basis of the book.

The empirical data on the management of Japanese com- panies in the UK came from four interrelated studies. The first, in chronological order, was a case study of decision making at a major trading company in the City of London. The second was the questionnaire study carried out by the International Centre for Economics and Related Disciplines (ICERD), of which the writer was a member, at the London School of Economics. The third consisted of interviews with personnel managers, general managers, and plant managers at thirty-nine companies. The fourth consisted of case studies at two banks, two manufacturing companies, and one further trading company.

The purpose of the questionnaire study was to obtain basic statistical information about the companies and their personnel which until that time had been lacking. The questionnaire itself was designed to obtain data on the relative numbers and positions of expatriates and local staff, in order to provide the quantitative, as well as qualitative, basis that a comparative study requires. Because of the problems of access and confidentiality, the questionnaire omitted any reference to potentially sensitive areas, such as industrial relations. The restriction of most questions to 'objective' quantitative data was also necessary in order to build up as accurate an 'objective' picture of the research field as possible; but the questionnaire did include one qualitative open-ended question and evaluative questions on the performance, attitudes, and time-keeping of local staff.

The press comments on the performance of Japanese companies in the UK, quoted in the preceding section, refer in most cases to the small minority of manufacturing companies; while the questionnaire study helped to put into better perspective the fact that as of 1982 there were no more than twenty manufacturing operations out of a total of approximately 280 companies of all types. Given public perceptions of the managerial and employee relations problems in British industry, media interest in the manufacturers may be understandable, but it is necessary to correct this one-sided impression. Directing attention to other types of firm, particularly the large number of commercial and financial firms concentrated in the City of London, also has the advantage of facilitating comparisons between different sectors, as well as between different firms in the same sector. It proved useful in drawing out certain typical contrasts between the commercial or financial, and manufacturing sectors, as will be seen in Chapter 4.

The questionnaire study provided an essential quantitative basis, without which it would have been dangerous to attempt to draw broad conclusions, but by itself the data would have been inadequate. To deal with such a complex subject as Japanese management, with the added complication of studying it in a non-Japanese environment, it was necessary to obtain as complete in-depth qualitative information as possible.

Business, employment, and industrial relations systems all deal with personnel, whose actions and perceptions cannot be treated in the same way as technology, machinery, and production systems—even if the latter are at the same time social products. To study communication or employee relations in any significant way it is necessary to obtain qualitative data by interview, which was the aim of the interviews held with personnel at the thirty-nine companies listed below. The (postal) questionnaire study excluded personal contact in most instances, but the rapport that can be established in interviews allows topics, sometimes including potentially sensitive ones, to be pursued in greater depth. Interviews with personnel managers and others also had the advantage of indicating whether a case study might eventually be acceptable.

The interviews with personnel managers and others, at the second stage of the ICERD study, were extremely valuable for the data they provided on management policy and attitudes; but it would clearly have been inadequate to construct the model of a company on the basis of one interview—and perhaps a tour round the plant or office. The research therefore moved on to the case studies, in which data in the greatest depth possible, both quantitative and qualitative, were sought where access was obtained.

In the case studies substantial samples of expatriate and local staff of all grades were interviewed and postal questionnaires were left for the remainder to complete at home. One other manufacturer, having declined interviews on grounds of time, took part in the postal questionnaire survey applicable to all grades of employees.

The selection of companies for case studies was designed to elicit whatever comparisons there might be between the commercial and manufacturing sectors, and to avoid the one-sided picture that a study of a single sector might give. In the commercial sector the banks and trading companies in the City of London are both the most numerous and the largest in the UK in terms of numbers of employees, and were therefore the most fruitful objects of study. The trading companies were also interesting because of their wide range of functions. The smaller number of mànufacturers that appear on the list below is still high in relation to the absolute total of firms. The large numbers of interviews held at sales and distribution companies provided much data on this numerically large but, from the viewpoint of managerial practice, less sharply differentiated category.

Throughout the research the minimum figure of fifty personnel was considered necessary for a study of managerial practices and the interaction of home country and host country personnel. The grounds for setting this minimum were that data that are significant in the present context cannot be obtained from, for example, 'representative offices'. Many of the latter have no more than two or three employees, and perhaps only one expatriate. Their business and personnel functions are limited and questions such as union recognition are unlikely to arise. In fact the companies in the case studies consisted of between one hundred and two hundred staff, with the exception of the chemical company, which had fifty. In comparison with local firms, these cannot be said to be large undertakings, but they are large as far as the majority of Japanese firms in Western Europe are concerned.

The initial questionnaire was highly structured, as already outlined, with the evaluative questions on a standard type of scale. The interviews at managerial level were semi-structured, to allow promising lines of inquiry to be followed up. In the case studies, the interviews and postal questionnaire covered identical ground. The only exception was the addition to the interview schedule of two open-ended questions on employee perceptions of the company. This type of question does not lend itself satisfactorily to short written answers, but where there is the possibility of discussion with the interviewee, richer and more precise data can be obtained. Following normal practice, all interviewees were volunteers, and it was possible to go into points where some had either special experience or particular views in more depth.

It is clear that differences among firms of Japanese, American, British, or other origin may be expected and that there is no such thing as 'a typical Japanese firm' in a strict sense, but for research purposes it is necessary to work with ideal typical models. In this case it is a question of looking for a nexus of findings, while seeing certain features at, for example, Okasa Engineering, which is known in Japan for its house style, in proportion. A nexus of findings that make up a coherent pattern should not be confused with one apparently striking feature, such as Okasa's savings scheme, when the implications of the data as a whole need to be considered.

Data from other Western European countries collected by ICERD show that the situation there is similar to that in the UK, although the UK cannot be taken as representative of the whole of Europe—let alone of 'the West'—an abstraction beloved by so many Japanese writers. On the other hand, whatever local differences there are in terms of legal institutions and custom and practice, the overriding business rationale of Japanese companies within the EEC area is the same. The British case is therefore relevant both in its European, or 'Western', context and in its implications for the internationalization of Japan's economy and society.

The problem for studies of Japanese companies abroad is that it is easier to find what home country practices are or are not being applied than it is to show what managerial strategies are being followed. The problem of access to companies for interview and questionnaire study purposes was largely overcome and the decision-making study at the first trading company provided valuable data on how decisions were made; but, as would be expected in business undertakings of other nationalities, what was being decided had to remain outside the scope of the investigation. It is also impossible to study 'upstream' decisions reached at head offices in Japan during a study being carried out in overseas branches, but the content of these decisions would normally be confidential in any case.

The constraint on research in terms of access to the content of decisions, observable in the work of Kidd and Teramoto (1981) for instance, is part of the research problem itself. Control of information is part of the managerial control, which, it is argued here, is a major determinant of the type of managerial practices used in branches in the UK. Tight managerial control in Japan, and in other societies where management enjoys greater control than it does in the UK, is interpreted in ideological terms by those who are at the same time propagating the ideology, and who are therefore anxious not to support other interpretations.

Control does not *a priori* exclude belief; and it is a common observation in countries as individualistic as the UK, USA, and France, that authoritarian organizations frequently succeed in attracting the commitment of believers. It can therefore be argued at a more general level that the prevalence of normative Japanese beliefs and group organization will result in action of

Table 1. Japanese companies studied in Britain

Banks	Trading Companies
Kiku Bank	Chuo Trading Co.
Moriguchi Bank	Ebisu Trading Co.*
Nippon Investment Bank	Maruyama Trading Co.
Ota Bank*	Morita Trading Co.
Sodo Bank	Nishi Trading Co.
Tanabe Bank*	Sanno Trading Co.
	Tanaka Trading Co.*
Securities Companies	
Fushimi Securities	Insurance Company
Kanto Securities	Kita Insurance Co.
Ohno Securities	
	Manufacturing Companies
Sales and Distribution Companies	Daito Engineering
Daimon Engineering	Higashi Chemical Co.
Daitoku Distribution	Kansai Electronics
Daitoku Electronics	Minami Chemical Co.*
Hito Engineering	Okasa Engineering
Horikawa Engineering	Saiin Engineering
Ishi Sales	Sono Engineering*
Kansai Distribution	
Kyoto Electronics	Transport
Miki Precision Products	Higashiyama Transport Co.
Morita Tractors	Nippon Transport Co.
Nishi Electric	Ueda Transport Co.
Toho-Morita Distribution	

*Case study.

a particularistic type such as exclusiveness and the absence of 'localization'. Japanese society is not totalitarian in the usual sense of the word, but there is a high level of uniformity in the values that its members hold, largely due to the strength of socialization processes in the school system and in the family (cf. De Vos, 1973). As Marsh and Mannari (1976, p. 179) have pointed out, personnel have already been fully exposed to these processes long before they enter a company. The values that they hold as a result may be important elements in their adoption of a management style and a given set of practices in overseas branches, but there would be methodological problems to overcome before such a hypothesis could be adequately tested. It would, for instance, be hard to quantify or to prove a causal link between values and social action.

Studies in specific areas cannot provide a total picture of

the entire research field, but it is hoped that they can stimulate further questions, and provide useful empirical data and conclusions based on the inductive method.

To preserve confidentiality, the thirty-nine Japanese companies studied in the UK are referred to by pseudonyms. These are listed in Table 1 according to type of business. Companies are only referred to under their real names in a few instances where material that has already been made public is quoted.

Notes

1. For example, Japan, Korea, Brazil, Kuwait?
2. Managerial control was discussed in Chapter 1. A concluding evaluation of control in Japanese companies in the UK is given at the end of Chapter 5.
3. Cf. Vernon's 'product cycle' argument above.
4. Order of the British Empire. A decoration awarded every year to civilians in recognition of achievements in many fields.

3 MANAGERIAL SYSTEMS IN JAPAN

3.1 Long-term employment

The so-called life-employment (*shushin koyo*) system is well known outside Japan as a conspicuously 'different' feature, either in the context of the commitment to the group it is said to reinforce or as a major ideological feature, often promoted by Japanese managers as a morally virtuous end in itself. A Japanese authority lists it as one of the major 'characteristics of Japanese labour management today', and one of 'the important aspects of the traditional patrimonial system that was carried over' (Hazama, n.d., pp. 11, 7).

It has been said that 'it is materially impossible to dissociate wage incentives from the pay policy and the pay policy from the personnel policy. Such a dissociation would, if it were possible, constitute a sociological error' (S. Hill and K. E. Thurley, *British Journal of Industrial Relations*, Vol. 12, 1974, p. 148). The Japanese seniority system, company welfare provisions, management ideology, and consensual processes of decision making belong with continuous employment in one company until retiring age. Because this age is 55 or 60, after which a less well paid job generally has to be found, the value-laden term 'life' employment is not strictly accurate. It is avoided here in favour of 'long-term employment'. It could also be expressed as a constraint on job changing and a dependency on one firm that gives management a powerful hold over employees, including managers. It is therefore an aspect of management as control.

According to Kahn 'a person first going to work as a regular employee is making a lifetime contract, or rather, both sides are at least morally committed to a contract. . . . Headhunting and job hopping towards advancement in a profession are unheard of' (Kahn, 1970, pp. 93, 96). The term 'contract', as in Maine's phrase 'the movement from status to contract', has a special meaning in this context. In legal systems based on Anglo-

Saxon law commercial contracts, leases, etc., give rise to legally binding relationships. In Japan, joining a company involves much more—entry into a situation bound by diffuse interpersonal relationships, induction into the group, and compliance with an extremely flexible task orientation.

New company entrants in Japan seldom sign an individual labour contract and, even if they sign an undertaking to abide by the employment regulations, they do not necessarily read them. 'If [they] show some interest in reading them, they may be suspected of being potential trouble-makers' (Inohara, 1977, p. 15). In Britain too, employment contracts are looser than commercial contracts. The employment relationship in Japan may be 'regular', in the case of full members of the permanent staff, or 'temporary'. The latter type of employee can be discharged at will and receives less favourable terms than a 'regular' employee. It is an exaggeration to assert that job changing among regular employees is unheard of in Japan, but it is less common among larger established enterprises.

The system of labour legislation in Japan has been based since the Second World War on American legal models, but resort to lawyers is low in comparison with the UK, and more especially with the USA. Legal action is generally seen in Japanese society as an admission of failure in the normal processes of informal negotiation involving interpersonal relationships, and in the company context as a failure of management: shameful in any circumstances. In spite of the instrumental aspects of the employment relationship, it may not be an exaggeration to assert that in Japan 'the relationship between employer and employee is not to be explained in contractual terms' (Nakane, 1973, p. 15). Kahn's use of the term 'contract', with its Anglo-Saxon connotations of a legal–rational order, is not very apt.

Japanese social norms, which apply to business among other contexts, emphasize the cultivation of diffuse interpersonal relationships of an open-ended kind. By comparison Anglo-American legal conceptions, especially where commercial contracts are concerned, appear 'cold'. In Japan, commercial contracts are brief and pragmatic in that they make little attempt to provide for specific or detailed eventualities. Many simply state that 'in the case of dispute, differences should be amicably settled by negotiation' (trading company legal department manager, personal communication).

Differing expectations underlie the views held by Japanese and British or American managers on the nature of the employment relationship, and it is thought of in very different terms in these countries. Nakane compares the Japanese employment relationship with that of lord and subject in feudal times and, although one may question the interpretation, it points to a high degree of managerial control. In Britain it is more explicitly the case that 'a job is a job' and a means to an end.

Abegglen saw long-term employment as 'the crucial difference between Japanese and American employment systems' (Abegglen, 1958, p. 11), although he did mention the option open to Japanese employers of sending employees home temporarily on 60 per cent of salary in a recession. He also noted that only directors and above can stay on after the official retiring age (ibid., pp. 58-9). Presidents can virtually appoint themselves chairmen.

Long-term employment is often popularized as a unique Japanese system, but it does not apply to small, financially insecure, firms. It is also found in the Civil Service, the police, the military, and publicly owned organizations in the UK and elsewhere, but it is not called 'life employment'.

Kahn and Abegglen disagree over the desirability of long-term employment, arguing that it may produce overmanning rather than commitment leading to performance (Abegglen, 1958, pp. 17-18, 20, 22-3); the debate on whether the practice can and should be preserved will be dealt with later. Given the technological changes that have taken place since the 1950s, Abegglen's argument on this point now seems insubstantial and the redeployment of labour appears less of a problem for management than he claimed.

In the shipbuilding slump of the 1970s, Mitsubishi Heavy Industries redeployed workers from the Nagasaki shipyard to their automobile plant at Kyoto and retrained them. In 1980, when the car plant had to suspend production of cars for Chrysler in the USA, Mitsubishi Motors announced that it would redeploy its surplus labour to another Mitsubishi Group company (*Financial Times*, 17 January 1981). Such examples show the degree of job flexibility and flexibility of deployment between related companies enjoyed by management in Japan. In addition, the vested relations of power, prestige, and financial leverage between major companies and their sub-contractors mean that 'in

recession the large firm reduces its purchases from its contrac-
tors, so posing the problem of adjustment to them' (Gibbs, 1980,
p. 25). Management in large companies enjoys greater elasticity
than originally suggested by Abegglen, thanks partly to the
vertical relations between the major firms and their dependent
sub-contractors.

Abegglen was criticized by Cole for 'relying almost entirely
on management sources' (Cole, 1971, p. 1), and it appears he
was sometimes given normative rather than empirical data by
his informants. In a pioneering work it may not have been possible to devote sufficient time to the importance in Japanese
society of outwardly proclaiming the *tatemae* ('rule' or 'principle'), while pragmatically allowing for the *honne* ('real' or
'underlying' motive), which often modifies the practical application of the theory. In societies with a stronger legal–rational
order a considerable divergence between formal and substantive
patterns might cause problems, but for Abegglen's informants
there would have been no difficulty in moving from formal,
ideological, description to pragmatically based action, however
contradictory this might appear. When discrepancies arise
between formal and informal managerial systems, they would
be implicitly recognized and tacitly agreed upon. It would be
superfluous to analyse or codify them further.

Cole, exceptionally, succeeded in being taken on as an employee at a Tokyo company employing 513 people at two plants
(Cole, 1971, p. 57). In the rules there were eight reasons given
for possible dismissal, including the need for redundancy in a
recession. This was a medium-sized firm, but Cole found that
the attitudes towards job-changing were similar to those in
Western industrialized societies. Other companies also poached
experienced labour from the firm.

Japanese Ministry of Labour statistics showed that job changers as a percentage of new hirings accounted for 44.7 per cent
in 1965 and that in the boom year of 1961 the figure had risen
to 58.8 per cent (ibid., pp. 127, 125). In 1975 the figure for
mid-career job changers in companies with over a thousand
employees was 40 per cent (Japanese Government, 1976, table
48). The oil crisis of 1973 obliged companies to shorten working hours and to discharge temporary and female workers,
although the situation recovered in 1975 (Japanese Government,
1980, p. 103).

These data show that the premise of long-term employment is not unvarying but it is prevalent in the large, financially strong, companies that set the tone. Banks and trading companies employing numbers of graduates, to whom they offer good life chances, approximate most closely to the ideal while automobile production lines show a higher rate of turnover in the first few years of a blue-collar worker's employment, before the wage curve rises significantly.

Bankruptcy may oblige staff to change jobs against their will or their employers'. In a severe recession even some well known firms shed staff. Yashica, the camera manufacturer, dismissed 900 employees out of a total of 2,200 in 1975 (Lyons, 1976, p. 217). In fact the Japanese employment system has been flexible enough to cater for a major shift away from agriculture and into manufacturing, trading, and banking since 1950. Whereas agriculture employed 48.3 per cent of the labour force in 1950, the figure had fallen to 19.3 per cent in 1970 (Sato, 1980, p. 91).

Women are also excluded from the long-term employment system. 'They cannot improve their job status . . . and should marry by thirty and leave' (Abegglen, 1958, p. 103). In 1965 women accounted for about 40 per cent of the total employed labour force but their work, except for doctors and teachers, etc., was generally of a basic type, lasting on average no more than 4.1 years.

Japanese unions have not made an issue of female employment, and the victory of a woman in the Tokyo District Court in 1966 over the Sumitomo Cement Co. on the grounds that dismissal on marriage was an infringement of the Constitution, does not appear to have materially altered the situation. In 1977 the president of Idemitsu Oil Co., a major oil company, described female employment as a brief interlude before marriage (Idemitsu, 1977, pp. 3-4).

Management also has the sanction of 'voluntary' retirement at its disposal. Great care is taken with selection procedures, especially in large companies, but employees who later prove to be unsatisfactory can be persuaded to retire by a number of means. They can be transferred, on the same salary, to a lower status job; or their social relations in the group, which are of major importance in Japanese society, can be disrupted by continual transfers. They can be offered more retirement money if they retire early. It is made plain, in spite of the euphemistic language, that they will receive less if they stay—and that they will not be promoted (Cole, 1971, p. 121).

After the 1973 oil crisis a new term became current in the language for people who were being eased out of the company by management. This was *madogiwazoku* ('people by the window') i.e. those placed by the window without any real function or, in the case of managers, subordinates. This ostracism or expulsion from the group can be very painful in Japanese society where 'the most important feature of Japanese company life is the quality of relations between one member of the company and the others with whom he interacts' (Inohara, personal communication). Cole considers that the mere threat of such action is often sufficient.

Although the premise of long-term employment is maintained, allowing management close control over the deployment, renumeration, and behaviour of employees, the exceptions to the rule are generally in management's favour, particularly regarding *de facto* dismissal. In 1974, for example, the shipbuilding industry had employed 280,000 workers, but in 1979 the figure had been reduced to 120,000. This was partly due to the bankruptcy of thirty-seven medium-sized yards, but also to voluntary retirement affecting thousands of employees. Aluminium, synthetic fibres, fertilizers, and other industries officially classed as 'depressed' in 1978 also made large reductions in capacity (*Financial Times*, 29 October 1980).

'Most large firms employ 10–20 per cent of temporary and part-time workers' (Gibbs, 1980, p. 24). Data from before the war show that in one major steel company 'some "temporary" workers were employed for fifteen years' (Taira, 1970, p. 161), at considerable financial saving to the company. Many workers at the present time in building and automobiles are temporary (Bennett and Ishino, 1963) and many in stevedoring are day labourers. In the view of the two Marxist critics 'they are nothing but an industrial reserve army of Japan, obliged to work under less than satisfactory conditions, laid off first when business becomes dull' (Halliday and McCormack, 1973, p. 171). The same authors assert that Nissan car workers were classified into four categories: permanent, probationary, provisional, and seasonal. 'Nissan keep these [seasonal] workers heavily segregated, engage regular staff to keep them under surveillance, and house them in barrack-style huts with an allocation of approximately two square metres of space per man . . . after the seasonal workers depart in spring they are replaced by those just emerging on to the labour market from the schools, of whom there is often a rapid turnover' (ibid., p. 182). If correct, this is a picture of strong managerial control that would require some modification of the 'happy worker hypothesis' in the Japanese context.

Another view of long-term employment is that 'the kind of lifetime commitment that exists is more a norm, that is, contingent, than a value. Commitment is conditional, not ultimate or absolute' (Marsh and Mannari, 1976, p. 243). This contrasts with Kahn's view of the commitment quoted above. Marsh and Mannari conclude that for all employees, security, and for higher-status employees, job satisfaction, are the main sources of long-term commitment on the employee's part (ibid., pp. 247, 245). They point to a universalistic instrumental orientation towards stable rewards, rather than to the particularistic value-laden orientation towards 'loyalty' asserted by Abegglen and Kahn.

The following table shows the effect on exit rates of the degree of financial strength of companies and of the life chances that they can offer:

Table 2. Annual exit rate of male workers in manufacturing industry in Tokyo (1968)

Size of firm (No. of employees)	Exit rate %
30–49	24.4
50–299	20.2
300–999	19.0
1,000 +	8.4

Source: Azumi, 1969, p. 38.

In a study of exit rates in 25 leading companies, such as Ajinomoto, Asahi Optical Co., Mitsubishi Corporation, and the Industrial Bank of Japan, the contrast between male and female patterns of employment in large Japanese companies was clearly apparent.

Abegglen detected little change in the rates between 1956 and

1966 (Ballon, 1969, pp. 114-19). Table 3 shows the greatest conformity, with the 'loyalty' model of long-term employment at the top end of the scale where many of those who represent the system in ideological terms would be expected to be. The dismissals took place almost exclusively in one company that had financial difficulties. This response shows the workings of pragmatism, but does not necessarily exclude a feeling of commitment.

Table 3. Exit rates in 25 major companies (1966)

	Top managers %	Middle managers %	Male employees %	Female employees %
Retirement at normal retirement age of 55	100	56	36	2
Voluntary retirement	0	25	54	97
Moved to related company	0	7	5	0
Discharged	0	13	5	1
				(N = 269,000)

Source: Abegglen, in Ballon , 1969, p. 102.

There are methodological problems in measuring how far employees are really committed to a norm like long-term employment and this may not be the type of question best answered with a simple affirmative or negative. Tables 4 and 5, however, suggest that employee commitment is less than the normative, or value-laden, model proposes.

Tables 4 and 5 show that, although employment is less stable in the more depressed shipbuilding sphere, there is little difference in the percentages of employees who understand an employee who changed jobs. Marsh and Mannari consider that Japanese workers stay with a firm for the same reasons of security as Western workers, although this does not imply that all their attitudes are similar. It is unlikely that criticisms of job changers would be expressed either in the same way or to the same extent. Cole found that some workers dreamed of independence but were deterred from setting up small businesses by a

Table 4. Employee perception of job changing in one electric and one shipbuilding company

	Electric company %	Shipbuilding company %
Question: What do you think of an employee who voluntarily leaves to work in another company?		
1. His behaviour is not Japanese	2.8	1.9
2. He is not sincere (*makoto*)	8.3	5.1
3. He is an unscrupulous opportunist	8.1	4.2
4. I understand him	70.6	73.0
5. I would do the same if I could	10.4	15.8

Source: Marsh and Mannari, 1976, p. 235.

Table 5. Previous employment in one electric and one shipbuilding company

Number of firms worked in prior to the present one	Electric company %	Shipbuilding company %
1. None (present firm is the first)	76.3	38.6
2. One previous firm	9.6	28.3
3. Two previous firms	3.1	20.0
4. Three or more previous firms	11.0	13.1

Source: Marsh and Mannari, 1976, p. 325.

lack of capital (Cole, 1971, pp. 133–4). In the meantime they had to submit to management control.

Employees in a white-collar firm complained about the long hours and degree of company control, but they appeared to be integrated into the organization and to perform their tasks conscientiously. Organization and task appeared to provide a reference point; another was the family, and it was possible to observe the informal systems and networks involving members of the group, suggesting that it could be a mistake to take grumbling as evidence of deep dissatisfaction.

In the tight labour market conditions of 1980 only 8.7 per cent of employees in permanent jobs voiced a desire for change. Reasons cited by 29.4 per cent were long hours and physical hardship; low pay by 24 per cent, and lack of prospects by 13.6 per cent (Anglo-Japanese Economic Institute, 1980, p. 2). In the 1970s the ratio for changing employers in Japan was less than half what it was in the USA (Marsh and Mannari, 1976, p. 116).

Rather than accepting ideological or cultural models of long-term employment, an examination of the origins of the practice may shed more light. Some see it as one type of employment structure found in the mid-nineteenth century in, for example, merchant households (Taira, 1970, pp. 190-3). In his account of 'Employers' Organisations against the Labour Market' (ibid., pp. 111-27) he shows how the cartel of spinning firms, the Federation of Japanese Cotton Manufacturers, realized that it would be in their interests to combine in order to regulate labour. Exit rates from textile mills in the late nineteenth and early twentieth centuries were high (Saxonhouse, in Patrick, 1976, pp. 97-126). Members of the Federation therefore agreed to restrict the mobility of labour and to refrain from poaching (Yoshino, 1968, pp. 72-3).

The 'Origins of the Japanese Employment System' (Dore, 1973, pp. 375-403) also shows that the restriction of the mobility of labour by employers was a conscious managerial strategy, in reply to the shortage of skilled labour following the decision to industrialize in 1868. Employers saw that the demands of new industries for skilled labour would lead to increased labour costs unless mobility of labour could be reduced by tying employees to the firm. The ideology of loyalty to one lord, or to one employer, was already to hand as a well-developed normative underpinning for this policy (Bellah, 1957, pp. 13-16 etc.). A writer on Japanese society who does not underplay culture or values gives substantially the same account as Dore, pointing to the development of the tendency from the turn of the century and its acceleration after 1918 (Nakane, 1973, p. 16). Another writer refers to 'the reaction of employers needing stable, trained workers against the employment instability of the early years of industrialisation' (Gibbs, 1980, p. 23), although he does not mention the earlier origins of the practice.

With so many social changes after 1868, it is possible to agree with Gibbs that this 'was not a straightforward carry-over from feudal times', but a managerial policy adopted with management advantage in view (cf. Abegglen's view above). As well as restraining the price of skilled labour, the advantages to management were a confident expectation of a return on investment in training, and a high degree of control over employees who were prevented from changing employers.

Employers and officials typically expressed the problem, for management, of job changing in ideological terms. The Annual Report for Factory Supervision in 1919 complained that 'the virtue of long and diligent service has been supplanted by a propensity to change jobs' (quoted in Taira, 1970, p. 132); management's strategy has had to overcome resistance. In fact 'any industrial society . . . must have devices to penalise movement out of the system; otherwise training and other related costs become unmanageable. . . . Labour market arrangements must guarantee some degree of employment tenure if they are to motivate workers' (Cole, 1971, p. 127). Arguably Japanese management has been more successful here in exerting control than most.

As a result, Marxist critics have attacked the Nissan management's company manuals for being 'aimed at the ideological formation of the workers'; one is bound to ask whether this would not be the case in societies of which these critics would presumably approve. A passage quoted from the manual is explicit in its statement of management's requirements and the sanctions that are at its disposal: 'After leaving school and finding a place in an enterprise, there comes a time when one tires of this work. . . . But whether pleasant or not one must do the work that one has to do. Perseverance is necessary . . . those not worthy of confidence cannot but be dropped by the enterprise' (Halliday and McCormack, 1973, p. 183). Is this very different from what an employer in Victorian England might have said?

During the period of reconstruction after 1945 the Japanese employment system entered a new phase: the American authorities promoted the unions as legal and more equal bargaining partners, and welfare benefits etc. came to be expected as of right rather than being granted as paternalistic privileges. In return for stable employment, employees undertook to submit to management control, and it can be argued that, while stable remuneration benefited employees, management profited from the bargain by ensuring a high degree of compliance with its prerogatives. 'The various dimensions of the Japanese work ethic rest ultimately on a fundamental power relationship that brooks no misunderstanding' (Cole, 1979, p. 252). It is in the light of this power relationship that the other managerial systems connected with long-term employment should be seen.

3.2 The seniority system

The development of long-term employment after the First World War required 'an additional device . . . to hold workers to the company, for example, the seniority payment system based on duration of service, age and educational qualifications, with the added lure of a handsome payment on retirement' (Nakane, 1973, p. 16). In this strategy employers had the advantage of existing patterns of asymmetrical relations at their disposal, and Nakane comments that even in the most modern-looking firms 'there is a tendency for the closed social group to resemble the Japanese household in its dynamics'.

The seniority ranking system, linked with the pay system, is based on the principle of *nenko joretsu* ('ranking by years of experience'), but it does not mean that all who enter the company on the same day receive the same wages (Cole, 1971, p. 79); nor does it create a gerontocracy (Gibbs, 1980, p. 24). 'A man on the day he enters the company can predict with fair accuracy his wage and position in that company at any given year in the future' (Brown, in Lebra and Lebra, 1974, p. 175). Brown's data show a close correlation between age and rank, especially for senior management. This fits the norms of Japanese society well, where it is generally considered that young but inexperienced people, no matter how brilliant, should not be put in authority over older people. To do so would be as shocking as putting the son in authority over the father[1] and would disturb the hierarchical order. But as in the case of long-term employment, there are devices by which management can effectively put unsatisfactory performers on one side and pass them over for promotion, once they have attained the minimum formal rank expected. To some extent this resembles the situation in the British Army, where officers may expect to attain the minimum rank of captain or major but can also be posted out of the main stream, and where the establishment for field marshals is as limited as that for presidents and managing directors in Japan. A further resemblance is that the standard ranks in Japanese companies and other organizations have a general, and not a

Table 6. Standard ranks in a manufacturing company

Rank	English Equivalent
Shacho	President (General Manager etc.)
Fukushacho	Vice-President
Senmu Torishimariyaku	Senior Managing Director
Jomu Torishimariyaku	Managing Director
Torishimariyaku	Director
Bucho	Department Manager
Jicho	Deputy Department Manager
Kacho	Section Chief
Kakaricho	Sub-section Chief
Hancho	Foreman
Hira-Shain	Ordinary Employee

Source: Clark, 1979, pp. 105-6.

functional or specific significance. They are easly recognized and understood by outsiders.

'As a man passed up the standard ranks he naturally received better pay. . . . The size of his desk . . . increased. But for the most part the variations in privilege were continuous. There were remarkably few privileges available only to those above a certain station. . . . These arrangements were reflected in informal behaviour. Everyone was acutely aware of relative rank' (Clark, 1979, pp. 109-10). But section chiefs are expected to take their people out to bars and restaurants, and despite the extreme consciousness of rank one is less conscious of the class type of social distance that is found in the UK (personal experience, Osaka, 1963-6). The fine gradation of ranks and status which, according to Clark, integrate all members into the organization, and the lack of social distance in face-to-face interaction are aspects of the often discussed social 'egalitarianism' in Japanese companies. The norms of a given rank bind those in senior positions just as much as subordinates, and personal aggrandisement or 'throwing one's weight around' is not appreciated; the correct behaviour is to fill the role.

Just as long-term employment secured management control over employees and the return on investment in training them, so the seniority system enabled management to motivate them. Competition in Japanese society as a whole is intense (Funaki, 1981), particularly where prestige and material rewards are at stake. It has not therefore been hard for management to harness this competition to promotion; and the amount of retirement money depends on the amount of salary, i.e. position attained, as well as on years of service. This policy has applied to both blue-collar and white-collar companies, and has helped management to profit from its investment in employees (Vogel, 1980, pp. 132–3). The related pay system has been designed so that employees 'would be penalised for entering the firm midway in their work cycle' (Cole, 1979, pp. 18–19), i.e. they would have to start again at the bottom of the scale—a strong incentive to be loyal.

In Cole's view 'the permanent employment policy', of which seniority is a component, 'came packaged in a traditional ideology which was consonant with the rural value system of recent migrants'. The policy is frequently described in terms of these values, but Cole argues that it 'should always be viewed against the background of management and government power'. A more extreme view is that the long-term employment nexus 'sapped the vigour of the labour movement by catering to aspirations for security and status that could not be met by most trade unions in inter-war Japan' (Large, 1976, p. 55).

Since the 1950s, the competence demonstrated by Japanese management, and the ability of the companies to meet the rising expectations of their employees, have tended to confirm the long-term employment model. Increasing Japanese economic success, and awareness of the problems facing business in the USA,[2] Japan's recent mentor, have increasingly satisfied Japanese management theorists of the rightness of the Japanese model (Vogel, 1980, p. 134). The British Civil Service long-term employment seniority model is often held to represent stagnation, but with an outwardly similar system Japanese management has been successful in motivating employees, in innovating and in attaining consistently high rates of expansion.

In the light of this achievement of its aims by management, the issue of how far employees may have 'internalised the ideology of management familism' appears marginal. 'In any case we must speak of the *degree* of internalisation; it is not an all or nothing proposition' (Cole, 1979, p. 20).

3.3 Recruitment and selection

The expectation that employees in established firms will stay until retirement means that 'in initially hiring employees, the company aims to be as merciless as entrance examinations in selecting people of quality' (Vogel, 1980, p. 149). But many firms proclaim that 'our greatest asset is our people' (trading company, personal experience), and pride themselves on the house style of 'the Tanaka man' or 'the Sato man'. The ideological concept is that firms hire the total man, not merely his productive capacity, and that he is 'completely enveloped' (*marugakae*) in the organization (Nakane, 1973, p. 15).

Companies typically recruit directly from school or university and then train or mould employees to fit the organization's needs, as conceived by management (cf. Dore, 1973, pp. 31–2, 61–2). Management maintains close links with the authorities in schools and colleges, enabling them to learn whether applicants have had good records, or whether they should not be recruited. As with other aspects of personnel work (Inohara, 1977), recruitment is not seen as a discrete task, isolated from other organizational structures (cf. Northcott, 1950, p. 322; Guest and Horwood, 1980, p. 28).

The higher status of manufacturing, engineering, and commerce in Japan, compared to the UK, is often discussed (cf. Mant, 1979, p. 28), and a distinguishing feature of Japanese policies is the large-scale induction of university graduates by the major firms. Table 7 shows the greater proportion in private firms of Japanese graduates, whose prestige is higher in Japan than the graduate in the UK.

Table 7. University graduates entering employment in Japan, UK, and the USA (percentages by types of employment)

Type of employer	Japan 1958		UK 1950	USA 1960	
	Male %	Female %	Male %	Male %	Female %
Private firm	67	29	40	55	23
Education	16	58	38	28	65
Government	13	12	12	11	8
Others	4	1	11	6	4

Source: Azumi, 1969, p. 90.

The background to these figures is the greater proportion over-all of university graduates in Japan. In 1950 Japan already had twice the proportion of students as compared with the UK. In 1960 this rose to nearly three times the proportion (Azumi, 1969, p. 25). The present situation in British universities is likely to increase the disparity.

From management's viewpoint the rationale of recruiting graduates is that they can be expected to have intellectual capacity and to be highly motivated to succeed in entering a 'good' university (ibid., pp. 25-6; Dore, 1973, p. 48). The best universities constitute an intellectual, rather than a social, elite (Halmos, 1966, p. 91). Their ranking order is widely recognized, and the pattern for leading companies to hire graduates almost entirely from a narrow range of leading universities has its origins in the Meiji period (1868-1912). Table 8 shows how the Mitsui Mining Co. evaluated and rewarded graduates from different grades of university in 1927.

Table 8. Comparative starting salaries of white collar graduate employees, 1927

From Imperial University (Tokyo, Kyoto etc.)	75 yen
From Waseda and Keio Universities	65 yen
From other private universities	60 yen
From Kobe Higher Commercial School	60 yen
From other higher commercial schools	55 yen

Source: Passin, in Livingston *et al.*, 1976, Vol. 1, p. 262.

In 1937 it was estimated that a graduate from a top Imperial university had twice the chance of finding a satisfactory post as had a graduate of equal ability from a less prestigious institution (Livingston *et al.*, 1976, p. 260), demonstrating the importance of the competition to enter such a university, and the link between competition and achievement at school and in the company (cf. McIntyre, 1978, p. 29). Long-term employment and the seniority system do not provide an automatic 'escalator', as some come close to thinking (Brown, in Lebra and Lebra, 1974, p. 175).

In recruitment, management therefore looks for the potential in applicants, since specific skills and ways of working will be taught in the company itself. Table 9 makes clear the preponderant weight put by interviewers on potential.

Table 9. Points investigated in interviews in 502 companies

	%
Personality	82
Attitude	81
Philosophy of life	71
Knowledge, culture	66
Family background	49
Ability to express oneself	46
Reason for choosing firm	22
Others	16

Source: Azumi, 1969, p. 87.

Companies commonly employ a private firm of investigators to conduct a 'family investigation' (*katei chosa*) to ensure that there is no mental instability, irregularity, etc. that might make the applicant a bad risk (Dore, 1973, p. 50). Such managerial power, also exercised for life insurance proposals (personal experience, 1963), is not at the disposal of British management. It is acceptable in Japanese society as a whole and is not regarded as an invasion of privacy.

Those graduating from university are expected to apply to companies through their university appointments office (Azumi, 1969, p. 51) rather than directly, and although some applicants can make use of connections, most companies have strict rules not to employ relatives.

The way in which interviewees should behave when approaching management is described in a manual mentioned by Azumi: 'Stop *at attention* at the entrance, bow once and wait .... Your head must be straight, chin slightly pulled in. . . . Bow to the examiners again . . . bend your body *about twenty degrees*. Bend your head slightly further etc.' (Azumi, 1969, p. 83). In spite of the social equality discussed above, no data could give a clearer impression of the position of management *vis-à-vis* applicants and employees.

A discussion of Japanese management as a meritocratic elite[3] would lead too far away from the present argument, but already in the Taisho period (1912–26) 'then, as now, the national universities were geared to the recruitment of a national elite' (Duus, in Livingston *et al.*, 1976, Vol. 1, p. 271). It is against this background that Japanese management in the post-war era formulated its recruitment policies and procedures, with the leading firms creaming off the elite.

This practice does not appear to have led to the problems of cleavage associated with UK management and society, partly because of the relatively high proportions of lower-income group members obtaining entry to the top government universities. Beliefs in the efficacy of willpower, rather than home background or innate intelligence (Gibbs, 1980, pp. 20-1), may reflect the chances that the post-war meritocracy has provided. This serves to reinforce the legitimacy of Japanese managers, who are generally regarded as owing their positions to their own achievements, and to make the power enjoyed by management more acceptable. Strong but competent management may avoid employee relations problems more easily than weak, less educated and less objectively legitimated management. In these respects Japanese management exhibits a high degree of rationality.

3.4 Salary and bonus systems

'In the paternalistic-lifetime commitment model of the Japanese firms, pay is based primarily on seniority, not on job classification' (Marsh and Mannari, 1976, p. 307). A large Japanese firm 'considers that it is buying, not a skill, but a lifetime's work' (Dore, 1973, p. 111). The salary curve for regular male employees rises slowly up to the expected age for marrying (mid- to late twenties), reaches its peak at age 40-4, when family responsibilities are likely to be heaviest, and declines (except for directors etc.) when children will usually be financially independent (cf. Japanese Government, 1976, p. 394).

Salaries for managers and blue-collar and white-collar employees are paid monthly, encouraging employees to take a long view (Ballon, 1969, p. 126). The payment of a lump sum on retirement reinforces this tendency and conceptually retirement money, bonuses, and salary belong together. All are regarded as part of earnings, not as something extra; while from management's point of view, bonuses and retirement money not only motivate employees and increase managerial control, but also represent the deferred payment of wages, which helps the cash flow. 'The Japanese employee has, because of the wage system, invested heavily in the enterprise' (ibid., p. 132). No wonder he is often described as feeling a strong commitment.

'Management sees many advantages in pinning down a work-force in which it has invested substantial amounts in training' (ibid., p. 164). In spite of management worries about the cost of long-term employment in the period of slower economic growth since the oil crisis, unions have been pressing for the raising of the retirement age. By 1978 one-third of firms had raised it to 60, while 40 per cent had kept it at 55 (Gibbs, 1980, p. 24). Although this is an increased cost to management, it reinforces managerial control by increasing the dependence of employees. This issue will be discussed further in the conclusion.

Pay in large companies in Japan is based on the factors shown in Table 10, and these principles are expressed in monthly salaries as shown in Table 11, where company involvement in provisions

Table 10. Determinants of pay in major Japanese companies

1. Educational achievement (determining starting pay)
2. Length of service
3. Age (largely coterminous with service, but separately recognized)
4. Sex
5. Merit (the supervisor's assessment of attitude, diligence, etc.)
6. Family responsibilities
7. Function in the firm (the newest determinant: an incentive component comparable with British differentials, 'If a market in labour existed')

Source: Dore, 1973, pp. 111–12.

Table 11. Components of pay in major Japanese companies

1. Basic pay (annual rate of increase negotiated by unions for all employ-ees, including management)
2. Adjustment pay (for rank)
3. Incentive pay (generally on group basis)
4. Attendance allowance (for each day worked: deducted for each day missed)
5. Family allowance (cf. British state system)
6. Regional allowance (e.g. Tokyo)
7. Travel allowance (fares to and from work, cf. British tax laws)
8. Housing allowance (if company housing not applicable, cf. British council housing)
9. Overtime (legal minimum 125%)
10. Miscellaneous (extra work, sick leave, etc.)

Source: Ballon, 1969, pp. 126–34.

for family and housing and management control of absenteeism by means of the attendance allowance may be noted. The latter also acts as a deterrent to taking the full theoretical entitlement of holidays, quite apart from the potential harm this would cause to an employee's promotion prospects. The average summer holiday is currently four to five days, while in the exceptional cases of companies such as Honda, Canon, and Ricoh, it is nine days (Anglo-Japanese Economic Institute, 1980). Japanese management has a high degree of control, but proclaims an ideology of the unity of the enterprise and the fulfilment of its common task; while British management, with a lower degree of control, blusters about 'management's right to manage'.

'To put in overtime willingly is regarded as a manifestation of loyalty to the enterprise; it is interpreted as a sign that one is eager to contribute to overall performance'(Ballon, 1969, p. 151). Overtime in Japan is the norm, even if it implies a mixture of social and work activity with colleagues (Vogel, 1980, p. 152). Work and leisure are less sharply differentiated than in the Anglo-American context (Whitehill and Takezawa, 1968, p. 347). Management evidently feels the financial cost is worth the control over employees it provides. The practice fosters the solidarity of the work group and therefore its potential team effort, and the converse also holds—taking holidays is selfish betrayal of the team (cf. Bellah, 1957, p. 36). But in spite of management propagation of the ideology of overtime and commitment there has been a rise in 'my homeism' (*mai homshugi*), or the concentration on private life (Vogel, 1969, pp. 35-7; Nakane, 1973, p. 132).

In one factory, senior employees were obliged to curtail their New Year holiday (the equivalent of Christmas in Britain and the USA) to come to work, 'but there was no point in their complaining at this treatment, because the company had so complete a control of their lives' (Clark, 1979, p. 186). 'The attitude [of middle-level employees financially dependent on a company in a tight situation] reflected their preoccupation with commitment, freedom and welfare, and was frequently a fiercely illogical combination of loyalty and resentment' (ibid., p. 187); an interesting example of ambivalence towards authority.

In addition to salaries, bonuses are paid at the New Year (the largest) and in the summer, not only by companies but by all established employing organizations. The English word is used but the meaning has been 'Japanized', and it is generally a flat rate applicable to all employees, based on the performance of the enterprise as a whole (JETRO, 1980, p. 18). The regularity of the bonus negotiations and payment throughout employing organizations, the regular entry into employment at the end of the academic year every April, and the regularity of the setting of the annual wage increase in the same month, are part of the national system of wage determination. Management planning is thus facilitated, and adds up to a rational, regular structure.

The total amount of bonuses may add up to another three months' salary, or more in a good year but less in a bad one. When salaries are correspondingly small 'the bonus is what enables the salaryman to keep the pot boiling' (sales company employee, Osaka, 1960s, personal communication). Table 12 shows the amounts of bonus with reference to educational background and length of service of male employees in one company.

Table 12. Bonus by educational background and length of service

Educational background	Age	Years of service	Amounts ¥	Monthly salary multiplied by
University	25	3	103,754	3.0
graduate	35	13	219,886	3.3
	50	27	453,095	3.8
High School	25	7	38,284	3.0
graduate	35	17	183,823	3.1
(white-collar)	50	33	369,249	3.6
Middle School	25	10	88,400	2.7
graduate	35	21	135,403	2.7
(blue-collar)	50	36	202,921	2.9

Source: Ballon, 1969, pp. 141–4.

It is inadmissible to think of recruitment, pay, promotion, and seniority systems as other than functionally integrated aspects of the same type of managerial control. The nature of these systems enable organizations to deal with situations where competent subordinates have to work under less competent superiors (Yoshino, 1968, p. 72). They know that they will be recognized at the right moment and in the meantime they do not threaten the position, prestige, or earnings of the superior (Vogel, 1980,

p. 143). Potential jealousy and lack of team cohesiveness is also avoided by the complexity—under the seniority, long-term employment type of pay system—of the different allowances. Employees are frequently unable to calculate how much their colleagues are earning (Dore, 1973, p. 318).

It would, of course, be wrong to have too rigid a conception of Japanese pay systems, particularly in view of the pragmatic realism that characterizes much of Japanese managerial activity. 'In recent years there has been a move towards pay systems which explicitly allow for ability and merit' (Gibbs, 1980, p. 22). This is not the same thing as a lessening of control because the determination of employee performance still depends on middle management. In 1958 retiring workers in manufacturing earned five and a half to six times as much as new entrants; by 1967 the ratio had declined to between four and a half and five (ibid.).

In 1966 Toyota changed its age and length of service-related pay system to one based on job content, ability, and cost of living, but in practice 'the measures are also vague enough to lead one to believe that informally seniority may play a significant role' (Cole, 1979, pp. 176-7). In the same year Ballon argued that technological change, shortages of certain types of personnel, and other factors, would compel management to increase the ability component of pay, although this would not be popular with older workers and could create difficulties with unions. At the same time he voiced the opinion that the firms where the long-term employment system was most deeply entrenched were those that had contributed the most to Japan's economic advance. He concluded that 'it is not likely that the guaranteed life income approach to the remuneration of industrial work will be abandoned altogether in Japan' (Ballon, 1969, pp. 164-5).

The problem for management is perhaps how to get the best of both worlds; how to get the performance that it is believed increasing attention to ability pay would foster, while retaining all the advantages of a stable, dependent workforce. Against its 'dread of the base-up' (the annual increase of basic salaries) (ibid., p. 164), management must balance its fears of the unintended consequences of modifying one part of the system. If employees are increasingly to be rewarded by individual ability pay, can management also appeal to their loyalty, their sense of commitment to the group, etc.? Some in any case see the 'pervasive, conservative influence' of the long-term employment seniority pattern as diluting the new schemes, as in Cole's example above (Patrick and Rosovsky, 1976, p. 870 *et seq.*).

Without going to the lengths of seeing some special 'inner consistency' (Abegglen, 1958) in Japanese managerial systems, it is clear that employment, recruitment, pay, and ideology, as discussed above, are intertwined and that it could be dangerous for management to modify one, unless it is prepared to run the risk of disturbing the other patterns that it has found to work to its advantage. Referring to British interest in adopting some aspects of Japanese managerial systems, Dore points to how such systems fit together and to the 'pitfalls of piecemeal borrowings' (Dore, 1973, p. 10).

The systems discussed so far reflect a high degree of managerial control, which it is not in management's interest to change. They aim at the training, motivation, and retention of employees in the context of the maximization of the individual's contribution to the task of his work group and company. Older staff, those who have already achieved promotion, and those who know they will achieve it under the present system, have a vested interest in preventing major changes. Such changes would require major modifications in ideology and values and, although it is wrong to be deterministic, it is hard to see what the net gain for management would be. Why jeopardize control?

3.5 Training and promotion

'Training' in Britain normally refers to technical training; in Japan it includes *seishinteki* (spiritual) training. In Japanese schools, universities, and companies, new entrants attend *nyushashiki* (an entrance ceremony). The president makes an admonitory address; the spokesman for the entrants reads a speech pledging the intake's best efforts. The degree of formality, reminiscent of religious or military ceremonial in the UK, makes an indelible impression on an observer. The purpose of the ceremony is 'consciously designed to reinforce the company spirit' (Noda, in Vogel, 1975, p. 141), and the 'handing over' of the young employee from the family to the company (Dore, 1973, p. 61) is part of the *rite de passage*. After the entrance ceremony, induction training starts. The premise, which is entirely congruent with the long-term employment seniority system, is that young employees starting work for the first time are 'more easily moulded to suit a company's requirements' (Nakane, 1973, p. 17).

Such an attitude may also apply to technical training where there is a specific approach to work organization and factory discipline. 'Sony likes to train its workers from scratch in its own way' (Lyons, 1976, p. 176); a point of view significant because Sony is famous as an innovator and, as a post-war firm, had no old house style to fall back on. Part of the Sony training system, found in other manufacturing companies, is that all new employees, including future managers, spend three months on the production line.

In banks and trading companies, graduates similarly start on the basic tasks and then, under a system of job rotation, are given work experience in different departments. This fosters their careers as generalists, or 'Tanaka men' and enables them to make personal contacts while learning from experienced superiors. On the general Japanese model of the *sensei* (teacher) and the *deshi* (pupil), the *sempai* (superior) has a diffuse responsibility for the progress and welfare of the *kohai* (junior), a relationship that persists into later life and which may help the erstwhile junior's subsequent career. The diffuse, blurred, open-ended nature of the relationship is characteristic of other relationships in Japanese society involving *on* ('a permanent obligation').

The duration and type of induction training depends on how much time management believes should be spent on it, and what methods it favours. At one bank, the course for male entrants was three months, while for women it was two weeks (Rohlen, 1974, pp. 192–211). The course culminated in a physically exhausting endurance run. Tasks such as cleaning, with room inspections by instructors, were emphasized.

At a manufacturing company, the persistent theme was 'fighting spirit', a slogan of the former Imperial Navy, interpreted as determination and group loyalty. Rohlen described the nature of the course as 'similar to the US Marine Corps but with greater emphasis on conformity and group loyalty' (in Lebra and Lebra, 1974, pp. 332–41).

The typical features of induction programmes in major companies are group residence, team activities, physical effort, and the indoctrination of the history, principles and *shaze*, *shakun* ('mottoes') of the firm. The aim is 'to make each employee realize that he is a member of an organization'. The training itself is similar to that 'imposed on recruits in more normative organisations, such as a military school or religious order' (Azumi, 1969, pp. 106-7); an unusual analogy for a Japanese writer to draw, although it would occur to members of British, American, or French society.

According to Nakane, and reflecting the prominence given to attitude in selection interviews, it has always been believed that the 'right' attitude greatly affects productive power. Since the 1960s many companies have sent new entrants to Zen temples or to the Ground Self-Defence Force (i.e. the Army) 'for periods of character building discipline' (T. Ishida, 1971, p. 42). Even a writer like Ishida (1971), who expresses some misgivings about other aspects of Japanese society, makes no comment on this use by private companies of Army facilities. Management, as in Rohlen's bank, may feel that post-war youth is getting 'soft' and that control needs reasserting.

It would be superfluous to quote the numerous remarks on the group orientation of Japanese social organization (Halmos, 1966, pp. 202-12, etc.). 'Japan was and largely still is a "groupish" society' (Dore, 1973, p. 230). Company induction training seeks to utilize mechanisms that are already available in the wider society, and an American observer notes 'the pervasiveness of collectivity orientation' in Japanese social life. This means that students, for example, are encouraged to think of themselves as members of a group rather than as individuals; and when they enter a company the lesson is restated with fresh emphasis, rather than being anything new. 'A company that has high solidarity among its employees can never take full credit for this, no matter how much it emphasizes group ideology in its company policy and practices' (Marsh and Mannari, 1976, p. 179) because of previous socialization processes (De Vos, 1973).

In one year no more than fifty-seven employees out of 85,000 were dismissed at Hitachi. While a rebel in a British factory may become a folk hero by 'acting out anti-authoritarian fantasies', similar behaviour in the 'totalitarian' atmosphere of a Japanese factory may lead workmates to 'shame or brainwash' the delinquent into behaving. Or he may leave voluntarily, unable 'to stand the moral pressure' (Dore, 1973, p. 186). On the other hand, interviews with workers showed that they perceived a distinction between their aims and the company's interests

(Marsh and Mannari, 1976, p. 210) and other accounts (e.g. Clark, 1979, pp. 159-164) provide evidence of scepticism despite training programmes.

Yet training provides the employee with communal experience of his new group and 'a basis for a feeling of competence' as a member of it (Vogel, 1971, p. 161). The *experience* of teamwork, competition, and team loyalty, rather than the one-sided process of being lectured at, is considered important by management (Tanaka, 1981). By investing money in it, management demonstrates its belief that this type of training contributes to organizational performance.

New entrants in larger firms learn the company song, which is sung in factories before work starts in the morning, when shopfloor workers pledge their best efforts, and on other official company occasions.

> *The Matsushita Company Song*
> For the building of a new Japan,
> Let's put our strength and mind together,
> Doing our best to promote production.
> Sending our goods to the people of the world,
> Endlessly and continuously,
> Like water gushing from a fountain,
> Grow, industry, grow, grow, grow!
> Harmony and sincerity!
> Matsushita Electric.
> (Quoted in Kahn, 1970, p. 252.)

'Building a new Japan' has been the ideal of a post-war society and the first line identifies the company with the patriotic aspect of industrial renewal and development. Management emphasis on productivity in 'to promote production' is explicit, as is the reference to the attitude and effort necessary to achieve it. 'The people of the world' refers to the ideals of internationalization and the raising of living standards, and also to the corporate goal of economic growth, stressed in the repetitive 'grow, grow, grow' (cf. Galbraith, 1972; Bendix, 1974, pp. 198-200, 434-6, 441-4). *Wa* (harmony) is a major value of Japanese social organization —specifically group harmony and harmony with 'the Japanese way'—to which *makoto* (sincerity) also refers. The wording of this type of song is therefore not fortuitous; it is a statement of managerial ideology.

In the Hitachi example 'training', in the English sense of the word, was dealt with by a fully developed system aimed at the progressive upgrading of employees' expertise at different levels. The system included Hitachi's own Industrial Training School, a School of Industrial Studies, and the placing of ten Hitachi students in overseas universities and eight domestically, most of the latter being engaged in contract research for the company (Dore, 1973, pp. 50-67). The rationale for such developed in-house schemes can be understood in the light of what has already been said about long-term employment.

A recent account of types of training in use (Sasaki, 1981, pp. 33-49) underlines the scant use of business departments belonging to Japanese universities. Only 16 per cent of universities have a department of business administration, and students registered with them account for only 7 per cent of enrolments. The reason is management belief in on-the-job training, or 'learning by doing', including the practice of job rotation already mentioned. Companies make use of short external courses, but on-the-job training has been practised in Japan since the early period of industrialization, when it was normal to become familiar with technology by such pragmatic processes.

The preference of major companies for their own training institutes, where they can design training to meet the needs of their company and no other, is a contributory factor in the failure of university business departments to develop further.[5] Large companies, as in the Toray example quoted by Sasaki, may organize training with considerable scope, but the figures in Table 13 suggest that on-the-job training suffers from lack of time.

Table 13. Duration of on-the-job training

	1 day %	1-3 days %	3-7 days %	7-28 days %	month+ %
Top executives	37	30	20	3	10
Managers	26	35	26	6	7
Specialists	20	25	40	5	10
Rank and file	15	26	40	4	15

Source: Institute of Business Administration and Management, Tokyo, 1974 (quoted in Sasaki, 1981, p. 45).

Table 14. Employees' satisfaction with company training programmes and reasons for dissatisfaction

	Technical specialists, researchers & managers %	Office workers %	Foremen & supervisors %	Skilled workers %	Ordinary workers %	Others %
Satisfied	22.8	18.7	42.4	27.7	26.0	23.3
Dissatisfied	48.8	40.3	32.5	40.3	33.6	28.8
Neither	24.9	33.2	19.7	25.2	34.9	32.9
No answer	3.5	7.9	5.3	6.9	5.5	15.1
Reasons for dissatisfaction						
Training only for the present job	15.7	19.6	19.2	35.2	38.8	38.1
No systematic training	61.4	54.7	51.5	36.3	37.5	47.6
To attend after working hours & on holidays	9.0	4.1	7.1	10.4	7.9	14.3
Limited number of trainees	7.1	7.4	10.1	12.6	11.3	—
Limited class of trainees	17.6	25.7	21.2	30.8	25.4	19.0
Others	16.7	8.8	13.1	6.0	13.8	28.6

Source: Japanese Ministry of Labour, 1972 (quoted in Sasaki, 1981, p. 46).

Considerable dissatisfaction with training at different levels is shown in Table 14. It will be noted that the principal cause of dissatisfaction is 'no systematic training'.

The major part played by on-the-job training in the case of managers is apparent in Table 15. Data on the aims of management training, from the same survey, show that the acquisition of specialist knowledge related to a specific function is not one of the highest priorities (see Table 16). Union relations appear to require little additional attention. For the technical and vocational training of ordinary employees there are also state schemes.

Table 15. Types of management training in Japanese enterprises

Method of training Number of employees	In-house group training %	On-the-job training %	Job rotation %	Business school & other training institute %	Subsidy for self-study %
Less than 300	34	38	2	4	19
300–999	34	35	5	3	23
1,000–2,999	43	38	4	1	13
3,000–9,999	38	44	5	1	10
More than 10,000	28	51	11	0	10
Total	37	40	5	2	15

Source: Keidanren (employers' organization, quoted in Funaki, 1981, p. 10).

Training and promotion are conceptually interlinked, but in large Japanese companies promotion is also determined by the ranking system and recruitment policies, especially in regard to graduates. Allowing for the four years spent at Japanese universities, Table 17 shows that graduates enjoy quicker promotion; it is asserted that few non-graduates will achieve such promotion in any case (Odaka, 1975, p. 56).[6] They would be especially unlikely to do so in the elite banks and trading companies, which employ graduates in regular annual intakes from the leading national and private universities generally regarded as the producers of the intellectual elite.

It was pointed out above that Japanese firms are not gerontocracies, in spite of deference to age in the wider society. Japanese

Table 16. Aims of management training in Japanese enterprises

	Would-be manager %	New manager %	Experienced manager %
Wider view	4	2.4	6.4
Specific job knowledge/ability	12.6	7.3	8.8
Decision making/problem solving	9.6	9.8	13.6
Managing change	3	1.6	5.4
Basic/advanced management knowledge	19.2	30.3	24.1
Deepen basic/advanced management knowledge	8.1	2.8	7.1
Motivating subordinates	11.6	6.9	7.5
Leadership and organization management	26.3	33.3	19.4
Union matters	2	3.7	3.4
Others	3.5	4.1	8.2

Source: Keidanren (employers' organization, quoted in Funaki, 1981, p. 11.

Table 17. Average number of years required for promotion

From joining firm to becoming:	Overall average in years	Firm with 10,000 + employees (N = 22)	Firm with up to 10,000 employees (N = 245)
Section Chief			
University graduates	8.6	10.5	7.7
Others	14.0	17.4	12.3
Department Manager			
University graduates	15.0	17.9	14.2
Others	23.0	26.5	21.2
Office Manager			
University graduates	23.9	26.2	23.5
Others	31.7	34.8	29.9

Note: Total N = 267 (Azumi, 1969, p. 42).

organizations contain their number of 'passengers', but employees know that their performance is constantly being monitored and that their next assignment depends on this assessment. Given the lack of functional differentiation between line and personnel managers, line managers spend much time evaluating their subordinates. The evaluation concentrates on the four criteria for promotion: ability, attendance, attitude or personality, and length of service. Each factor carries equal weight, resulting in ability being outweighed by the three others (ability is equivalent to technical competence).

According to the workings of the ranking system already described, members of an intake entering the company in a given year should be promoted as far as a certain minimum level at a determined time, but when slower economic growth results in fewer positions being available, alternative strategies have to be adopted. These include the conscious proliferation of, largely honorific, intermediate titles, or the creation of teams and *ad hoc* specialist work groups (Inohara, 1977, pp. 20–1). As with 'lifetime' employment, management has methods of ensuring the necessary elasticity while preserving the formal premise and structure of the system. Given the importance of status, or 'face', in Japanese society, these techniques can be essential in prestige and value terms. The expectations of members of the firm must be met, and management must be seen to be running it in a traditional way. At the same time, the acute consciousness of rank, mentioned above, and the political skill of organization members in identifying where power resides, make it unlikely that status and authority will be confused.

Following the arguments of Abegglen and others that the long-term employment system is not rational in terms of production, similar questions could be raised about the promotion system, which has an element of the same 'length of service' principle. If the Japanese promotion system were based almost entirely on length of service this would be a valid objection, but the reality does not follow such a stereotype. Where management closely controls and assesses employees, where competition is keen, and where employees are highly motivated, because of the structural and peer group pressures already described, length of service is a functional criterion. Employees who are motivated and controlled increase their technical competence, human relations skills,[7] leadership qualities, and status in the eyes of fellow members of the organization during their company careers. 'Like the wage system the *nenko* ('years of experience') promotion system is not inherently irrational' (Cole, 1971, p. 101).

3.6 Welfare paternalism and welfare corporatism

In 1898 Shimura Gentaro, a director of the Industrial Bank of Japan, urged managers to profit from the example of industrialism in the West. He recommended 'socially responsible patterns of management' i.e. enlightened self-interest, and 'family like relationships, which we have at present in Japan', i.e. the selective reinterpretation of traditional social behaviour and values. Having considered conditions in Western industrial societies, his aim was 'to prevent the kind of antagonism between capitalists and workers which results in such things as strikes' (quoted in Dore, 1973, p. 393).

Such a conscious managerial strategy was initiated by Muto Sanji, general manager of the Kanegafuchi Spinning Company (Kanebo), between 1902 and 1907, whose aim was to reduce high desertion rates[8] (Saxonhouse, in Patrick, 1976, pp. 76-126). Many of the schemes were modelled on those of Western firms. The sick pay, pension, and welfare fund was patterned after Krupp's, a firm known in Germany until recent times for company welfare and employee loyalty. Other features were inspired by the National Cash Register Corporation in the USA (Dore, 1973, p. 395) and welfare schemes at Cadbury and Lever in the UK (Hazama, n.d., pp. 13-14). Muto's 'welfare paternalism' attracted considerable attention, but its success was limited; the desertion rate of 68.5 per cent for female employees in 1914 was higher than that reported in 1897, before the scheme was introduced.

As late as 1910 'management faced the task of creating what Bendix (1974, p. 204) has called "an internalized ethic of work performance"' (Yoshino, 1968, p. 77). One way to do this was to stress the reciprocity of the employee's duty to the enterprise in return for the welfare paternalism that it provided. The strategy had the advantage of providing a modern analogy of the reciprocity that ideally existed between superior and subordinate prior to industrialization: benevolence in return for loyally carrying out wishes or commands (cf. Bellah, 1957).

'In many large companies the adoption of corporatist welfare devices was a relatively late and conscious event'. The devices were known generically as 'the American Plan',[9] clearly revealing their foreign origin. The promotion of the Plan in the 1920s was accompanied by the propagation of an ideology: 'observing the lack of government social security and appealing to what was still mainly a rural, family-based society' (Patrick, 1976, p. 486). Management adopted the Plan as a pragmatic solution to problems of control, while describing it as a form of familism or benevolence, 'yet . . . the continued existence of pre-industrial values and practices made management choice of these policies, and worker acceptance of them, more likely' (Cole, 1971, p. 175). As in the case of other Japanese managerial systems, expediency was not the whole explanation, which can only be completed by taking 'value rationality' into account, referring to the existing society.

In post-war Japan the expression 'welfare paternalism' is no longer appropriate for managerially controlled corporations; 'welfare corporatism' is more suitable. Companies provide housing, sports and hobby facilites, medical care, subsidized concert tickets, outings, holiday bonus, shops where goods (especially those produced by the company or its associates) are sold at competitive prices, a marriage-arranging service, etc. They pay statutory and non-statutory welfare costs, such as health insurance, and make occasional payments of the traditional type on births, deaths, and marriages (Ballon, 1969, pp. 127-33, 146-8). At Hitachi the total expenditure on welfare, including housing, medical care, recreation, and occasional payments, was 8.5 per cent of total labour costs; in the median British firm in the sample it was 2.5 per cent *including sick pay* (Dore, 1973, p. 203).

Young employees may be sceptical of company welfare schemes, but once settled with a family etc. they are locked into the system. Company savings schemes, such as that mentioned in 'The Cycle of Goodness', directly benefit companies by providing low-cost finance, although control has been tightened as a result of the scandals that occurred in the 1960s, when several bankrupt companies lost their employees' savings (Cole, 1971, p. 175). The relatively low level of government social welfare provisions (Iida, 1981), leading to high rates of personal saving (Patrick, 1976, p. 450), indirectly provides investment capital for business (Cole, 1979, p. 247). Thrift was an officially promoted value in pre-industrial Japan, which government and management could later invoke, and it created a pattern of accumulation[10] (Bellah, 1957, pp. 126, 144–6).

Company welfare fosters dependence on the company, as government welfare in the UK fosters dependence on the state or the bureaucracy. Self-reliance in the form of personal savings in Japan and individualism in Britain coexist with structures and ideologies of dependency, but welfare corporatism is not identical with fringe benefits. It is more of a conscious policy aimed at the control and motivation of employees. They are first impelled to compete to enter the company, then to achieve its aims and to continue to do so in order to enjoy the benefits that accrue to them. Leisure activities subsidized by Japanese companies, such as martial arts for male employees and tea ceremony and flower arrangement lessons for women, enable the company to pervade non-working hours. 'Competing for the employee's time is a key management issue' (Noda, in Vogel, 1975, p. 140). Management 'envelops' the employee in the company.

British entrepreneurial deviants, such as Owen, Cadbury, and Rowntree, are often dismissed as 'exceptions' or as being too 'idealistic'; but it may be asked whether, from the viewpoint of managerial control, the Japanese welfare corporatist strategy is not in the long run more 'rational'. In the relative absence of government welfare, public housing, and a more mobile type of labour market, management takes the initiative in binding the employee to the firm and in providing strong material incentives for him to perform well in it, so that he can finally collect the full amount of retirement money and/or pension due to him.

3.7 Decision-making processes

In the preceding discussion of the long-term employment, seniority, welfare-corporatism model, it has been argued that functionalism, taken as a concept unrelated to a specific social context, tends to break down because what is functional in a Japanese organizational or social context may well be dysfunctional in a similar British, American, or French context. This principle can be applied to decision making in particular.

It has been asserted by a Japanese authority that the traditional view of organizations is to see them as 'organic unities' or 'natural phenomena' instead of human or social products. This view provides the organizations with 'an all-embracing tendency' that generates solidarity but which leads to the simultaneous weakness of an *appearance* of participation. 'The activity is not spontaneous. It is rather the result of passive obedience to the leader or to the principle of group conformity. Behind the outward appearance of activity lies a certain apathy' (T. Ishida, 1971, pp. 62-3).

Ishida considers that the theory of the natural development of the will of the organization from the members' conformity has led to a blindness towards the empirical nature of decision making. He sees '*carte blanch* leadership . . . based on the unconditional and unanimous dependence of the rank and file on their leader'. By definition this is an authoritarian concept, consistent with the structure and process of managerial control discussed above. He points out that formal organizational procedures, based on the decision of the majority and the right of the minority to be heard, have not been considered important (ibid., pp. 100, 63-4).

Without embracing the synchronic cultural pattern (Benedict, 1961) concept, Ishida's assertions make it necessary to investigate decision making in its social context, instead of merely regarding it as a technical or functional procedure. The ideal typical structure of a Japanese corporation and its ideal typical decision-making processes are empirically linked, and they continually act and react on one another.

The main official type of corporate decision-making process is the consensual, collective model (Yoshino, 1968, pp. 254-72; Glazer, in Ballon, 1969, pp. 88-90) known as *ringi* ('submitting a proposal to a superior and receiving his approval; deliberation and discussions'). It is commonly referred to as a system, but the term is too static or mechanical. In the real world its dynamics cannot be taken for granted, and it is preferable to refer to it as a 'process'. In practice *ringi* is not a single system but a principle that allows management the choice of a selection of pragmatic options. Too much emphasis on the *making* of decisions may also obscure the equally important point of how they are, or are not, implemented.[11] The problem is to decide to what extent decision making in Japanese corporations, compared with Anglo-American types, represents differences of degree or differences of kind.

Ringi has often been seen as a contributory factor in the

taking of correct decisions commanding wide support and as an illustration of 'the group nature of the Japanese decision-making process and, in general, the group nature of Japanese society' (Glazer, op. cit., p. 88). A British authority argues that business organizations do not exist in a social vacuum, and that differences in employment systems, which affect decision making, are significantly related to societal differences (Dore, 1973, pp. 13, 280), even though the precise relationship is not a deterministic one and should not be stereotyped by some sort of 'catch-all' explanation. 'Belongingness as the ultimate need of the individual', for example, has been discussed in an American corporate context (Whyte, 1960, pp. 11, 48–76 etc.). Other societies also show tendencies of 'mechanical solidarity' (Durkheim, 1966, pp. 70–132).

In the *ringi* model the *kiansha* ('initiator') of a proposal is typically a section chief (see position on Table 6). Section members research the subject and discuss it with him. When he is satisfied, he passes it up the line. Participation of junior employees is a major factor in training and motivation, and is a reason for the model being described as 'bottom up' decision making, in contrast to the 'top down', Anglo-American, model (Noda, in Vogel, 1975, pp. 127–8). The *ringi* document is stamped with managers' formal seals at ascending levels on its progress up to the final authority, the president—although, as will be discussed, the allocation of responsibility is ambiguous (Brown, in Lebra and Lebra, 1974, pp. 180–1 etc.). Whether the formal stamping of the document means 'seen', 'consulted', or 'approved', etc., only those with an inside knowledge of a given organization can tell.

Such formal descriptions of the ideal operation of the model unfortunately omit the informal processes of bargaining, persuasion, the seeking of support, the long-term trading of favours, and reciprocal obligations etc., that are frequently the crucial part of the process. Generically these activities are termed *nemawashi* ('binding up the roots'): the image of a tree that will survive transplanting only if everything is adequately prepared first. The proposal is only committed to paper in the formal shape of the *ringi* document when the negotiation process is complete. Approval of the document should at that stage be a formality, though this is not always so in practice. The use of personal relationships and the long-term trading of favours, resembling the establishment of credit that can be called in even much later, is specific to Japanese society and assumes long-term membership in the same organization. Analogous personal contacts, among, for example, merchant bankers, are not unknown in British society, but their scale is restricted by comparison (Teramoto, personal communication). Nor do they refer to a widely recognized social code of obligation and the duty to repay favours on a commensurate scale.

A president may have to call for a compromise if an inter-departmental dispute arises, or reject a proposal altogether if it is financially unsound. In principle *ringi* should be applied to all types of decision: prolonged *nemawashi* is required in the case of major issues, but trivia are dealt with without such discussion (Dore, 1973, p. 248).

The formal resemblances between *ringi* and procedures in the British Civil Service etc. have led some to question its efficiency, but this interpretation would appear to overlook the significance of the informal processes, as well as the apparent ability of Japanese corporations to make good decisions and to carry them through (cf. Fukutake, 1974, p. 79; Patrick, 1976, p. 456). It can be argued that the major corporations, who are the greatest users of *ringi*, are among those who have contributed the most to post-war economic advance.

Japanese managers are indefatigable students of the works of Western management theorists like Drucker, McGregor, Likert, Herzberg, etc. (Cole, 1979, pp. 130–2) and they have pragmatically adopted some features of American systems, such as Quality Circles and Zero Defect strategies; but after the American-inspired 'management boom' of the 1960s many companies that had tried to supplant *ringi* restored it in full. Possibly they felt increasing self-confidence in Japanese methods as a result of Japan's economic success. *Ringi* may also be a more rational and effective way of making decisions than it appears in formal logic. In Western companies with a Galbraithian (1972) 'techno-structure', there is considerable use of decision making by committee, involving functional specialists rather than all departments as in Japan, but both in Japanese and Western corporations 'decision making can be more or less collective according to what is being decided and in what context' (Clark, 1979, p. 127). The difference is that a meeting of individuals in the British or American sense, called together at a given moment for a specific purpose, is not identical with a group in a Japanese context, to which the members are bound without limitation on time or commitment.

In practice *ringi* can be short circuited in case of urgency. The president, perhaps with some senior managers, takes the decision and circulates the information afterwards. Including all managers is essential if the unity of the management team is to be maintained; a manager who feels left out will create difficulties and can do much covert damage. 'The more urgent a decision, the more likely it will be made according to hierarchy' (Rohlen, 1974, p. 107). There could scarcely be a clearer indication of where power lies.

According to the ideological collectivist model, one-man control is not traditional, and even respected journals like the *Nihon Keizai Shimbun*, the Japanese *Economist*, tend to point to 'the weakness of an autocratic one-man system' (Clark, 1979, p. 132) as the cause of unsound decision making, leading to bankruptcy. The empirical evidence however shows the importance of individual decision makers in firms such as YKK,[12] Honda, Idemitsu, and Toray.

Decision making is also a political activity, affecting not only organizational performance or business success, as some popular accounts appear to argue, but primarily the members of the organization themselves, their standing and their careers. The president of a Japanese company enjoys 'the fiction of absolute authority' (Dore, 1973, p. 227), and forceful personalities endowed with political skill can translate the fiction 'into something near reality' (Clark, op. cit., p. 131). Members of Japanese organizations often become highly sensitized not only to the ranking but also to the amount of power of particular managers. It is 'typical of Japanese political arrangements that power is veiled and indirect, but nevertheless ever-present' (Rohlen, 1974, p. 140). Collectivist ideology cloaks power relationships and the analytical methods of Western social science are uncongenial to it.[13]

The use of *de facto* 'top down', or authoritarian, decision making in Japanese companies shows that managers are quite capable of making individual decisions, and that they may be bound only by the formality and not the substance of the collectivity or consensus orientation. Noda considers that the process is frequently more active and vigorous than a search for unanimity appears to imply (in Vogel, 1975, p. 145). Ishida's pessimistic[14] view of *carte blanche* leadership, with its apathetic or disenchanted followers, is that such a state of affairs is likely to continue and that 'to "force" someone to be free is a contradiction in terms' (T. Ishida, 1971, pp. 99–101, 128). Regarding the affective side of decision making, Noda asserts that 'Japanese executives give great attention to problems of morale and human relations' (op. cit., p. 140). Once again it is clear that this attention moves downward from the top of the organization.

During the management boom of the 1960s some firms tried to streamline procedures by reducing the number of participants or allowing direct access to senior management in urgent cases, while others established authorized levels of expenditure for given ranks, but only where capital expenditure had been already approved in the budget (Yoshino, 1968, pp. 262–72). In one case a deputy department manager, theoretically responsible for production in a factory, was given an authorization of ¥30,000, only about £65 at current rates (Clark, 1979, p. 132).

In implementation, collective decision making largely protects individuals (Yoshino, op. cit., p. 259). This is consistent with long-term employment, which makes dismissal for mistakes in decision making and implementation problematical, with the concept of the generalist who performs any task ordered, and with the principles of flexibility and redeployment inherent in membership[15] in an enterprise, instead of the allocation of precise job descriptions. Critics have attacked *ringi* as 'collective irresponsibility', but it allows top management freedom of action while mobilizing those lower down the organization, giving it dynamic movement. According to Brown, 'The difficulty in grasping the locus of authority really comes from attempting to discover what corresponds to the Western concept of authority in a non-Western social organization. The *ringi* system shows the course of the decision-making process, but does not establish it' (in Lebra and Lebra, 1974, p. 182).

Ideologically *ringi* may be described as traditional, with the normative values that this implies, but historically it was first employed by the Japanese Civil Service after 1868 (Yoshino, 1968, p. 256). Given the close connections between government and industry that existed, and continue to exist, and that the Meiji government itself promoted new industries and then sold them to private enterprise, the spread of *ringi* from the

Civil Service to private industry is less surprising (cf. Norman, in Livingston *et al.*, 1976, Vol. 1, pp. 116–22).

At a formal level, Anglo-American concepts of answerability (Lamb and Turner, 1969, pp. 161–2; Dore, 1973, p. 229); of a 'science' of decision making (Simon, 1960); of managers in decision-making roles, and of techniques such as 'decision trees' (Mintzberg, 1973), seem to suggest that Japanese decision making is irrational, even chaotic. Science has become the dominant universalistic value of the West (cf. Bendix, 1974, pp. 206–7) and has led to an intellectual approach at variance with Japanese pragmatism. Taylorism separated thinking and acting (Strauss and Sayles, 1972, p. 30) in a way inconsistent with Japanese management's control of the social group and the task; but *ringi* is not theoretically based on science. It is rooted in social relations, power, and values, and has arguably been validated to a considerable extent by Japanese organizational success.[16] It must therefore be asked whether *ringi*, *nemawashi*, *ato-ringi* ('approval afterwards'), and Japanese decision-making processes are substantially as irrational as the formal criteria imply. The concept of the 'inefficiency' of Japanese decision making may be increasingly untenable in the light of comparative economic performance.

The *de facto* use of top down decision making in Japanese corporations, when management judges this to be necessary, shows that the difference from the Anglo-American model is one of degree rather than kind; as such it is universalistic. The difference in the processes and implications of such practices as *nemawashi* refers specifically to Japanese corporations in their social context. Their concomitant emotional climate, ideology, etc., are differences of kind. It would be misleading to attempt to separate them from the long-term employment model or from social mechanisms prevalent in the wider society. As such they are particularistic; though this does not necessarily make them irrational, in the sense that they frequently appear to be well adapted to achieving the result desired by management. Managers appear to be able to shift without difficulty from top down to bottom up as they judge the circumstances dictate. This flexibility could be more rational in its adaptation of the requisite means to an end than 'scientific' Anglo-American methods based on abstract principles,[17] and it is a symptom of a greater degree of managerial control, which should not be reified as 'cultural'.

3.8 Enterprise unionism

Ideological accounts of Japanese unionism stress the integration of the members of an enterprise into a unified interest group, or social community, ignoring the period preceding the Occupation reforms, which took place after 1945. They tend to play down this external stimulus.

The first strikes in a modern industry took place in spinning companies in 1886 and 1894. The Japanese Machine Operators' Union was set up in 1897 and the Railwaymen's and the Printers' Unions in 1898. In 1897 there were thirty-two disputes, involving 3,510 workers; the following year there were fifty-three disputes, involving 6,293. In 1919, the time of the rice riots during the period of post-war inflation, there were 497 disputes involving 63,000 workers. May Day was first celebrated in 1920, and in 1926 there were 488 unions, with 350,000 members (Halmos, 1966, pp. 78-9). The Public Peace Preservation Laws of 1925 were used against union members and officials who were considered by the authorities to constitute a danger to the state. The *Tokko* (Special Higher Police) arrested those suspected of *kiken shiso* ('dangerous thoughts'), while the 1928 Act provided the death penalty for the organization of secret associations dedicated to changing the national constitution. In 1940 the unions, together with the political parties, were absorbed into the Imperial Rule Assistance Association (T. Ishida, 1971, p. 62). At factory level, the unions became 'labour fronts' on the German model (Grunberger, 1977, pp. 241, 249-57), dedicated to increasing productivity and patriotic sentiment.

After 1945 legalization of unions was part of the policy of democratization pursued by the American authorities, many of whom were liberal supporters of Roosevelt's New Deal (Dore, 1973, p. 116). The quickest way to re-establish the unions was to take the existing factory-based labour fronts and to put them on a more democratic footing. This is the historical origin of enterprise-based unionism from the time of the Occupation onwards, in contrast to the ahistorical assertion of ideology stressing the unitary nature of enterprises. It is doubtful whether this move would have been instituted without American influence. The present Japanese Constitution, for example, was drawn up by the Occupation authorities after the majority party had failed to produce a draft (Von Mehren, 1963, pp. 445-6).

According to the legal expert Ishikawa 'labour law did not exist in any meaningful sense' until Article 28 of the new Constitution established 'the right of workers to organise and to bargain and act collectively'. Subsequent American-inspired legislation paralleled the Wagner Act of 1935 and the Taft–Hartley Act of 1947. The former regulated bargaining relations and the latter provided for management and labour to 'bargain in good faith'. 'Unfair labour practice' would incur legal sanctions (Whitehill and Takezawa, 1968, p. 64). After labour had been granted the freedom to organize and to bargain by the United States authorities[18] in 1946, union membership rapidly increased. In 1959 enterprise unions accounted for 88 per cent of all unions, with 6.6 per cent for craft unions and 3.1 per cent for industrial organizations (Cole, 1971, p. 225).[19] 'In the post-war period, when the Japanese unions took shape, no employer dared question the unions' right to exist' (Dore, 1973, p. 415). The choice of the word 'dared' suggests that Occupation policy was the reason for management's low profile.

Wartime destruction, the demobilization of the army and navy, the repatriation of Japanese settlers from Manchuria, Taiwan, and Korea, the eviction of the Japanese population from Russian-occupied Sakhalin, and the cessation of war production, created a post-war economic crisis of major proportions. High unemployment and low wages dictated union preoccupation with job security, remuneration in accord with the cost of living and family needs, and the enterprise's ability to pay.

In return for a guarantee of no lay-offs (except temporary workers) unions accepted management control and the need for productivity. Long-term employment, at a moment when it appeared to constrain management, eventually served management's purpose well. Employees with no alternative possibility of employment needed to produce the results that alone could ensure the enterprise's ability to pay. By a Weberian 'unintended consequence' the democratization by the American authorities of workshop-based or enterprise unions also resulted in a more permanent binding of employees to the company, from whom the union members received their salaries and allowances. Payment of family allowances confirmed the company's position as provider for the family and strengthened the seniority-ranking pay system, with its implications of managerial control. During the deflationary period of the Dodge Plan of 1948–50 there was large-scale disruption, which was in part a reaction after the repression of the 1930s and 1940s; but in the absence of a welfare state and in the severe economic conditions noted by Reischauer there was a widespread pragmatic recognition that employees were dependent for their livelihood on their employers, and that if the company collapsed they would go down with it.[20]

Some observers, such as Abegglen and Rohlen, see this recognition as an example of a particular value orientation, which prompted a rejoinder from Nakayama, president of the Japan Institute of Labour. He attacked scholars who had drawn attention to the aspects of Japanese industrial relations which they 'thought to be peculiar to Japan in the light of Western criteria. All these assessments . . . seem to us Japanese[21] considerably exaggerated. Some of them even give us the impression that they regard these characteristics as merits, to be preserved more or less permanently, whatever the changes in our industrial society' (*British Journal of Industrial Relations*, Vol. 3, 1965, p. 225). The inference is that what is a 'merit' in management's view is not necessarily one in a union leader's view.

In 1980 there were 71,780 unions, with a total membership of 12.3 million, of whom 8,573,000 were in private enterprises. Of the latter, more than half, 4,841,000, were in the large corporations (over a thousand employees) in the dominant part of the economy (*Anglo-Japanese Economic Institute Review*, No. 72, 1980, pp. 30-2). Strikes by public service workers, first forbidden during the disruption of 1948, are still illegal, and severely sanctioned when they occur, for example, on the railways. The issue remains a political problem (Kochiro, in Nishikawa, 1980, pp. 236-54).

Temporary workers also remain an exception to the general pattern (cf. Levine, in Dore, 1971, pp. 255-62). In spite of the politically-inspired rhetoric of employee solidarity, the interests of union members do not coincide with those of non-unionized temporary workers, or employees of small firms. Some see the preservation, if not the enlargement, of the dual economy of large corporations, offering high wages and full welfare benefits, and small businesses, which cannot afford them, as resting on 'a tacit understanding between management and organized labour' (Whitehill and Takezawa, 1968, p. 323).

In spite of pre-war distinctions between blue-collar and

white-collar employees, all are now included together as equal members of enterprise unions. Management cannot negotiate separately with the two categories, and the union gains from the numerical strength of blue-collar workers and the knowledge and ability to search out and interpret data on wage levels etc. of white-collar employees. All employees up to a given rank are union members, but on attaining this rank they automatically become management. Reflecting the separation of ownership and control, the rise of professional managers and the single status systems in Japanese corporations, the rate of managers' annual salary increases also depends on union negotiations. The discussion of the ranking system above referred to the large numbers of fine gradations between ranks, rather than abrupt cleavages, and this sociological factor also applies to union organization. The comparative absence of class (in the popular British sense) cleavages between managers, supervisors, and employees, is apparent.

The enterprise-based union is the unit of negotiation and from a structural point of view cannot be compared with British or American unions (Whitehill and Takezawa, 1968, p. 38). The will of workers to resist management and to assert their rights is weakened by employee identification, for reasons discussed above, with the company, and 'because the authority of the Japanese employer has been almost absolute throughout industrialization, even with post-war democratisation' (Cole, 1971, p. 226). Some unionists can only find the moral courage to oppose management by adopting the rival ideology of Marxism, which, in the 1960s, led Ota, president of the Sohyo union federation, to complain that the political theorizing of Marxist scholars was distracting people from the basic issue of the low wages and low occupational status of workers (Von Mehren, 1963, p. 473).

By law, unions must hold an annual convention, although typically conventions are held more frequently, allowing leaders to test the balance of power and to rally support (T. Shirai, in *British Journal of Industrial Relations*, Vol. 3, 1965, pp. 201–9). Shirai sees the necessity for this in the danger of factionalism (T. Ishida, 1971, pp. 64–9; Passin, 1965, p. 125). Factions may form around different interest groups: white-collar and blue-collar, young single men and older men with families, senior and less senior, the loyal and the less loyal, etc. Factionalism contrasts with the ideology of consensus.

At the convention a quorum is normally two-thirds of the membership, and meetings are held at a convenient time and place: on company premises during the lunch hour or immediately after work. Meetings are well attended and peer group pressure to join the group is strong (Dore, 1973, pp. 122, 127-8).

The convention evaluates the actions of the executive committee, to which the president of the union cannot belong. The committee members are responsible for specific areas of activity. Shirai considers that this diffusion of power is a cause of weakness, exacerbated by 'the marked group orientation of Japanese organizations', in which the members expect the leaders to follow 'the mass line' and try to reconcile different interests without overt conflict (op. cit., p. 175). Cole and others quote employee criticisms of officials' lack of interest in their affairs and allegations that officials have implicitly 'sold out' to management.

A period as a union official is often part of a managerial career and no role conflict is perceived. The risk of possible antagonism is reduced because the annual union negotiation over the amounts of the bonuses and the regular annual salary increase also apply to managers, as already noted (Dore, 1973, pp. 168-73). Officials who are on their way up the promotion ladder and managers who have been officials in their time are less likely to see each other as 'them and us'. In the Japanese context, 'us' means the members of our group, or company, and 'them' means rival groups or companies, competitors at home and abroad.

According to Dore, the Hitachi union explicitly subscribed to the values of hard work, skill, and productivity. He also gives the example of a union leader who by 'cheating in the taking of holidays' also understood the imposition of an unfair burden on colleagues. Several union officials spoke of their feeling of guilt at putting extra work on others when they attended meetings in working hours (ibid., pp. 185, 189-90).

Dore mentions the concern of the shop floor that officials should be acceptable to management, and describes the informal discussions by which this was ensured. Such features have led some to accuse Japanese unions of being 'fully integrated with management'. Halliday and McCormack, for example, attack the Nissan union as acting 'on behalf of management, as watchdog of capital and accomplice in the efficient exploitation

of workers'. The evidence given is the close parallel between the
hierarchies of supervision and union, demanding equal qualifications etc.; the statement in the union handbook not to demand
'unreasonable amounts'; a 1971 survey in Kansai (Western
Japan) showing the preponderance of middle- and upper-rank
employees among union officials; that 40 per cent of supervisory staff had been officials and that supervisors would automatically move on to the union committee (Halliday and McCormack,
1973, pp. 183–6). Cole (1971) quoted workers who alleged that
sums had been agreed before official bargaining started, but that
'it would not have looked right' for the negotiators not to 'go
through the motions'. Abegglen criticizes what he sees as the
'irrationality' of Japanese wage bargaining, but Dore points to
the accepted legitimacy of unions, removing potential causes of
dispute, and to the rationality of fixed bargaining periods. He
also evaluated the Hitachi union, with its impressive use of data,
as a 'generally more efficient, formally well thought out, and
more literate organisation than its British counterpart' (op. cit.,
pp. 137–8). Table 18 shows the levels of satisfaction among
different categories of employees.

Table 18. Workers' self-evaluation of their present status*

	Very satisfied %	Satisfied %	Dis- satisfied %	Very dis- satisfied %	Don't know & not certain %	N
Managerial workers	7	67	24	1	1	287
White-collar workers	3	51	41	4	1	2,467
Blue-collar workers	3	45	44	7	2	2,604

Source: *Japan Labour Bulletin*, 1 April 1971, p. 7.

* 'Status' here refers to life chances, income and living conditions. For blue-
collar workers promotion chances and 'job motivation', or satisfaction, are significant.

Table 19 shows that 'the great majority of blue-collar workers
identifies with the middle-class stratum', and Table 20 shows a
preponderance of responses for 'work as a duty', compared to
the more 'instrumental' orientations.

Table 19. Workers' class identification

Class identification by occupation and sex	Upper %	Upper middle %	Middle %	Lower middle %	Lowest %	Uncertain %	N
Management	–	16.7	66.7	11.9	–	5.6	18
Males							
Professional & Technical	1.7	8.1	61.8	22.0	4.6	1.7	173
Clerical	0.7	11.7	67.1	16.1	2.0	2.3	684
Sales & Services	0.6	9.3	59.3	23.5	5.4	1.8	332
Labour	0.4	4.0	55.3	30.5	6.7	3.0	810
Others	–	7.1	71.4	17.9	–	3.6	28
Females							
Managerial	1.4	16.2	71.6	9.5	1.4	–	74
Professional & Technical	1.1	11.5	70.1	14.9	1.1	1.1	87
Clerical	0.5	14.1	62.5	19.0	3.3	0.5	184
Sales & Services	–	9.4	58.8	25.9	4.7	1.2	85
Labour	–	3.6	57.0	29.1	9.2	1.2	337
Others	–	14.3	71.4	14.3	–	–	14

Source: Japan Labour Bulletin, 1 April 1971, p. 8.

Table 20. Attitudes about the meaning of work

Type of work	Everyone has a duty to work. Hard work is important	Working is a good opportunity to demon-strate one's ability	Work is only a means to obtain money or social status	Others incl. not certain	
	%	%	%	%	N
Managerial workers	72	17	11	—	92
White-collar workers	61	22	14	3	1,545
Blue-collar workers	59	16	22	3	1,142
Age					
16–19	54	20	23	3	231
20–24	54	25	17	4	992
25–29	61	18	18	3	822
30–39	67	16	15	2	461
40–49	73	12	14	1	320
Educational level					
College	55	31	12	2	2,229
Senior high school	58	22	17	4	1,220
Junior high school	56	15	24	5	526

Source: Japan Labour Bulletin, 1 April 1971, p. 9.

A simplistic interpretation of such data might suggest that management would have everything its own way, but this can be disputed. The immediate post-war thrust of union activity directed at preventing redundancy has been superseded by a regular pattern of pay bargaining, referred to in the discussion of salary and bonus systems.

The major nationally institutionalized bargaining period is the *Shunto* ('Spring Labour Offensive'), approximately coincid-ing with the school or academic year in April. The *Shunto* applies to all major employing organizations and determines the amount of increase in basic salary rates. It is often accompanied by symbolic acts, such as the wearing of red armbands. The negotiations for the amount of bonus are held in the summer and at the end of the year. The unquestioned right of unions to negotiate at these times, their access to information, and their hiring of professors to provide information on economic trends etc., suggests that enterprise unions are not as weak as some stereotyped accounts have argued.

Plant unions belonging to the same company gain support

from the federation of their company's unions and may also be affiliated to one of the national federations. The most influential are Sohyo, linked to the left-wing Japan Socialist Party, and Domei, connected with the Democratic Socialist Party. Neither has the power of the Trades Union Congress in Britain, although there is some tension between bottom up and top down pressures. The enterprise union at plant level has the members, the funds, and the local interest; the federation cannot bargain at the crucial plant or company level (Levine, in Dore, 1971, pp. 263-77). The federation may propose a 'line' during the Spring Labour Offensive, but this may be ignored at plant level once the enterprise union has achieved its goals. The line was better maintained before 1975; since then greater variation in settlements at workplace level has occurred (Thurley, personal communication).

In cases where management–union relations deteriorate into a confrontation, management may promote a *dainii kumiai* ('second union'). In one example, creditors of a company in financial difficulties had demanded a return to work as a precondition for wage negotiations. A three-year 'peace stabilization plan', involving a no-strike commitment, was then agreed. Many left the company in disgust, while the management promoted a 'second union' with the assistance of foremen. It was 'dedicated to cooperation with the company' (Cole, 1971, p. 189).

The expression 'second union' has no meaning in Britain or the USA, but it is well understood in Japan. The formation of a second union is often accompanied by factional, and perhaps violent, struggles (Ishikawa, in Von Mehren, 1963, p. 461). Halliday and McCormack report a uniformed squad of company and union men mobilized to deal with troublemakers (Halliday and McCormack, 1973, p. 185). Such data are inconsistent with ideological images of 'harmony'. Makino asserts that since union membership is automatic up to a given rank, unions contain a proportion of workers whose support is lukewarm. He sees this as liable to cause a split, as in the second union process, when leaders propose a radical course (Halmos, 1966, p. 9). If this is so, it would be to management's advantage.

Table 21 puts the Japanese record of working days lost into perspective. Although the record is one of the best, it is surpassed by West Germany, the Netherlands, Sweden, Switzerland, and Norway.

Table 21. Working days lost through industrial disputes per 1,000 employees in selected industries* (mining, manufacturing, construction and transport) 1970–9

	1970	1971	1972	1973	1974	1975	1976	1977	1978	1979†	Average for 10 years 70–79	Average for 5 years 70–74	Average for 5 years 75–79
United Kingdom	740	1,190	2,160	570	1,270	540	300	840	840	2,430	1,088	1,186	990
Australia‡	1,040	1,300	880	1,080	2,670	1,390	1,430	670	960	1,560	1,298	1,394	1,202
Belgium	830	720	190	520	340	340	560	420	650	320	489	520	458
Canada	2,190	800	1,420	1,660	2,550	2,810	2,550	830	1,930	1,660	1,840	1,724	1,956
Denmark§	170	30	40	4,440	330	110	220	240	90	140	581	1,002	160
Finland	270	3,300	520	2,530	470	310	1,310	2,360	160	270	1,150	1,418	882
France	180	440	300	330	250	390	420	260	200	350	312	300	324
Germany (FR)	10	340	10	40	60	10	40	—	370	40	92	92	92
India	1,440	1,100	1,330	1,330	2,480	1,450	830	1,510	1,650	2,180	1,527	1,530	1,524
Irish Republic	490	670	600	410	1,240	810	840	1,040	1,610	3,920	1,163	682	1,644

Italy**	1,730	1,060	1,670	2,470	1,800	1,730	2,310	1,560	890	2,560	1,778	1,746	1,810
Japan	200	310	270	210	450	390	150	70	60	40	215	288	142
Netherlands	140	50	70	330	–	–	10	140	–	..	82	118	38
New Zealand	470	350	300	530	360	390	950	810	790	..	550	402	735
Norway	70	10	–	10	490	10	70	40	90	..	88	116	53
Spain	240	190	120	210	310	370	2,540	3,350	1,820	3,260	1,241	214	2,268
Sweden¶	40	240	10	10	30	20	20	20	10	20	42	66	18
Switzerland**	–	10	–	–	–	–	20	–	–	–	3	2	4
United States**	2,210	1,600	860	750	1,480	990	1,070	1,070	890		1,211	1,380	1,042

Source: International Labour Office, see Department of Employment, 1981.

Notes:

* The figures are restricted mainly to these four relatively strike-prone industry groups by the ILO to reduce the effects of different industrial structures & improve the basis of comparison of strike rates between the countries.　　　　† Provisional figures.

‡ Including electricity & gas; excluding communication.

§ For Denmark, figures up to 1974 relate only to manufacturing, and are therefore not fully comparable with later figures which include construction and transport.　　　　** Including gas, electricity and water.

¶ For Sweden, figures for 1970 and 1971 relate to all sectors and are therefore not fully comparable with those for later years: — = negligible/less than five; .. = not available. Averages relate to those years for which figures are available.

Glazer sees a similar attitude to employers on the part of British and American unions (Patrick and Rosovsky, 1976, p. 882), based on a differentiation of interests (Whitehill and Takezawa, 1968, p. 350). Glazer appears to underestimate the significance of Japanese management's power and to overstate the significance of 'cultural' elements (Patrick and Rosovsky, 1976, pp. 816-21), in distinction to Cole, Clark, and others. Abegglen went as far as to assert that employment in a Japanese company was 'a system of shared obligations. Loyalty to the group and an interchange of responsibilities take the place of the economic basis of the employment of workers by the firm' (Abegglen, 1958, pp. 17, 98-100). This interpretation may be correct at an ideological level and may partially explain certain types of action, but it can hardly replace employees' concern for their livelihood and prospects (cf. Table 17). The assertion is not supported by the data of Marsh and Mannari.

It was shown above that enterprise unions were freed from the constraints of repressive legislation and policies by the American Occupation, which a Japanese government might not have done. Unions enjoy a high degree of legitimacy and the established right to bargain.[22] They have access to management and company information. It is reasonable to argue that the constant rise in employee living standards since the war has been due in part to union pressure. This pressure is institutionalized in the form of regular bargaining over the 'base up' and the amount of bonus, and as such is a rational method of regulating pay. It also works to management's advantage, as do the deferred payment of salaries in the form of bonuses and retirement money. The middle-class orientation of the majority of employees and the perception of work as a 'duty' or something 'important' imply a relative lack of militancy that again favours management. The post-war bargain struck between unions and management, under the eyes of the Occupation authorities, confirmed management as the provider of essential employee welfare benefits, thereby confirming management's leverage over employees, or 'right to manage' in British parlance.

The organizational weakness in union structure described by Shirai and the tendency towards factionalism are 'passive' factors that favour management and can be more actively used in pursuit of a second-union strategy. Management enjoys an advantage in dealing with enterprise unions consisting solely of its own employees and in its success in ensuring the interchange-ability of supervisory and union personnel, often as part of a normal career progression. But this structural factor alone would be unlikely to assure management's desired degree of control in another society. In the Japanese case it is linked with the rest of the employment system, including the close communication and the type of interpersonal relations that are cultivated within the enterprise.

There are qualitative and quantitative problems in arriving at a satisfactory evaluation of two such different structures and processes as the Japanese and the British; but as a generalization it can be asserted that unions in the Japanese case, largely because of management's own efforts, do not pose such a threat to managerial control. Given the intrusion of Occupation policy, management has been able to settle for a system of recognition, regular bargaining, and institutionalized management–union relations with a considerable degree of rationality, removing a great deal of uncertainty from business operations and assisting management in the planning and execution of its long-term strategies.

As a generalization, it seems safe to say that the ideological and highly particularistic aspect of union–management relations and employee dependency on the firm (i.e. management) have misled some writers into underestimating the relevance of struc-tural, or universalistic, factors. The last word is left to a Japanese expert: 'There seems to be a theory that Japan is different and requires certain unique interpretations [but] . . . the postulates of economic theory and the logic of the labour market are not "culture bound" to the West' (Taira, 1970, p. x).

Notes

1. Although traditionally the son has had authority over his widowed mother.
2. Not to mention the problems facing British business.
3. Cf. poorly educated British managers (Thurley, 1975, p. 8).
4. The standard translation but inadequate because of the different con-notation. *Makoto* is not a transcendentally based ethic, but refers to normative behaviour in Japanese society. At a meeting, Japanese and American businessmen exhorted each other to be 'sincere', each doubt-less believing that they already were.
5. Companies may feel that training remote from the workplace is not

realistic enough. Cf. Mant's view of comparable training in the UK (Mant, 1979, pp. 159–71).

6. An analogy is the Civil Service in Britain. Entry to the Administrative, Executive, and Clerical grades is determined by educational achievement, as in companies in Japan, and movement between grades is difficult. Other public and private organizations in the UK and the USA have long-term career structures, but nothing comparable to what is really a national recruitment structure in Japan.

7. Human relations skills are important in Japanese companies in, for instance, group work and decision making. A 'wet' (warm) atmosphere is a group ideal. Ability to handle interpersonal relations harmoniously is crucial for managerial promotion.

8. That is, quitting without notice during a fixed-term contract, typically made between textile companies and the parents of operatives from rural areas. (Cf. Orchard in Livingston *et al.*, 1976, Vol. 1, pp. 307–10).

9. The corporatist welfare movement in the United States failed to develop further because of the slump of 1929 (Whitehill and Takezawa, 1968, p. 237).

10. Hence the analogy with *The Protestant Ethic and the Spirit of Capitalism* (Weber, 1947). For contrasting views see Bellah (1957) and Hirschmeier and Yui (1981). The analogy is closer in relation to accumulation than to ethics. The Tokugawa merchants were not Calvinists.

11. Even the best decisions can 'disappear into a porridge of inertia', or be sabotaged at the implementation stage by those who have not been consulted because under Western functional differentiation their participation is considered unnecessary. (Cf. *Financial Times*, 3 December 1980.)

12. YKK (Yoshida Kogyo Kaisha) is a privately owned company with strong personal leadership. In 1950 Toyo Rayon's president decided to purchase nylon technology from Du Pont for US$3m. Yoshino (1968, p. 261) says this was a personal decision. A manager in London considered such a decision, like other strategic decisions, would have been reached after consultation with an executive committee of senior directors. In any event, this entrepreneurial decision gave Toray the lead in nylon production and made it highly profitable.

13. Power relationships exist in industrial societies under different political systems and not only under those described as 'capitalist' by e.g. Halliday and McCormack.

14. Pessimistic in the light of his values.

15. At YKK all employees are officially called 'members'.

16. Cf. British organizations with weak cohesion and little overall sense of direction. Competent individuals work in isolation and optimum organizational performance is not achieved.

17. According to Simon (1960) many American managers in fact use 'rule of thumb'. In Britain 'muddling through' is well known. Yet many Japanese believe Western societies are dominated by 'logic'.

18. The 'capitalists' in the conception of Nakase and others.

19. Two notable exceptions to the enterprise-based principle are the Teachers' Union and the All-Japan Seamen's Union.

20. There is some disagreement over how far the democratization of unions went. Under the Occupation, left-wing union leaders and politicians were released from prison. After the strikes and violence of 1946-7, a 'reverse course' was instituted to prevent liberalization degenerating into disorder (cf. Livingston *et al.*, 1976, Vol. 2, pp. 139-86).

21. The expression 'we Japanese' is often heard in Japanese society.

22. But there is widespread public agreement on the bounds of legitimate action. Most railway strikes are short (one day or less), but on other occasions railwaymen have been physically attacked when people feel they have gone beyond the accepted limit. Many Japanese are perplexed that there seems to be no comparable limit in the UK.

4 JAPANESE MANAGEMENT IN THE UK

4.1 Development

Mitsui & Co. opened their London branch in 1880 and were the first Japanese company to be admitted to membership of the Baltic Exchange in 1910. By 1940 the branch had 120 staff; and 225 in 1978 (Mitsui, 1976, p. 4). The Yokohama Specie Bank, forerunner of the present Bank of Tokyo, established its London branch in 1881. The then Mitsubishi Trading Co. opened its London office in 1915.

The early arrival of such commercial firms reflected the need of a City of London base from which to handle Anglo-Japanese trade. Their role was restricted compared to the present, but trade expanded and after 1931 there was 'a boom in Japanese exports' (Lockwood, 1954, pp. 64-8, 70-5). Manufacturing firms did not begin to arrive until the 1970s.

The Second World War caused a suspension of activity and Japan's domestic economic difficulties after 1945 prevented an immediate reopening. From 1949 onwards the overseas activities of Japanese companies were strictly controlled by the Foreign Exchange Control Law (Ozawa, 1979, p. 13). In 1949 a body that has exerted decisive influences on industrial policy, including overseas operations, was established (Magaziner and Hout, 1980, pp. 31-5). This was the Ministry of International Trade and Industry (MITI). The other ministry with major influence over foreign investment etc. was the Ministry of Finance (MOF). The Bank of Tokyo reopened in London in 1952; Kawasaki, the shipping line in 1956, and Mitsui & Co. in 1957. Honda opened its office in 1965.

In 1969 the Bank of Japan granted automatic approval for overseas investments up to $200,000. In 1970 this limit was raised to $1 million and it was abolished altogether in July 1971 (Ozawa, 1979, p. 16).

According to Ozawa, applications under the 1949 Foreign

Exchange Control Law were subject to 'case-by-case screening'. It was tacitly understood that: 1. Direct foreign investment should either promote Japanese exports or develop overseas resources vital to Japanese industry; 2. Foreign investment should not jeopardize the competitive position of Japanese firms at home; 3. Foreign investment should not interfere with domestic monetary policy. 'The official attitude towards overseas investment was clearly ethnocentric, even mercantilistic', although this later changed to a more global orientation (ibid., p. 13). It is often claimed in the West that 'Japan was a highly protected market until the late 1960s and many of the mental attitudes acquired before that seem to live on' (B. Thorne, 'The reasons behind Japan's closed market', *Financial Times*, 27 February 1981). Tables 22 and 23 show Japan's comparatively low import ratio of manufactured goods but its industry's dependence on imported raw materials.

In spite of the oil crisis of 1973, the Japanese economy has continued to grow and to become more widely involved internationally (cf. Murakami, 1981). Table 24 shows that the Japanese economy consistently had the highest rate of growth between 1973 and 1978, except for 1974, compared to other industrialized countries.

The growth of Japanese foreign trade has been conspicuous, and has had clear implications for the increase in the number of Japanese firms in the UK and elsewhere and for managerial strategies. A comparison between 1960 and 1979 is dramatic. In terms of millions of US dollars, exports rose from 4,055 to 103,032; imports increased from 4,491 to 110,672. In 1978

Table 22. Import ratios of manufactured goods in developed countries (1976)

	%
Japan	19.8
USA	54.2
UK	52.0
FRG	54.6
France	63.7
EC (Ex. intra-regional)	39.6

Source: O.E.C.D. Statistics (quoted in Japanese Embassy, 1977, p. 7).

Table 23. Overseas dependency on primary products (1974)

Items	Country					
	USA	West Germany	France	UK	Italy	Japan
Beef	4.2	10.2	0	17.1	32.0	15.7
Wheat	0	13.9	0	32.2	20.7	95.9
Maize	0	85.7	0	100.0	45.0	99.6
Greasy wool	10.3	90.0	82.0	53.2	82.4	100.0
Cotton	0	100.0	100.0	100.0	99.6	100.0
Wood	0.3	12.7	3.1	77.6	43.9	41.2
Copper	26.1	99.8	99.9	100.0	99.7	90.1
Lead	41.5	88.5	88.2	88.5	88.9	80.3
Zinc	61.8	70.1	95.3	98.9	61.6	64.5
Bauxite	60.9	99.8	0	100.0	91.0	100.0
Tin	100.0	100.0	98.2	80.8	100.0	98.5
Nickel	93.5	100.0	100.0	100.0	100.0	100.0
Iron ore	34.1	94.1	8.8	80.3	97.9	99.4
Coal (incl. coking coal)	0	0	37.2	0	93.5	72.2
Crude oil	26.2	94.3	99.1	99.9	99.2	99.7

Source: F.A.O. Statistics, Metal Statistics, World Energy Supplies, Iron and Steel Statistics (quoted in Japanese Embassy, 1977, p. 7).

Notes:

(1) Overseas Dependence $= \dfrac{\text{Import} - \text{Export}}{\text{Production} + \text{Import} - \text{Export}}$

For: Copper, Lead, Zinc, Bauxite, Tin $= 1 - \dfrac{\text{Production (Ore)}}{\text{Consumption (Metal)}}$

(2) Wood, Coal, Crude oil, in 1973. Others, in 1974.

Table 24. Economic growth rates

	1973 %	1974 %	1975 %	1976 %	1977 %	1978 %
Japan	10.0	−0.3	1.4	6.5	5.4	5.6
UK	7.9	−1.8	−1.7	3.6	1.2	3.2
USA	5.4	−1.3	−1.0	5.5	4.8	4.0
Canada	7.5	3.5	1.2	5.8	2.9	3.4
France	5.4	3.2	0.3	4.6	3.1	3.3
Germany (West)	4.9	0.5	−2.1	5.6	2.8	3.1
Italy	6.9	4.2	−3.5	5.7	1.7	2.6

Source: Japanese Government, 1980, p. 28.

Japan was third, behind the USA and West Germany, in world exports and imports. The Japanese economy accounted for 8.3 per cent of world exports and 6.5 per cent of world imports.

Table 25 shows the consistent increases in both exports and imports, accompanied by fluctuations in the balance of trade.

Table 25. Trend of Japanese foreign trade (US$ million)

	Exports	Imports	Balance
1960	4,055	4,491	−437
1965	8,452	8,169	283
1970	19,318	18,881	437
1973	36,930	38,314	1,384
1974	55,536	62,110	−6,575
1975	55,753	57,863	−2,110
1977	80,495	70,809	9,686
1978	97,543	79,343	18,200
1979	103,032	110,672	−7,505

Source: Japanese Government, 1980, p. 80.

To date, Japanese investment in Europe has not achieved the levels that it has either in Asia or North America, but the significant extent of its involvement in the commercial sector is clear from the comparison in Table 26.

In spite of post-war economic difficulties and heavy initial dependence on the USA for capital, technology, and markets (Ozawa, 1979, p. 77), Japan has become one of the four major capital exporting economies. Direct foreign investment increased fivefold between 1968 and 1973, and by 1979 was sixteen times that of 1968 (Allen, 1981, pp. 2-3).

Japanese investment in the UK has not matched this significant progression, partly because of management worries about personnel and industrial relations problems (*Oriental Economist*, 1979, pp. 47-57). Table 27 shows Japanese investment in the UK, on a Bank of Japan approval basis. The total represents 20 per cent of Japanese direct investment in Europe. 'Great Britain has not been a particularly attractive market for Japanese corporations' despite investment incentives, comparatively low labour costs, etc. (ibid.).

In London in 1980 there were 180 major firms belonging to the Japanese Chamber of Commerce and listed in their directory. Other smaller firms, including representative and liaison

Table 26. Overseas investment by Japan, the USA, and West Germany (amount outstanding in %)

	Japan (Mar. 1977)	USA (End 1976)	West Germany (End 1977)
Region			
North America	25.2	24.7	19.7
Central & S. America	17.6	17.1	14.1
Europe	13.9	40.7	55.3
Asia	27.4		
Japan	—	2.8	0.6
Oceania	5.5	4.3	0.6
Middle East	6.1		
Africa	4.3		5.9
Other developing areas		5.2	3.8
Others		5.1	
Sector			
Agriculture	2.6		0.7
Mining	21.5	5.1	
Oil products, etc.		21.6	6.5
Food products		3.7	
Chemicals	6.7	8.8	18.0
Textiles	5.8		
Metal & metal products		2.8	
Iron & non-ferrous metals	5.2		
Iron & steel			7.8
Machinery		12.4	7.8
Transport machinery		7.1	6.4
Electric machinery	4.2		
Electric & electronic machinery			10.8
Other manufacturing	11.9	9.7	19.3
Commerce, public service, insurance, finance, etc.	41.2	28.8	22.7

Source: Ministry of International Trade and Industry (MITI), *Wagakuni Kigyo no Kaigai Jigyo Katsudo*, 1978, quoted in Nakase, 1980a, p. 3. (The above table allows for different official criteria in the classification of, e.g. 'machinery'.)

Table 27. Japanese direct investment in the UK

Final year	No. of cases	Value (US$)
1972–3	48	817
1973–4	58	62
1974–5	34	38
1975–6	34	46
1976–7	44	88
1977–8	48	50
1978–9	87	66
Total	351	1,167

Source: *Oriental Economist*, 1979.

offices are listed in the directory of the Anglo-Japanese Economic Institute. The breakdown of Japanese firms in 1980 is given
in Table 28, totalling all firms:

Table 28. Total number of Japanese firms in the UK

Sales operations	82
Transport, resources, services	60
Banks	31
Trading companies	28
Manufacturing operations	19
Insurance	14
Other commercial and financial	13
Total	247
Total manufacturing, including joint ventures	21

Sources: Japanese Chamber of Commerce, Anglo-Japanese
Economic Institute, 1980.

The preponderance of firms in the City of London and the
limited number of manufacturing operations stand out. Journalistic accounts of the manufacturers have tended to produce
a distorted picture of the distribution of companies. It is significant that whereas some Japanese firms have been operating in
the UK since the nineteenth century, their managerial systems
have only recently begun to attract interest, and yet those systems or structures are not entirely post-war products. Table 29
puts the date of establishment of firms in the UK into perspective.

Table 29. Dates of Establishment of Japanese firms in the UK

Type of organization	Number	No. starting pre-1970	No. starting post-1970	(% post-1970)
Local manufacture and sales	17	—	17	100
Manufacturers sales and distribution	45	12	33	73
Trading companies	5	3	2	40
Banking	18	3	15	83
Transport and resources	6	1	5	83
Insurance	10	2	8	80
Other commercial	7	1	6	86
Total	108	22	86	80

Source: Thurley *et al.*, 1980, p. 37.

The growth of popular perceptions of Japanese firms in the UK would therefore appear to be connected with the post-1970s increase in the number of firms, as well as with increasing penetration of the British market. It has been estimated that 6,414 personnel are employed in Japanese commercial firms in the UK, compared with 3,876 in manufacturing. The latter total is reduced if only wholly-owned subsidiaries, as opposed to joint ventures, are included (Thurley *et al.*, 1980, p. 38).[1]

By itself, the total of 247 firms in the UK does not adequately express the situation in terms of managerial sytems. Such systems and work organization may vary between large and small firms (Cunnison, 1966; Lupton, 1963; Warner, 1973). Small branches of large Japanese firms may show variations due to size, as well as to other factors such as the local environment, their mixed personnel etc. Table 30 shows the preponderance of small branches and, with the exception of the joint enterprises, even the 'large' Japanese operations seldom have more than 300 employees.

The managerial systems in use in the UK branches must also be seen in the wider context of Japan's industrial structure (Sato, 1980), industrial policy (Magaziner and Hout, 1980), and the development of Japanese overseas investment and operations (Ozawa, 1979; Sekiguchi, 1979). This explains the relative numbers of manufacturing operations, commercial firms, etc. in the UK, the USA, and areas such as South East Asia respectively.

Table 30. Size of Japanese firms in the UK

Type of organization	No. of employees per firm (% of firms)				
	1–10	11–50	51–100	101 & over	No. of firms
Local manufacture & sales	5	35	12	47	17*
Manufacturers sales & distribution	48	35	5	12	70
Trading companies	59	18	5	18	22
Banking	16	65	16	4	26
Transport & resources	64	22	10	4	44
Insurance	100	–	–	–	13
Other commercial	50	42	8	–	12
All firms (%)	48.5	32.8	7.4	11.3	204
No. of firms	99	67	15	23*	204

Source: Thurley *et al.*, 1980, p. 39.

* Including two large joint enterprises with more than 1,000 employees.

'Perhaps no other country is so bent on reorganizing its industrial structure as Japan' (Ozawa, op. cit., pp. 65, 234). Overseas investment is a way of upgrading the industrial structure and of promoting economic growth via assembly and manufacturing. MITI intends that Japanese industry should be broadly competitive, instead of relying on a 'laser beam' strategy in selected industries (Horsley, 1981), and should be more integrated into the world economy: hence the rhetoric of 'internationalization' (Lehmann, in Thurley *et al.*, 1981, pp. 51–2).

The best analysis of the frequently discussed relations between government (e.g. MITI) and industry in Japan is probably that of Magaziner and Hout. Contrary to the stereotype of Japan Inc, it shows the continual process of bargaining, compromise, and the trading of favours in these relations, in which private industries sometimes successfully defy MITI. The pattern is one of the continual search for advantage, and MITI—which is only one actor, along with MOF, the Foreign Ministry, and the companies and their federations—does not have unlimited power at its disposal. The strength of its administrative guidance depends on the power it can muster in specific instances (cf. Befu, in

Lebra and Lebra, 1974, pp. 208-24). It can be argued that the
Japanese economy is neither a free market nor a planned economy, but a 'guided' economy (cf. Ueno, in Sato, 1980, p. 387).
The model could be a pointer to those seeking to avoid the dis-
advantages of the other two types. In Reischauer's view 'the
Japanese system might be called post-capitalistic, in its leadership by salaried "business bureaucrats" and its orientation to
national service and growth rather than merely to profits. It
does not submit itself entirely to the unseen hand of the market,
but accepts government guidance' (1977, p. 194). Guidance is
more pragmatic and flexible than planning connected with political dogma, as found in eastern Europe and supported by some
members of the Labour Party in Britain.

These points are not always apparent to people competing
with Japanese exports. The head of the British Electrical and
Allied Manufacturing Association (BEAMA) was reported as
saying 'Japan's entire [sic] industrial structure was essentially
predatory and defied international relations which were based
on the principle of reciprocal world trade' (Financial Times, 25
May 1981). Union and management opposition obliged Hitachi
to drop its plan for a wholly owned operation and to establish a
joint venture, which has been less satisfactory (Thurley, personal communication). The bad press that Japanese industry sometimes receives in the UK helps to explain management's generally
low profile and the reluctance to invest in the UK referred to
by the Oriental Economist above.

Though MITI has overall strategic aims at macro level, individual firms have their own priorities and plans, and there is no
evidence of a grand plan of Japanese investment in the UK, any
more than there is evidence of a uniform managerial system
throughout the firms that have been established there. Japanese
firms come to the City of London for its advantages as a financial centre, and to the UK in general in order to have a base
within the tariff walls of the EEC, to protect markets, to compete with rivals as a part of their corporate strategy, and, especially for smaller firms, to expand overseas when domestic
conditions are constrained (cf. Sekiguchi, 1979, p. 128). Some
City offices are also regional headquarters for Europe, Africa,
or the Middle East. The attraction of the City, over several continental centres, is the expertise available and the centralization
of established financial markets, for example, in insurance

(Japanese insurance company general manager, personal communication).

According to S. Matsukawa, MOF wants Japanese banks to be more competitive internationally, and their overseas assets now amount to between 20 and 30 per cent of their total assets (*Financial Times*, 27 May 1981). According to R. C. Hanson, the overseas percentage of Japanese direct corporate capital raising has advanced from 0.7 per cent in 1973-4 to 26.7 per cent in 1980-1, a significant increase (*Financial Times*, 21 July 1981).

These data materially affect the business side of the Japanese banks in London, posing the problem of whether this necessarily results in changes in personnel policies or managerial practices; Chapter 5 will enlarge upon this point. In the 1950s the main function of the banks was to service Japanese customers. In the 1960s they became increasingly involved in the Eurodollar market, centred on the City. From the time of the 1973 oil crisis they have been endeavouring to increase business with British and other Western firms. These have been 'the three stages of the internationalization of Japanese banking' (deputy general manager, Sodo Bank, personal communication). In 1980 Euro-credits accounted for 60 per cent of his bank's loans; 30 per cent represented loans to Japanese companies: the remaining 10 per cent went to British and other companies. The insurance manager already quoted aimed to pursue profitability 'without national considerations'. He stated that although it was his company's duty to assist Japanese clients, he did not welcome this business; it brought in little profit, since Japanese clients expected the same high standard in London as they received in Japan.

The thirteen insurance companies pursue non-life business, but only four write exclusively Japanese business. Nine are incorporated as UK companies, outside the formal control of MOF. The trading companies also need to be seen in the context of their global operations. Mitsui, for example, has over 130 offices in nearly 80 countries and, although London is an important centre, it is not comparable to the head office. The latter is the centre of the global communications and information networks.

Since the emphasis on import–export business in the 1950s, the internationalization of the traders' business has been analogous to that of the banks. They have become organizers, financiers, and the coordinators of major international projects. The companies are keenly aware that they must offer new services, based on their particular expertise, in order to preserve their advantage as middlemen between producers and purchasers. Despite the recession they have increased their turnover, as Table 31 shows. Sumitomo Corporation, which increased its offshore business by 143.9 per cent, registered the best all-round performance. The discrepancy between the respective figures for sales and profit refer to heavy interest payments, Marubeni's unprofitable affiliates, etc.

Table 31. Trading company performance

	Sales ¥bn	Change on year %	Operating profit ¥bn	Change on year %	Net profit ¥bn	Change on year %
Mitsubishi	6,892	+28.7	21.31	+ 5.1	10.81	+ 18.4
Mitsui	6,302	+24.2	17.12	+ 2.0	7.18	+ 19.7
C. Itoh	5,220	+29.7	11.66	+44.1	2.40	− 38.5
Marubeni	4,721	+26.7	8.41	−43.3	4.67	− 14.8
Sumitomo	4,704	+42.1	14.36	+14.3	5.56	+ 23.2
Nissho Iwai	3,285	+26.9	6.02	+ 4.7	2.44	+ 10.4
Toyo Menka	1,604	+23.9	1.49	+38.8	0.78	+ 2.6
Nichimen	1,208	+19.9	2.57	+48.8	1.70	+138.8
Kanematsu Gosho	1,511	+21.5	0.44	−20.0	0.11	− 1.8

Source: *Financial Times*, 21 November 1980.

* Half year April–September 1980.

The predominance of the City firms underlines the contrast with the situation in Ireland, where there are seven companies engaged in production, but no banks and only two small offices belonging to trading companies. Asahi Chemical Co. is said to have invested £45 million, in a continuous process plant and spinning company.

'Japanese corporations usually advance into Great Britain in the hope of obtaining a viable foothold in the EEC' (*Oriental Economist*, 1979). The investment incentives of the development areas are an attraction in South Wales and the north east of England. Companies carry out detailed feasibility studies— which some British managers claim has not always been the case —and bodies such as the Invest in Britain Bureau of the UK

Department of Industry and the regional development corporations exert a 'pull' effect.[2] The Welsh Development Agency has attracted a cluster of firms (Sony, Matsushita, Sekisui, Takiron, Aiwa, Hoya, Yuasa), and this success has produced a 'follow my leader' effect. Companies are more confident in an area where they know other Japanese firms are satisfied. On the other hand, one development corporation finds Japanese feasibility-study missions over-punctilious and repetitive, and in some areas isolated Japanese firms have not been followed by others. But in analysing the development of Japanese companies in the UK the pull effect of, for example, demands for investment where an important market exists should not be ignored. They may affect operations such as ball-bearing firms who do some greasing and packaging in order to qualify as producers, and 'screwdriver' operations in fields such as hi-fi and instruments.

A 'push' effect frequently comes from corporate strategy. 'Because Sony did this, National and Hitachi had to do the same' (Funaki, 1981, p. 11). This effect particularly applies to the manufacturers of colour T.V. sets, who constitute the major part of the manufacturing sector in the UK. Banks, trading companies, and manufacturers are engaged in global competition, particularly in view of the strategy of corporate growth, and they cannot afford to let a competitor get ahead. Japanese firms in the UK employing no more than fifty people, such as Minami Chemical Co., are none the less offshoots of major firms and groups in Japan. Other small firms can advance overseas because they are backed up by the expertise of the trading companies (Technova, 1980, Vol. 1, p. 50). This resource is not available to comparable small British or American firms. A small Japanese operation in the UK may or may not belong to a small company in Japan, and it is unwise to pay too much attention to branch size at the expense of data relating to the parent company.

Advance into the British market can also be based on a new type of product or process. Saiin Engineering in the Midlands, for instance, is building its operation around new types of measuring equipment developed by the scientist-founder of the firm. The territory of the UK operation covers Spain, Portugal, and the Middle East, but it is integrated into a European strategy involving branches in Germany and Switzerland; it is strong in the USA.

Minami Chemical Co. produces a finer grade of product than

other British firms in the same market, and is connected with a European sales company in Switzerland and another production centre in Holland. Higashi Chemical Co. was the first firm to produce the new product that it manufactures in the UK. Hito Engineering is the largest manufacturer in its field anywhere in the world, and produces items of a dimension no longer being produced by any British manufacturer. It competes strategically with one American firm, which took over the last British firm in the field and rivals in France, Germany, and Switzerland. From its UK sales office it controls direct sales in the UK, Ireland, and the Netherlands and sales agents in France and Sweden. The manager interviewed during the study was experienced in the setting up of overseas operations, in which he had been involved in Singapore and the USA.

Strategies such as the defence of markets, the avoidance of threats of protectionism, corporate competition, and the exploitation of technical advantage are not necessarily mutually exclusive. The significant factor is the long-term strategy, described by some Japanese managers as 'putting down the seeds' (Sony). No major firms have voluntarily withdrawn. One oil-related company was forced to withdraw by the bankruptcy of the parent. A small fashion company that was losing money was sold to a British firm. One distributor, which had started operations in a militant London area and experienced a strike, closed the establishment down, dismissed the workforce, and moved to a more suitable location.

Compared to the 1950s, companies now have a body of knowledge and experience of UK operations at their disposal, and should be able to avoid initial mistakes due to lack of familiarity with the environment, including investment incentives that conceal other problems. Their advance has been a reflection of the increased strength of the Japanes economy and of the increase in Japan's trade, detailed above. It is part of the process referred to as the 'internationalization' of the Japanese economy, influenced at the macro level by MITI strategy, and at the enterprise level by corporate strategy.

A Japanese critic of this spread sees three phases in post-war advances overseas. The period 1950–65 was one of 'resumption and briskness of overseas expansion; between 1965 and the oil crisis of 1973 there was 'the period of full-scale overseas expansion'; the third, present, period is one of 'reorganization of overseas expansion and transformation towards the 1980s (after the 1974-5 panic)' (Nakase, 1980, pp. 36-9). The underlying strategy is maintained, continuing the momentum through all three stages, but the pace and tactics are adapted to fit recession conditions such as lower growth.[3]

Nakase quotes a report from the administrative division of Mitsui & Co. entitled 'General Studies on Multinational Enterprises—including the Present Situation and an Overview of the Internationalization of Overseas Enterprises', comparing Japanese and American multinationals in the 1980s. The report predicted that 'by 1985, two hundred to three hundred global enterprises will dominate 80 per cent of the total production of the free nations'. Mitsui intended to play a leading part by promoting the Global Industrial System Constellation concept (GISC). The strategy was based on: (1) the optimum distribution of global resources; (2) the diffusion and exchange of new technology; (3) the profits of investment-receiving countries; (4) the profits of investing countries; (5) the profits of the multinational enterprises themselves (ibid., p. 32). The broad scope of this long-range vision characterizes Japanese thinking at both the enterprise and the government level.

Nakase concludes that the current trends of Japanese multinational enterprises are: (1) to establish full-scale multinational networks (major banks, trading companies, and manufacturers have already gone a long way to creating these) to facilitate 'the global division of labour inside the multinational enterprises'; (2) to re-allocate management resources such as personnel, goods, capital, and information (Mitsui's own global operations were reorganized on a quadripolar basis: Asia, the Americas, Europe, and Australia/Oceania. Within the London office, Mitsui & Co., Europe, is the quadripolar controlling all European and African operations); (3) to promote the vertical integration of industries; (4) to adjust their activities and plans to systematize 'the global division of labour inside the world's financial [capital] concerns'. Nakase considers that the global concept and the international distribution and utilization of all types of resources will enable the head office to reap maximum profits, but this is not consistent with views of Japanese corporations as growth- as well as profit-oriented (ibid., pp. 44-6). Symbolizing the trends discussed above and demonstrating the new corporate strategy, Mitsubishi Trading Co. was renamed

Mitsubishi Corporation in 1971 and Sumitomo Trading Co. became Sumitomo Corporation in 1978.

Other major corporations have similar plans for the future that are likely to affect the UK, although it would be an error to consider the situation in the UK deterministically. Nissan, which may establish a British production operation, plans to increase its world market share from 5.7 per cent in 1981 to 8.5 per cent by 1990. The proposed British investment would be between £200 and £300 million.[4] Other plans are for a $500 million plant in Tennessee; a ¥60 billion expansion in Mexico; acquisition of a 37 per cent stake in a Spanish manufacturer for ¥6 billion; an investment of ¥3 billion in a joint venture with Alfa Romeo, and a ¥20 billion expansion in Australia. If successful, Nissan would be building 30 per cent of its cars outside Japan by the mid 1980s (*Financial Times*, 24 February 1981). This programme would have major implications both for the internationalization of the Japanese economy and for the spread of Japanese managerial systems.

Nissan is said to be 'the Ford of Japan', and its major competitor, Toyota, 'the General Motors of Japan'. Toyota is a Kansai (western Japan) firm, with strong elements of personal leadership. Its operations are centred on its plants and satellite sub-contractors in the Nagoya area, where it operates the *kamban* system (cf. Hirschmeier and Yui, 1981, p. 338). This depends on continual punctual deliveries of components to the production lines by the sub-contractors, saving the expense etc. of warehouse stocks. The company doubts whether overseas plants could match the efficiency of its plants in Japan.

It has eleven overseas assembly operations, but does not manufacture even in the advanced industrial countries. Between 1981 and 1984 it aims to invest $1.5 billion every year on plant and equipment. It does not publicize its goals, but it is believed to want to increase its 1981 world market share of 8.4 per cent to 10 per cent by 1985. It already has 37.3 per cent of the Japanese market, but wants to raise this to 40 per cent by 1985. Under protectionist pressure it commissioned think tank feasibility studies in the USA. Two out of the three studies, regarding a car or commercial vehicle plant in the USA, were negative, and talks with Ford collapsed (*Financial Times*, 24 August 1981).

These contrasting examples demonstrate that even competitors in the same industry may make different managerial choices;

that there is not necessarily an iron logic of internationalization; and that it is dangerous to attempt to interpret moves
directed towards internationalization on rigidly functional
grounds, probably in the above cases only possible *after* the
event anyway.

The depth of analysis, the vision and clarity of overall aim of
these long-range strategies are impressive, while the well known
pragmatism of Japanese management can cater for the flexibility required to deal with unforeseeable circumstances.

At an empirical level, Inohara stresses that Japanese manufacturing operations in Europe he had visited are long-term
ventures, of which several would already have been considered
'bankrupt' by Western firms (in Thurley *et al.*, 1981, p. 28).

Stopford sees no major economic differences between Japanese companies investing in Europe and other multinationals
with regard to investment strategies, industrial structure, and
effects on trade. In this view, there is a parallel between American multinational advance into Europe in the 1950s and 1960s
and the Japanese advance in the 1970s and 1980s; both of
which have provoked political reactions (ibid., p. 8). The business strategies and economic data discussed above furnish the
context of managerial systems, but it would be deterministic
to argue that they exclude managerial choice and other priorities such as the maintenance of the company structure and its
home employment systems. The latter are linked with the
structure of Japanese society as a whole, in areas such as socialization, education, competition, and the distribution of power.
It is not clear that Japanese power holders would wish to
change domestic structures in order to benefit the foreign employees of Japanese corporations operating internationally.
Tables 32 and 33 show that, in spite of the dramatic increase in
Japanese overseas investment in the 1960s and 1970s, affiliated
overseas companies remain small in terms of personnel, sales,
and assets.

According to Sekiguchi 'Japanese direct foreign investment is
expected to increase steadily, overall. . . . In Western Europe
and South East Asia, where trade friction has already been
serious, investment will have to shift from export sales activities
to manufacturing' (Sekiguchi, 1979, pp. 136–7). If correct, this
could have major implications for the situation in the UK and
for the types of managerial systems in use. For British or

Table 32. Position of Japanese affiliated companies overseas in relation to the head office

Total assets overseas as percentage of total assets of the mother company	4.7%
Total fixed assets overseas as percentage of total fixed assets of the mother company	3.2%
Percentage of sales made overseas	8.2%
Percentage of employees engaged overseas	6.4%
Percentage of overseas employees dispatched from the mother companies	2.5%

Source: Export–Import Bank of Japan Overseas Research Centre, Management of Japan's Overseas Business (1978), p. 18. (Quoted in Nakase, 1980, p. 35.)

Table 33. Amount of direct overseas investments of Japanese enterprises on the approval basis (US$ million)

	Total	% invested in New Industrial Countries (NICs)
1968	5.6	5.8
1969	6.7	11.4
1970	9.0	9.5
1971	8.6	26.7
1972	23.4	18.8
1973	34.9	26.9
1974	24.0	20.3
1975	32.8	18.0
1976	34.6	15.6
1977	28.1	20.8
1978	46.0	19.8
1979	50.0	32.3

Source: Ministry of Finance, in Ministry of International Trade & Industry, 1981, p. 127.

American policy makers who wish to attract investment the implication appears to be that they should apply pressure in certain cases, to which Japanese management could be expected to make a pragmatic response.

In order to understand the current situation it is necessary to investigate the staffing of Japanese enterprises in the UK, which is arguably a fundamental indicator of the types of strategy being pursued.

4.2 Staffing, recruitment, and selection

Table 34 shows that just over one-quarter of the personnel of Japanese enterprises in the UK are expatriates, but that the typical ratio of expatriates to locals varies between sectors.

Table 34. Nationalities in different types of firm

Type of organization	British %	Japanese %	Other nationalities %
Local manufacturers	87.8	12.2	—
Manufacturers' sales	86.7	12.5	0.8
Trading companies	64.1	33.3	4.6
Banking	62.1	36.1	1.8
Transport & resources	36.7	58.6	4.7
Insurance	20.0	80.0	—
Other commercial	46.3	50.0	3.7
All firms	72.2	26.9	1.9

Source: Thurley *et al.*, 1980, p. 40.

Ratios of expatriates to locals also vary within the same sector. At Tanabe Bank 25 per cent are expatriates, compared with 15 per cent at Ota Bank. Ebisu Trading Co. has an above average figure of 43 per cent, the average being one-third, and the figure has recently risen due to the tighter centralized control management considers necessary to overcome the recession (Ebisu personnel manager, personal communication, 1981). At Tanaka Trading Co. the figure of 37 per cent is not markedly above average. These variations suggest the range of varying managerial strategies.

Under Department of Employment regulations non-EEC staff require work permits. Established firms report little difficulty in ensuring the regular replacement of their expatriate staff, but additional applications can cause problems. The criterion that no expatriate should have a function that local staff could fulfil is easily met on grounds of language, accounting procedures, reporting to head office, etc.; but at a time of high local unemployment Japanese managers fear a curtailment of expatriate staff.

In sales and manufacturing, local expertise is needed in functions such as selling in the local market and industrial relations.

The proportion of expatriates is correspondingly lower, although they typically occupy the key positions, providing a contrast with the trading companies and banks, many of which have a higher proportion of expatriates than American or continental banks. It also shows the danger of stereotyping Japanese firms and their managerial systems.

The expatriate ratios for commercial firms mentioned above do not necessarily correlate simply with size. Ota Bank, with fewer expatriates, is not smaller than Tanabe Bank. Ebisu Trading Co., with a higher proportion, is not larger than Tanaka Trading Co. At Ota Bank the declared policy is 'localization', i.e. that local personnel should, as far as possible, staff the organization.

Daito Engineering Co., like Minami Chemical Co., has only one expatriate, but in the former case his function is engineering, while in the latter it is accounting. Sono Engineering has nine expatriates in key managerial and engineering positions, while Saiin Engineering is the limiting case of a small manufacturer with no expatriates at all, although it is visited every six months by a director from head office. The variation again suggests differing managerial strategies.

With some exceptions, it is usual for an expatriate to hold the top executive position. In the banks and commercial firms all senior posts are held by expatriates, and at trading companies such as those referred to above this extends down to the majority of section heads. Sections in London are classified as 'departments', but the title of department manager is an inflated equivalent of the Japanese *Kacho* ('Section Chief'). These arrangements increase the top-heavy appearance of organization charts and prompts local comments of 'too many chiefs and not enough Indians'. The degree and specific function of direct expatriate managerial control can be inferred from organization charts, in which the preponderance of expatriates in managerial positions in the City firms is noteworthy.

In evaluating titles, care is necessary: the use of the term 'sub-manager' for 'supervisor' at one City firm, and the inflation of 'section chief' to 'department manager', are examples. 'Counsellor' or *Komun* ('advisor') sounds more prestigious in English, while in Japan this title, and that of 'researcher', may be given to those who have been passed over for promotion. At one trading company a British manager, whose performance did not satisfy his expatriate supervisors, was given the honorific title of 'adviser', evidently unaware of its connotation in Japan. Tanaka Trading Co. and the two banks studied each have a British assistant general manager, but there may be several expatriates with the same title and the title is of less significance than the position they occupy in relation to substantive decision making.

Titles can proliferate in Japanese organizations to the point where they lose meaning, except in prestige terms. 'Deputy general manager' may suggest a single office in English, but at one bank in the City there is a 'senior deputy general manager'. Because a rank does not illustrate an unambiguous function it is necessary to investigate what a given title means in a particular organization. A 'chief clerk' at one trading company stated that technically his rank was 'senior chief clerk' but that he felt embarrassed to use it, while a colleague asserted that the use of words depended on the principle of: 'A word means what I want it to mean, when I want it to mean it.' The proliferation of titles, discussed earlier in the context of promotion and the company ranking system is acceptable in Japan, but not among the local staff of Japanese firms in the UK. In this case the firms are applying a practice used at home to the London branches, in the evident expectation that it will solve a problem in the same way.[5]

Major corporations of the type found in the City have a policy of no redundancies in Japan; consequently the pressure of personnel recruited on a large scale in boom years (e.g. the 1960s) becomes acute during a recession. This phenomenon is alleged to account in part for the high proportion of expatriates in the City firms, described by a British personnel manager as 'exporting unemployment'. Anglo-American assumptions about the meaning of words and principles such as 'say what you mean and mean what you say' (Pascale, 1978, p. 156), categorize the imprecise use of titles as unethical. This judgement refers to absolute values, whereas Japanese values are rooted in concrete social relations, without a transcendental basis. A firm must satisfy its members' expectations of promotion and status, both to motivate them and to avoid the criticism of not being a good employer. If business conditions make this impossible, then they must do the next best thing.

The branches of the banks and trading companies in Europe

are under tight head office control and have virtually no autonomy (Japanese commercial official, Düsseldorf, personal communication). General managers are given a level of authorization
by the head office, which is periodically reviewed to allow for
inflation etc. There are strict rules for credit management in the
branches, and at Tanaka Trading Co. all new types of transac-
tion, all business in 'risk' areas, and all transactions above the
general manager's level of authorization must be referred to the
head office.

The Japanese practice of maintaining close informal links
with colleagues at head office, for career reasons, ensures constant consultation by telephone and telex (Inohara, personal
communication). The distinction between informing the head
office and consulting it in order to obtain approval is blurred,
and it is unlikely that significant transactions (even within the
limit) would be initiated without the head office being informed/
consulted by, for instance, *Kohai* (juniors) in the branch tele-
phoning to their *Sempai* (seniors) in Japan. As Inohara has said,
'Looking at the surface and the formal structure of Japanese
organisations does not provide many lessons' (in Thurley *et al.*,
1981, p. 29). This cannot be repeated too often.

In the overseas branches of firms of any nationality there is
likely to be competition between expatriates and locals for
career positions. 'Considerable rivalry exists among Japanese
middle managers in the UK and potential British managers who
might also jeopardise their promotion prospects' (N. Kagami,
former director, Nomura Research Institute, London, in Thurley *et al.*, 1980, part 2, p. 9).

Local staff are virtually excluded from the type of telephone
contact with the head office referred to; firstly, because they
have no diffuse relations of the Japanese type with personnel
there; secondly, because they are not familiar with Japanese
business and do not 'know their way around' the organization,
and so cannot cultivate the right relationships in their centrally
controlled companies; and thirdly, because they suffer from
linguistic and other social handicaps in the Japanese context.
This isolates them from the expatriate group in the branch,
which maintains its control whatever titles may be given to
local staff.

The British personnel manager at Ebisu Trading Co. has secured
formal approval for a complete set of British job descriptions,

assessment, and promotion criteria, with definitions of terms used, so as to make them unambiguous, but it has been impossible to have them implemented (personal communication). Criteria for promotion of local staff exist at Tanaka Trading Co., but it is alleged that the demands for linguistic skills and familiarity with the business relations of the company make it impossible for local personnel, however competent in a given business field, to be accepted. To expatriate managers this is a 'functional' reason, while to the local staff it is a self-fulfilling prophecy.

Japanese companies have long been aware of the need to avoid conflict with their local employees (Thurley *et al.*, 1976, p. 113). The commercial firms are conscious of the problem and employ a number of strategies to accommodate it, but the training of local staff for senior or even middle management positions has hardly been attempted. According to Kagami, a manager with considerable overseas experience and an 'international' outlook, 'the problem lies with top management. Individual Japanese managers in the UK cannot deal with it on their own' (ibid., p. 10). It is a question of head office control and head office policy.

The above discussion shows why it is logical to treat staffing, recruitment, and selection together: all are determined by the head office policy regarding local staff. Kagami's remark confirms the Düsseldorf official's comment on the lack of branch autonomy.[6]

Many commercial firms, such as Oka Transport Co., Ueda Transport Co., and Maruyama Trading Co., have one long-serving British manager, with anything up to twenty-five years' service. They are important as 'go-betweens', a characteristically Japanese institution, between the expatriate management and the local staff, but they are not integrated into the former. The manager fulfilling this role at Maruyama Trading Co. is a trained engineer who worked in Japan, but those at Moriguchi Bank, Ota Bank, Toho-Morita Distribution etc., have pursued a steady career in the same field. Their attitude, their ability to act as go-betweens, especially regarding personnel administration, and their specific expertise, in that order, are their main qualifications.

They also provide an element of continuity, while expatriates are replaced on average every four to five years. Discussions of the ideal type of life employment in Japan distract attention from the empirical situation in the London branches, where the longer-serving locals are the 'permanent staff', and the continually circulating expatriates the transients. Young expatriates must to some extent defer to older British managers of the 'go-between' type, even if the latter cannot hope to attain the positions open to the former. Age and long service, especially when accompanied by competence, are respected in Japanese society. Such older managers may be useful to the firm on the personnel side to explain local custom and practice, employment law and official regulations with which expatriates are unfamiliar. Table 35 shows the small proportions of older long-serving local staff compared to the more mobile younger age groups.

Table 35. Age distribution of local staff

Age Groups	Men	%	Women	%	Total	%
Under 20	176	10.1	235	16.2	411	12.8
20–29	654	37.4	645	44.5	1299	40.6
30–39	504	28.8	340	23.5	844	26.4
40–49	209	11.9	155	10.7	364	11.4
50–59	152	8.7	52	3.6	204	6.4
Over 60	53	3.0	23	1.6	76	2.4
Total	1748	99.9	1450	100.0	3198	100.0

Source: Thurley et al., 1980, p. 43.

Virtually all male expatriates are posted to London by the head office, but few females. Locally recruited Japanese males are rare, except in travel agencies and in cases where they have studied and/or married locally. A Japanese Cambridge graduate, for instance, is employed at Toho-Morita Distribution. The predominance of male over female expatriates is a further index of the senior status of Japanese staff, in view of the patterns of female employment in Japan discussed above. In spite of this, many female staff have useful linguistic skills. They are evaluated as more conscientious workers than their local counterparts, and can more easily be persuaded to do overtime. Tables 36 and 37 show these data statistically.

General managers of banks and trading companies may stay only two to three years in London because the head office requires their knowledge before it becomes outdated. Trainees stay

Table 36. Origins of expatriates in UK branches

	Men		Women		Total	
	No.	%	No.	%	No.	%
Sent from Japan	993	93	53	16.5	1,046	75.2
Recruited locally	75	7	269	83.5	344	24.7
Total Japanese	1,068	100	322	100	1,390	99.9

Source: Thurley *et al.*, 1980, p. 41.

Table 37. Nationality and sex of employees of UK branches

Nationality	Men	%	Women	%	Total
Japanese	1,068	76.8	322	23.2	1,390
British	1,992	54.0	1,695	46.0	3,687
Other	44	45.8	52	54.2	96
Totals	3,104	60.0	2,069	40.0	5,173

Source: Thurley *et al.*, 1980, p. 40.

approximately two and a half years. Manufacturing company managers may stay longer, depending on the stage of development of the company, or any special needs.

The posting system is 'Japan-centred', and the continuous replacement of expatriate personnel leads to problems of familiarization and the adaptation of local staff to the style of a new manager. Many local staff in the City assert that it is a cause of lower levels of organizational performance, but they are hardly in a position to know the priorities of the head office which are the decisive factor. For expatriates themselves, service overseas creates the anxiety of losing touch with the 'main stream' in the head office, and of being disadvantaged in their careers. They also face problems with children who are older than kindergarten age because of the pressures of the Japanese education system (cf. Funaki, 1981, pp. 10–11).

An 'internationalist' expatriate at Tanaka Trading Co. argued that it would be more rational to select expatriates who are willing to serve long periods overseas, and to reward them accordingly;

this would provide continuity and good management. Few inter-viewees supported this view and it is doubtful whether there would be enough volunteers, but it does show that there are internationalists, as well as traditionalists and the merely acqui-escent, among Japanese managers. The manager in question was competent, ambitious, and experienced in overseas operations.

The City firms are typically staffed by expatriates from assis-tant manager (deputy section chief) to general manager level, but in the sales and manufacturing companies there is typically a smaller proportion, consisting of senior managers and func-tional specialists. The latter are typically responsible for engineer-ing, quality control, finance and administration, purchasing from and liaison with Japan: different types of control function, re-flecting head office policy. Sales, personnel, and industrial rela-tions are typically local responsibilities. Distribution firms with 100–300 employees, such as Daitoku Distribution, Daitoku Electronics, and Kansai Distribution, have Institute of Personnel Management (IPM) qualified personnel managers; until recently there was no such example in the City. There are a few Japanese managers with personnel department experience acting as per-sonnel directors in the larger trading companies, and one in a manufacturing company in Ireland that has faced personnel problems, but their assignment overseas by the head office is exceptional.

At Kansai Electronics the functions allotted under company policy to expatriates are in senior management (control) and engineering and quality control. At Sono Engineering each of the British quality inspection leaders and production section leaders is 'covered' by a Japanese engineer. Arguably, the head office fears that quality standards could drop if responsibility were handed over to local staff, but it can then be asked why the company does not recruit the grade of staff in which it would have confidence. This could be due either to policy on salary levels or to policy on the employment of home personnel. Inohara stresses Japanese manufacturers' emphasis on quality, punctual delivery, and productivity, in that order (Thurley *et al.*, 1981, p. 28). One manufacturer in Ireland with quality and productivity problems has brought in an expatriate task force under its senior technical expert, but this has not improved relations with local staff.

It is emphasized that staffing policies vary between firms in the same field. Daito Engineering replaced all its expatriates in 1981 except for the managing director and one engineer. The managing director is also responsible for sales and is one of the few expatriates likely to stay permanently. He has a British wife and was recruited for his present post by the trading company connected with the firm. He could have career and social difficulties in re-entering a company he had left. His chances might be better with Daito in Japan, but from their management's point of view he is more useful in the UK.

One firm in Ireland also has a long-serving expatriate managing director, who joined it before start-up, and whose experience in Ireland is therefore valuable to the company. He has been successful in overseeing the Irish operation, but his career prospects are similarly constrained by having come from another firm. In these two cases the managing directors enjoy higher status than they had in their original firms and they are not in a good position to request a transfer. In the first case the manager is probably content to remain in Europe, but it was our impression (confirmed by a Japanese colleague) that the second manager was less willing.

Other smaller manufacturers have fewer expatriates. Minami Chemical Co. has a managing director to control policy from the sales office, but on site there is only a middle-ranking accountant. Higashi Chemical Co. has an expatriate managing director and a sales manager, the latter to be replaced by a British graduate. Sales were first handled by Ebisu Trading Co. There is a locally recruited female expatriate purchasing manager, who appears likely to remain. A key role in the firm is that of the British director,[7] an Oxford chemistry graduate. These two chemical firms both employ approximately fifty staff. Saiin Engineering, employing twenty, has no expatriate staff, although its activities are coordinated by a visiting director and a European operations centre. One other small assembler in Scotland now also has no expatriate staff.

Kyoto Electronics, a distribution firm with sixty-nine employees, is run by one expatriate and two local managers, one of whom is from another EEC country. Daimon Engineering and Hito Engineering both distribute ball bearings. The former is managed by a local man, who replaced an expatriate, and the latter by an expatriate experienced in overseas operations. Hito Engineering has engaged competent British sales staff, formerly employed by a British competitor. Under expatriate control, they are given local autonomy. The career prospects of such managers in distribution firms are superior to those in the City firms.

The preliminary study of Japanese companies in the UK reported that, on the basis of Dore's definition of Japanese employment policies, there was little evidence that such principles were important. 'Recruitment, for example, used the channels of advertisements in newspapers, personal contacts and notification of vacancies to job centres and private agencies. Only in the case of Company D (a manufacturer) was recruitment from schools important' (Thurley et al., 1976, p. 103). This pattern has not changed greatly. Firms use national newspaper advertising for a few more senior specialized posts (in, for example, personnel management) and local papers for others. Companies such as Ota Bank use a standard application form and a screening interview, with a final interview held by the department manager concerned. Like others in the manufacturing field, it has had mixed experiences with staff provided by agencies; the same also applies to the government-run Job Centres.

Most commercial firms require local staff for routine administrative, clerical, or technical, e.g. computer, work. The distribution of local staff at the lower end of the occupational hierarchy and their low educational levels are apparent from Tables 38 and 39.[8]

Table 38. Occupational status groups of local staff

	Men	%	Women	%	Total	%
Managerial*	181	7.4	7	0.5	188	4.8
Administrative/technical	887	36.5	246	17.0	1,133	29.2
Supervisory	243	10.0	34	2.3	277	7.1
Clerical	461	19.0	944	64.2	1,405	36.2
Manual/ancillary	659	27.1	216	14.9	875	22.6
	2,431	100.0	1,447	99.9	3,878	99.9

Source: Thurley et al., 1980, p. 42.

* It must be stressed that the term 'managerial' used above was applied by the companies themselves.

Table 39. Educational qualifications of local staff

	Men	%	Women	%	Total	%
University education	101	5.1	29	1.7	130	3.6
A-levels or H.N.C./H.N.D.	259	13.0	98	5.8	357	9.6
4 O-levels	382	19.1	268	15.8	650	17.6
	742	37.2	395	23.3	1,137	30.0

Source: Thurley *et al.*, 1980, p. 44.

Some development areas, where manufacturers are situated, have high levels of unemployment, but this does not apply to the City. White-collar staff pursue individual managerial or clerical careers, seeking prospects of promotion and reward and creating considerable job mobility. This does not accord with the pattern of long service that the firms in the City follow in Japan. Companies like Tanaka Trading Co. avoid discharging long-serving staff, but they have no policy of attempting to implement the full Japanese pattern in the City's fluid labour market. Turnover is considerable. Companies will reward individuals whose attitude and performance meet their needs, especially of the 'go-between' type; this encouragement of 'loyal' staff is seen at Tanabe Bank, Tanaka Trading Co., and others.

At Ota Bank, nearly half the local staff surveyed had served for more than five years, with a considerable number in the one-to-five year category. At Tanabe slightly more than one-fifth of local staff surveyed had served more than five years, but there were more in the six-months-to-a-year category than in the one-to-five year. At Ebisu Trading Co. annual turnover was over 40 per cent, but was reduced to single figures after the engagement of a British personnel manager. Part of his strategy was to cease recruiting typists in the volatile 20–6 age group and to recruit either more stable, mature staff, or school leavers who might be socialized into the organization. The British manager at Moriguchi Bank with personnel responsibility had also built up recruiting connections with schools.

Many employees at manufacturers in South Wales and other development areas have come from older firms that have closed down or laid off staff. The exceptions are Sono Engineering and two television manufacturers, which maintain contact with schools and train their high proportions of young workers in their own way. Nearly two-thirds of the workforce of Sono Engineering are under 25, and most of the remainder are under 35. For 31 per cent of the workforce it is their first work experience after school. At Kansai Electronics half the workforce are female: 90 per cent of them at the operator level, as could be expected in Japan. About 70 per cent of the workforce are aged between 20 and 39. These three companies, whose employment practices most resemble those in Japan, as described by Dore and others, are relatively isolated examples in a labour market characterized by considerable movement. Sono Engineering has been commercially successful, exporting 80 per cent of its production and investing in new lines even during the recession, but managers are aware that they face promotion problems in a few years' time because the bulk of young employees are of similar age. This situation resembles the problem for the commercial companies in Japan discussed above.

Table 39 showed the small proportion of British graduates in Japanese firms in the UK. Ota Bank, an 'internationalist' firm with a low (15 per cent) proportion of expatriates, has one graduate loan officer, classified as an assistant manager. At Tanabe Trading Co. there are two graduate trainee traders. Another graduate, with a degree in Japanese and who negotiated with the company to be sent to Japan for a year, left the company since the study began. Many firms do not employ graduates, and it is questionable how far the few that there are can participate in, e.g., decision making, as opposed to fulfilling a specific function for which it is not necessary to be a graduate.

The issue of graduate recruitment is frequently discussed. Manufacturing firms such as Kansai Electronics and Sono Engineering do not recruit local engineering graduates, and there are few exceptions to this principle in either Britain or Ireland. The British director at Higashi Chemical Co., an Irish laboratory manager, and an Irish plant manager (directly under an expatriate) with PhDs are exceptional. Companies like Sono Engineering are extremely quality conscious, but there the British manager (again under an expatriate) is an *assistant* quality control manager because he has a lower formal qualification instead of the degree which would confer the full status in expatriate eyes. His position in relation to his *de facto* expatriate superior is not clear from the formal organization chart.

Other manufacturing and distribution firms visited also had no local graduates. Does this mean that in the UK there are insufficient qualified engineers to staff the Japanese companies? Or is it company policy not to recruit them?

Some argue that local engineers are not 'trusted', in the sense that Japanese engineers were formerly not trusted as technicians. Engineers in Japanese companies in Japan receive in-house training on the particular system in use, but this does not appear to apply in the EEC. It is not adequate to argue *ex post facto* that the presence of expatriate engineers proves that they are functionally essential, even if they are convenient for the companies.[9]

Regarding the centralization versus decentralization problem, the City companies are in a different situation to the manufacturers and sales companies, but there is an analogous problem with graduates. Japanese graduates frequently study subjects as 'impractical' as those studied by British arts graduates but, unlike the British, they change quickly to the new role they are expected to play in the company. 'The Japanese look upon man as a being subordinated to a specific and limited human nexus; they conceive him in terms of human relations' (Nakamura, 1971, p. 311). British arts graduates tend to regard business as 'inferior' (Mant, 1979); they are in any case more 'individualistic' and, until the recession, had high expectations of a career.

The pull of the City for Japanese companies and its success as an earner of invisibles suggest that there is local expertise present, including graduate expertise. The insurance companies, for example, are content to let British agency companies do business for them, a fact which explains why the largest of the thirteen companies has only five staff.

At companies like Tanaka Trading Co. three types of local staff can be identified. They are, firstly, the 'old type', i.e. long-serving staff with low educational qualifications recruited from the 1950s onwards as clerks, with no suggestion that they were management material, although some have honorific titles. In spite of (critics would say because of) their poor performance, the company will not discharge them. Secondly, there is the 'new type': near graduates and other better educated local staff. They are restricted to specific trading areas in the business sections and are not found in the crucial support sections, such as credit control. This restricts their promotion, but they are more competent than the old type of local staff. Thirdly, there are the graduates, recruited on the Japanese pattern from prestigious universities in the 1970s, in theory to be groomed for managerial roles. Inevitably this led to mutual bad feeling with the old type of clerical staff.

The measure of the problem was that many interviewees referred to the graduate recruitment scheme as 'window dressing', partly because no consistent training or career progression could be identified. It was asserted that expatriate managers whose main, and in most cases only, experience of local staff was with the old type of staff whose promotion was blocked, concluded that local staff in general were incompetent, poorly motivated, and unsuitable for promotion. 'Incompetence' therefore became a self-fulfilling prophecy, when the root cause was the recruitment and staffing policy.

Some expatriate managers, including the personnel manager who had promoted the scheme, were in favour of this internationalist approach, while traditionalists opposed it. The latter were in the majority and, since this probably reflected the head office view, it is not surprising that the scheme was discontinued.

Individual graduates were sent to Japan at different times, but the problem was less how to recruit them than how to retain them. Most eventually left for promotion reasons.

Some expatriate managers, including the general manager of Morita Trading Co., appeared to think that recruitment of graduates straight from the most prestigious universities would operate in the UK as in Japan, and were not easily convinced that this would not be the case. The British personnel manager at Ebisu Trading Co. believed it would be more practicable to train graduates in Japanese as businessmen than vice versa, but traditionally Japanese studies in the UK have been oriented towards the arts, although there are recent exceptions. Tanaka Trading Co. had been disappointed not to get a more positive response from university appointments boards, leading to a closer relationship.

Sanno Trading Co. had a graduate who was proficient at reading Japanese telexes, but when he left he was not replaced. It was explained that such expertise was no longer necessary because the English of expatriates had improved, a point which the interviews confirmed. One female graduate with a first-class degree in Japanese is employed on secretarial work in an insurance company, and another female graduate was employed for a short period as a personnel assistant at a retail company, but none of the present studies has revealed a demand for local staff with a knowledge of Japanese. Indeed some local staff believe this skill is not wanted because Japanese may be useful as a confidential language. In theory a knowledge of Japanese is a criterion for the promotion of local graduates, together with competence, familiarity with the company's operations in Japan and overseas, and the ability to entertain Japanese clients etc. To date no one has met these criteria.

One Tanaka Trading Co. manager saw the solution in splitting the London operation into 'Japan-oriented' and 'Europe-oriented' parts, but the latter would have to 'be aware of human relations with Japanese mills, producers etc.'. His view was that 'British staff can't adapt to the Japanese system and make it work efficiently. The crucial difference is the social background.' He saw the latter specifically as the familistic organization of the merchant houses from the Tokugawa period onwards. It should be emphasized that he had been in London for ten years and had a son who had graduated from a British university. His solution included the promotion of competent graduates in joint ventures, while the old type of staff could be employed on routine clerical work in the Japan-oriented company. His standpoint was traditionalist, but it contained a more frank assessment of staffing problems than many expatriates were prepared to discuss. With regard to 'competence', local graduates should have the advantage in dealing with Western firms or government bodies compared to expatriate managers whose stay in London is limited.

A further problem is that local graduates expect to be rewarded by faster promotion than is the norm in Japan. When it is not granted, they leave. This shows the difficulty of reconciling the ideal typical Japanese long-service promotion model with its gradual progression before the high fliers are separated out, with the British pattern of job mobility and individual career development based on performance, without a minimum formal age for a given rank. The manager quoted above proposed that the way round the problem would be to post potential local managers to, for example, Canada or Australia, and then back to London so that they would be old enough to be acceptable to expatriates as managers.[10]

A sceptical Japanese comment was that the graduates were clever to get experience of Japanese business and then to move up to a better career position in a local firm. One graduate expressed the view that the internationalization of business would have to include personnel and that there would be local graduate managers by the late 1980s, but this interpretation appeared to ignore the interests of the head office.

To some extent a company like Tanaka has moved up market away from the old type of local clerical staff but it was unsuccessful in retaining graduates, and others have not attempted a similar scheme. One graduate stated that 'London is moving towards autonomy but Tanaka is very conservative.[11] The Japanese in London are not international and are still thinking of Tokyo. The Japanese won't accept good local staff's knowledge of local conditions.[12] To work here one must accept that the Japanese basically make all the decisions. At whatever age they come in, local staff come in as trainee traders, not managers.'

Another graduate stated that 'Tanaka is geared to be Japanese, not multinational; it will take time to evolve and it does not exist in a vacuum. The stronger, more creative Japanese who have been abroad support internationalization and bringing more Europeans to Japan, but all this is the dream of a few people. There should be a European personnel adviser in Tokyo to push multinationalization, but the function of the personnel department in Tokyo is to train Japanese personnel abroad.' This is a statement of the policy of the 'Tokyo-centred' head office, showing where its priorities lie and why change is 'the dream of a few people'.

The ICERD study revealed several ill-defined *ad hoc* compromises in the personnel field. Tanabe Bank stated that it wanted local staff 'with a deep sense of responsibility', and warned that 'brilliant but awkward people would not fit in'. This stress on fitting in (to the Japanese organization) reflects the concern with attitude previously discussed. At the formal level Ebisu Trading Co. had clear assessment procedures and promotion criteria, but these were modified in practice by informal variations. For local staff, success in the Japanese companies remains on the organization's terms and these do not cater for job changing and career paths—concepts opposed to the organization-centredness and task orientation of Japanese firms.

How far expatriate and local selection criteria might be interchangeable does not appear to have received consistent attention. As with competence, the differences in connotation may be so great as to render the concept useless. In many City firms selection is a joint responsibility, with the expatriate managers in senior positions having the greatest say. On the other hand, Ota Bank clearly stated that it required 'professionalism' from its local staff. In the ICERD survey, 68 per cent of the banks and 56 per cent of the trading companies stated that they hired males with specific job experience.

The comparison of staffing and recruitment in the City firms with that in the sales and manufacturing firms shows that those succeeding in exerting the greatest control in the local environment are manufacturers like Sono Engineering and the television makers. The volatile City labour market forces the commercial firms to compromise and to settle for a lower level of control over local staff than they are accustomed to. At the same time they maintain tight, separate control over home country staff by operating the same career and reward system as in Japan. This is the 'dual employment system' found in all Japanese companies in the UK, but which becomes conspicuous in the City firms because of the large number of expatriates they employ.

Local staff cannot move from one part of the dual employment system to the other. If they are prepared to fit into the organization on its terms they may be rewarded for fulfilling the basically routine tasks required of them. If they are not prepared to acquiesce, they generally leave. Either way the organization avoids disruption and fulfils its aims. Expatriates and their assignment and training are the head office's priority. They are the full members of the organization, selected in the proper way, who, barring accidents, can be expected to stay with the company until retirement. They are the personnel controlled most closely by the head office, on whom the head office and their own colleagues can place the greatest reliance, and from whom the company can expect the most highly motivated service because their own careers are at stake.

4.3 Training, promotion, and rewards

Only thirteen companies, of which five were manufacturers, stated in the ICERD questionnaire study that they had induction training for local staff (Thurley *et al.*, 1980, p. 47).

The course at Ebisu Trading Co. is one of the most developed, but it lasts only three to four hours and can be held only twice a year, when sufficient participants have been assembled. The course outlines the organization and activities of the trading companies, especially Ebisu. There is a general discussion about Japan, a company film and slides. Changes were necessary in some of the materials provided by the head office because 'the company man image is not appreciated' (personnel manager, personal communication). Ebisu runs functional courses for telex, computer accounting, and business: the latter for possible candidates for promotion.

Japanese managers receive a general orientation for overseas, not geared to any particular area, before leaving Japan. They then attend a short external course on familiarization with the UK at a British management consultant's centre. Training at Ebisu 'is in its infancy' (personnel manager), but the company is doing more than most City firms. The majority provide no orientation training for expatriates at all (Thurley *et al.*, loc cit.).

Ebisu and a few other City firms, but no sales organizations or manufacturers as far as is known, provide voluntary Japanese language lessons, paid for by the company, except for text books. They are held in the office. The purpose is to acquaint local staff with Japanese life and thought, not, however, for use in business, where the complexity of the written language makes even reading telexes difficult.

Individual Japanese managers may attempt to communicate something of the corporate culture to local staff but little is done through official training programmes. There are several possible reasons. Most firms are small and local staff are generally recruited as clerks, telex operators, secretaries, etc., and not as potential managers. Provided they fulfil their functions adequately and fit in to some extent with the organization, there is no need to train them further, particularly as they may leave the company for alternative employment. Given the significance of informal systems in companies, which local staff have not experienced by analogy in the wider society and cannot recognize, there may be limited value in formal instruction. Time is a constraint and companies prefer tight manning and the use of overtime.[13]

Training requires instructors and it is not clear how many expatriate managers would be able to operate as communicators and trainers in a non-Japanese environment. The host society does not provide the social and ideological supports available to trainees in Japan, and it must be asked how many expatriate managers are sufficiently well acquainted with the local society to know what staff require to learn. Expatriate managers complain of the apathy, lack of initiative, and narrow occupational consciousness of local staff and criticize the failure to share information, without always being aware of the social background of occupational boundaries and their connection with local career structures. The personnel director at Toho-Morita Distribution considers 'the problem is the way of thinking. Japanese are not requested to do things. They get on by themselves and find things to do; but British wait for orders, so top management must order everything in detail. Some key locals are beginning to understand what is needed.' Japanese who are (relatively) secure in an organization, and have been trained to be flexible as well as loyal, have a different perspective from local staff, who have experienced a different type of authority and have learnt not to infringe a superior's prerogative. But how many expatriates are in the UK long enough, or have the time and inclination, to grapple with such concepts?

Outside the City, Japan Air Lines is one of the few companies that has a developed training programme, with formally organized courses in passenger sales etc. Most City firms use on-the-job training, and it seems unlikely that they would be willing to expand training during a recession.

According to Inohara, unprogrammed on-the-job training in Japanese firms in Europe in general follows the principle of 'you learn by being with us' (in Thurley et al., 1981, p. 28). The prevalence of on-the-job training in Japan itself has been discussed already, and in this respect the companies are following home practice, although for the reasons stated the solution is more ad hoc abroad. Job rotation (cf. Ouchi, 1981, pp. 51-5; Sasaki, 1981, p. 37) is less common because of local functional specialization and because it is not necessary to use this training method with staff who will not be promoted as generalists. Local staff generally remain in the function for which they were recruited.

Unprogrammed on-the-job training may appear to lack employer commitment and the case studies showed that training and promotion were the areas of greatest local staff dissatisfaction. Reports on other EEC countries presented at the 1981

ICERD conference on Japanese Management in Western Europe indicated that this was not confined to the UK.

Consistent with the pattern of recruitment, especially of young employees, a limited number of larger manufacturers of precision products, such as Sono Engineering and the television makers referred to, are the firms with the most developed training schemes. At the start-up Sono Engineering followed normal practice and brought in a large group of (fifty) expatriates to train local personnel. The study showed that 84 per cent of supervisors and 53 per cent of operators had been trained by expatriates and that they had appreciated the training. Japanese engineers, whose English is generally weaker than that of trading company personnel, had succeeded in demonstrating the production processes to local employees. The expatriate company secretary still acts as an unofficial interpreter when necessary.

This informal training at operator level, and the way Japanese engineers would run through the whole procedure, is warmly remembered at Sono Engineering and Minami Chemical Co. Sono has also sent two groups of eight or nine managers and supervisors to Japan for four-month periods of mainly technical training, with some insight into man management in Japanese plants. This training was appreciated, although eight of the first group were sent two days after joining the company and found that not everything was ready. In 1977 a party of eighteen supervisors in a chemical company in Ireland were sent to Japan for training, but half have now left. This is disappointing for management and unlikely to persuade them that training in Japan is cost effective.

At Higashi Chemical Co. new operators train with experienced operators. Workers with leadership potential are trained by local staff as foremen but, as in most companies, this is 'technical, not philosophical, training—we don't use Japanese policies here' (local production manager, personal communication). This contrasts with the situation in Sono, where there is a more Japanese emphasis on quality and the prestige of the product, and with the Japanese climate in the television factories (Takamiya, 1979a).

At Sono Engineering employees are appraised three times a year, and if their performance is satisfactory they will be trained as section leaders or chargehands, and upgraded. This is a conscious motivational policy and was appreciated by the workforce.

It struck researchers who visited one industrial estate as rare because in most of the British and other firms 'there was no appreciation that developed appraisal and promotion systems could be linked to motivation' (Anderson *et al.*, 1980, p. 62).

At Minami Chemical Co. half the workforce and all but one of the ten managers and supervisors stated that they had received training from expatriates during the start-up period. The British plant manager's policy is to train operators for other jobs, using on-the-job instruction, and 61 per cent of the workforce stated they had experienced job rotation. The aim is to motivate the workforce by the satisfaction inherent in job rotation, which differs from the Japanese tendency to use it as training *per se*. The average age of shopfloor workers, recruited on the basis of their qualifications and experience, is thirty-five, and they are older than at Sono. The basis of recruitment and the training system are more British than at Sono.

Together with Sono, the television makers studied by Takamiya were the firms whose training systems most closely approximated those in use in Japan. At Daitoku all new entrants, whether shopfloor, engineering, clerical, or managerial staff, follow a basic production course in soldering, colour coding, and assembly.[14] Office staff work for several days in different departments before joining the one to which they are assigned. Engineers spend an initial six months as repairmen, familiarizing themselves with the work of each section on the production line. The standpoint is that 'for a good engineering job, acquiring down to earth knowledge of the production line is far more important than marginally improving your engineering skills by modern sophisticated theories' (local engineer, quoted in Takamiya, 1979a, p. 11). The plant manager sees the shopfloor as the centre of the company because it produces what the company sells. He has less interest in the cleaner, in Britain usually higher status, office. But in spite of these training programmes, researchers found the training function of the personnel department in two Japanese companies 'underdeveloped' (Bennett *et al.*, 1979, p. 99).

In Takamiya's example, job rotation applied to managers as well as to the shopfloor. Its purpose was to break down departmental barriers and improve coordination. A manager was obliged by his Japanese superior to find out from other departments what the consequences for them of his reports and

proposals might be. This took him time, but in the end he commented favourably on the concept, which was similar to that
of *ringi* in the commercial firms discussed below.

Such training, in which locals are being incorporated to some
extent into a Japanese system, contrasts with the situation in
the City, where locals may be given on-the-job training in a
specific function but remain more isolated from the expatriate
system. A third variant, in firms with few expatriates, is for
technical training on the British pattern to be given. This applies
to craftsmen at Miki Precision Products and technicians and
engineers at Daitoku Electronics.

City firms, such as Kiku Bank, have sent local staff to Japan
to combine business with an opportunity to see the functioning of the head office, but this cannot be considered training in
any structured sense. Some firms send long-serving local managers to Japan on seminars, as a reward rather than as training,
and at Ota Bank this is a regular practice for those about to
retire. In view of the recession and the high costs, it is not surprising that few companies use visits to Japan to train and motivate employees, and to accustom them to working in closer
accordance with home country practice, but in most cases it is
impossible to find any evidence that such training has been con-
templated or that organized courses are available.

In training, the Japanese organization- and task-centred
approach contrasts with local individual- and career-centred
approaches. City firms are unwilling to send staff on external
courses unless they are directly relevant to the employee's function in the company. There is no interest in training staff for
a career outside the company, which might increase the likelihood of them leaving. The interview question 'How far is the
company willing to help you with your future career?' prompted
several respondents to ask whether this meant inside the company or outside it. Many stated that the companies would do
anything necessary for the organization, but were not interested
in furthering individual careers, especially where competitors
might reap the benefit.

This is consistent with the argument developed earlier that
management in Japan controls its employees through long-term
employment, enabling it to recover the costs and inputs of training. The functional objection to job mobility was that it reduced
work group cohesiveness and organizational performance, while

the ideological objection was that it represented 'disloyalty', 'selfishness', etc. The moral tone of some interviewees' comments on the sense of obligation employees should feel for training received was striking.

Expatriates and local staff tend to persist with their usual ideas and ideologies. At a successful electronics factory in Ireland, for instance, the management, who might be described as benevolent traditionalists, were keenly aware of the risk of losing ambitious managerial and technical staff, but saw a dilemma. If they replaced expatriates by local managers, there was no guarantee that they might not be tempted away by better prospects elsewhere. Continuity would be lost and in the worst case the operation might collapse. Here it can be argued that the operative factor was not so much 'loyalty' but the cost to the firm of staff in a more competitive labour market than exists in Japan, where the problem would not arise for the management of this type of established firm. The labour market as a factor in pushing up wage costs, especially in a booming industry such as electronics, and in reducing the level of managerial control, is a doubly unattractive prospect for the companies. The data also suggest that the career problems of local staff in manufacturing may not be so dissimilar from those in the commercial firms after all. Managers and technicians at this plant voiced the same complaints, in almost identical terms, as those in the City firms, although the ceiling on promotion was higher. The shopfloor appeared well contented and working conditions, canteen, etc., were excellent, but expatriate management appeared more worried about them than about local managers and technicians, who were potentially a greater problem because of their possible opportunities in rival electronics firms.

The Irish factory was one of several instances where the expectations of expatriate managers and their perceptions of the local situation diverged from the empirical data. Lack of orientation training results in stereotyped and inadequate knowledge of local conditions. Having heard about British and Irish unions, militancy, demarcation, etc., Japanese managers expect trouble from the blue-collar workforce. They do not seem to appreciate that such workers, with their solidaristic orientation and lower job mobility, and their desire for 'egalitarian' treatment (which Japanese manufacturers practice), are in fact easier to handle than white-collar and managerial staff. Conversely, management expects the latter to be loyal, motivated, and task-oriented, and is at a loss how to deal with individualistic, upwardly mobile, career seekers. This situation is no longer new and yet there is little evidence that orientation training for expatriates is considered necessary or that the above stereotypes badly need revising.

The sole clear exception on the matter of external courses was Ota Bank, which encourages local staff to take the Institute of Bankers' exams and rewards those who are successful. In fact few take the opportunity, even though this would help them in their careers in other banks (personnel manager, personal communication). One shipping line subsidizes employees who take the Institute of Chartered Shipbrokers' exams, but 'this is up to the individual; we do not deliberately encourage them'. Both examples show British rather than Japanese practice. Unlike most City firms, especially the smaller ones, the bank has a grading system and an annual appraisal, with a self-appraisal element.

The ceiling on promotion is most constraining in the City firms, where all substantive managerial posts are held by expatriates. In sales companies, such as Toho-Morita Distribution and Morita Tractors—both connected with the same trading company—local managers, including general affairs or personnel managers, are under direct expatriate control.

In other sales firms, such as Daitoku Distribution, local managers can sometimes gain the upper hand. A qualified employee at Daitoku, trained in the firm, left for a similar post with a rival, Kansai. Shortly afterwards he telephoned to the British personnel manager, asking to be taken back. Subsequently he was re-employed. The personnel manager was put under extreme pressure by expatriate colleagues, embarrassed by telephone calls from Kansai protesting about 'poaching by a fellow-Japanese firm' and requesting the employee's return. But the personnel manager adamantly declared, 'We've trained him and if he wants to come back then he's ours.' The willingness of his expatriate colleagues to hand back a 'defector' underlines this classic instance of the gap in perceptions and values of local and expatriate personnel and the incompatibility, in present conditions, of the two types of employment system.

There are British managing directors at Daitoku and Daitoku Electronics, but purchasing from Japan is in expatriate hands. At Hito Engineering the managing director is Japanese and the sales manager under him British. Such firms offer promotion up to a certain level, but no cases have been reported of promotion outside the local branch.

The ceiling on promotion is less constraining in sales and manufacturing, but the examples of Sono Engineering and Kansai Electronics show that it still exists. The exceptions are small (fifty employees) branches, such as Minami and Higashi Chemical companies,[15] with their British production management, and the limiting cases of Saiin Engineering (twenty employees) and an assembler in Scotland with all-local staffs.

The new policy of 'this is a British company' was announced personally by the president of Daito Engineering from Japan. Although under the control of a 'permanent' expatriate, in contact with the head office, it is entering a new phase. Previously there had been a gap between local and expatriate management, resulting in pressure for localization, and as a result the company had evidently decided to adopt this policy. It withdrew its expatriates, probably at a considerable financial saving. The company's licensing agreement is due to expire and to deal with responsibility for its own engineering it has engaged a qualified engineer with an electronics background; but he is a Member of the Institute of Electrical Engineers, not a university graduate.

In small firms, a shortage of expatriate managers, the high cost of maintaining expatriates and their families in the UK, the type of technology, and specific company policies, are factors affecting the degree of localization. The amount of control over promotion that manufacturers exert varies, but few have gone as far as Daito or Saiin. Sono and the television makers have not yet indicated a move in the same direction.[16]

The ceiling on promotion, determined ultimately by head office control, is the context in which the underdeveloped state of most training needs to be seen. There is no point in training staff for posts which are not open to them. To do so would lead to increased dissatisfaction and turnover, adversely affecting the productivity the companies are anxious to ensure.

It has been claimed that the success of Japanese firms overseas has been the result of advanced technology and levels of pay and fringe benefits, following the 'happy worker' hypothesis. This theory was disputed by Takamiya, who found in his electronics study that the Japanese companies provided 'much poorer incentives than those traditionally used in the West' (Takamiya, 1979, p. 6).[17] In general Japanese managers are sensitive to the possible reactions of local employers and do not wish to be criticized for creaming off labour by offering higher wages.[18] In development areas, where most manufacturers are situated, there is in any case no need. Sono Engineering had no sick pay scheme for blue-collar workers, because of fears of abuse, until 1981, when dissatisfaction led to its introduction.

British sales managers in firms like Hito Engineering enjoy good pay and conditions, including a more up-market car than that normally supplied to representatives. The same principle applies to professional personnel managers in sales firms such as Daitoku and Kansai. The latter regarded their careers as following the British pattern, though the Daitoku manager spoke warmly of the company. Such professionals can move elsewhere in pursuit of promotion.

Several City managers interviewed asserted it was company policy to offer rates slightly above those in comparable local firms, in order to attract staff who might feel there were difficulties in a 'different' environment. Many companies can decide the rate locally, although the head office would be likely to question more than a certain increase. Replies to job satisfaction questions showed that satisfaction with pay is higher than with training and promotion, but that it is not exceptionally high or high enough to substantiate the 'happy worker' hypothesis. The data showed that satisfaction with pay was higher at Sono Engineering, a very Japanese firm in work organization terms, than at other firms on the same industrial estate.

Starting pay at Sodo Bank is based on age, qualifications, and achievement, and then on performance as evaluated by department managers. As in most City firms with fewer than a hundred employees, there is no formal system of regular appraisal. Two bonuses a year are paid, although their scale is not as large as in Japan. Ebisu Trading Co. bases starting pay on qualifications and age, but has had to include length of service to prevent newcomers from receiving higher salaries than longer-serving staff due to inflation. It does not represent a Japanese policy despite the superficial resemblance.

The British tax system renders inoperable most of the welfare benefits that bind the employee to the company in Japan. Nishi Trading, which attempted to pay employees' fares to work, was accused of trying to get round the pay code during a period of restraint.

Sodo Bank operates a good non-contributory pension scheme but dropped a scheme for free health checks. Tanaka Trading Co. was said to have one of the best pension schemes in the City and the banks and trading companies are well placed to offer assistance with mortgages, concessionary loans, etc. At Ota Bank and others there is normally a minimum qualifying period, and fringe benefits are not necessarily automatic. At Ebisu Trading Co. luncheon vouchers are given strictly for days worked. Their cost can be set against tax.

These examples show some use of fringe benefits in motivation and control, but it is questionable how far they represent a good investment, given the type of labour market. The line between benefits that are willingly accepted and an 'invasion of privacy', defined as a perceived attempt to exert control outside the workplace, may be a fine one.

Fringe benefits are attractive to long-serving British 'go-betweens' and to personnel like the old type of Tanaka clerical staff, but the latter are not a good investment in performance terms. Because of the ceiling on promotion, only a few local staff can expect a well paid post in a Japanese company, and there is no evidence to suggest that they are paying over the odds. The introduction of a union in two City firms and the formation of an unofficial staff association in another were prompted by dissatisfaction over pay.

The responses to job satisfaction questions showed that satisfaction with fringe benefits was highest in the commercial firms but that it did not differ significantly in the British and other firms on the industrial estate. The data also showed a low figure at Sono Engineering, a very Japanese company, apparently supporting Takamiya's findings at the two electronics companies. The figures for the two chemical manufacturers did not differ greatly either. Methodologically, it may be unwise to attach too much importance to such figures at a given moment, because of inflation and the temporary effects of pay settlements, but the data tended to confirm the superficiality of the stereotyped 'happy worker' hypothesis.

The dual employment system, in the exceptional conditions of overseas operations, modifies the systems of training, promotion, and reward that would be expected in home country operations. This deviation from Japanese practice (Inohara, in Thurley et al., 1981, p. 29) results from head office policy and there is little to suggest an impending change, despite the problems of morale and performance that managers are aware of.

'Power and authority in Japanese establishments have by no means shifted away from Japanese expatriates to local European management' (Thurley *et al.*, 1981, p. 48). The ceiling on promotion remains and it is said that the greater climate in favour of localization in the 1970s has been replaced by a policy of tighter head office control. This is in part because the head offices believe that the recession necessitates it, and in part because Japan's continued economic success validates Japanese management methods, the converse being true of UK management. This begs the question of why more local managers are not being trained to manage in the Japanese way.

The ICERD study showed that Japanese firms followed local practice for wages and salaries, and were not using a high wage policy (ibid., p. 49). The pay of expatriates and locals, like the career structures, are entirely separate. Banks like Ota link bonuses to individual performance, and the companies are able to use the dual employment system to exercise differing degrees of control over their two categories of staff. This policy reflects their scheme of priorities.[19]

4.4 Decision-making processes

Formal organization

Open-plan office layout in the City firms closely resembles that in Japan, down to the grey steel furniture and the different status chairs, with or without arms etc. The physical layout reflects the structure and social organization of the company, just as the separate offices and closed doors in many British companies do.

In a large company in Japan an open-plan arrangement for one department can cover an entire floor, while at Tanaka Trading and other branches in London, several departments are on the same floor. As in Japan, the desks and chairs are arranged in strict hierarchical order, with the most recent entrant at the bottom of the table.

Open-plan arrangements naturally mean that staff work in close proximity, and Sasaki sees this type of layout as suiting 'the requirements of an information process required to promote group consensus, as well as the Japanese mentality, which is fond of teamwork based on collectivism. The Japanese office operates as if it were a factory to produce decisions' (Sasaki, 1981, p. 72). The proximity of working areas and the fine grading of positions fits the company structure of standard ranks, listed in Chapter 3 in the context of the seniority system.

Open-plan offices are normal in Japan. 'Communication and mutual understanding are easier if managers can see each other at work and access is not screened by personal secretaries' (Howard and Teramoto, 1981, p. 8). 'Face-to-face communication is more important in Japan, and written less so, than in the West. . . . The total volume of communication is higher than in a Western firm' (ibid., p. 7). Pascale and Athos consider the working relationship among colleagues in Japan as comparable to that between managers and their secretaries in the USA and the UK (op. cit., pp. 137–8).

But the appearance of similarity in office layout between the company in Japan and the London branch cannot determine that the dynamics of decision making are equally similar. Howard and Teramoto assert that 'Japanese culture imparts a non-theoretical, intuitive understanding of *nemawashi* processes' (op. cit., p. 2). Indeed the types of authority, control, and assumptions about decision making in Japan throw into question whether the same processes can operate in the host society.

Apart from business confidentiality, decision making is difficult to research because it is a political process. It reveals who has power in the organization, and in the Japanese case involves the linking 'of different kinds of issues through complex subjective book-keeping *"kashi"* (lending) and *"kari"* (borrowing)' (op. cit., p. 63). Discrepancies between formal authority and substantive power make it harder to disentangle the process from the myth.

It is important not merely to impose intellectual categories on the data. Teramoto asserts that 'top down', 'bottom up', or 'middle up' are ideal types of decision making, differing only in degree in real-life situations. In Japanese companies 'it is a very important point that most of the lower and middle managers think and believe a very significant part of the decision-making process is done through this middle-up process. . . . It serves to induce a high contribution and commitment to every decision. And it succeeds in generating very strong obligations in the

implementation process of the decisions' (loc. cit.). His assertion expresses a Weberian effect of beliefs as motivators of
action, which it can be argued is highly relevant to decision
making in Japanese companies.

The original decision-making case study at Tanaka Trading
Co. revealed that there was one type outside the branch (head
office authorization) and three internal: *ringi*, routine procedures, and some delegation to individual managers. The latter
was not very important.

Head office authorization is the major determinant of business policy, but because it is an upstream datum involving confidential decisions outside the branch it cannot satisfactorily be
studied in London; it involves no local staff.

Tanaka officially describes *ringi* as the standard procedure for
important decisions in large companies, the orthodox process.
The official explanation, for local staff, describes the circulation
of the proposal and its eventual passing up the line, on the
normative pattern. The need for teamwork is stressed, although
some local informants claimed that departments resemble separate 'kingdoms' in practice. The explanation describes the functional rationale of *ringi*, such as the need for credit control and
other support departments to be involved in even the simplest
types of business.

The official *ringi* form (*ringi sho*) used in London is the same
as in Japan, and business departments must send a copy of
every contract report to the head office. Copies also go to the
support departments, who monitor performance. The head
office controls the branch; and the support departments, such
as credit control, exercise control over the business departments.
They are therefore more prestigious.

Ringi is used in London for major branch decisions; the fre-
quency varies thus among different departments. Most expatriates interviewed had a conception of how 'bottom up' and 'top
down' processes differed, but many local staff had little knowledge or experience of *ringi*.

The highest number of *ringi* reported in a year was 150 'unprogrammed' decisions in a support department. The proposals
were normally in Japanese, which not more than one or two
local staff could have understood. Language as well as position
can exclude local staff from decision making (cf. Kidd and Teramoto, 1981, p. 39), leading to cleavages in the organization and

allegations of the use of a 'secret language'. Only expatriates can communicate with the head office, and one graduate hesitated to use Japanese because of what his British colleagues might imagine.

Some Japanese internationalists are keen to promote English but, although telex messages are supposed to be in English, they tend to be in Japanese, especially when confidential. One department had a rule that all reports were to be in English, which cost one Japanese manager considerable time, but this is exceptional. It was said that there was a commitment to extending the use of English, but no programme for its implementation could be detected. Where facsimile machines are in use the danger of local staff isolation becomes greater; one British manager at a joint venture, Horikawa Engineering, therefore flies regularly to Japan to make contact on his own initiative with the head office. This *fait accompli* is accepted.

The support department manager referred to earlier dealt with another hundred *ringi* a year for credit approval. They did not necessitate the full *nemawashi* process because they were on the routine basis of established credit lines, or limits.

A British graduate said that in his business department they typically had four *ringi* a year for new business and two or three for large transactions. Proposals took much longer to prepare than in the routine credit approval process. To many local staff *ringi* was one aspect of 'the Tanaka system' and it involved much more than the official company outline given earlier.

The Japanese manager of a department (section) engaged in routine business stated that he did not normally need to use full *ringi* and that he could only remember one instance of new business where it was necessary. Several local staff engaged in routine business made similar remarks. One Japanese manager explained that routine business without significant decision making could be left to expatriates because they would undertake all tasks as part of their company career and as fulfilment of their obligations. He considered it would be unsuitable for British graduates; he saw the challenge necessary to hold them in areas of greater intrinsic interest like long-term planning, decisions on plant exports, and long-term overseas projects.

In spite of some local perceptions of 'the Tanaka system' as consisting of mountains of paperwork, routine procedures are characteristic of bureaucracies in general. Management consultants found that expatriates did not find 'the system' oppressive, though local staff did. This reaction can be explained partly by a difference in expectations and partly by the greater readiness of local staff to voice criticisms.[20] Expatriates are more skilled and experienced at negotiating the system, as a result of their previous socialization into a society whose dynamics and values are broadly reflected in company decision-making processes. Some local staff claimed they could manipulate or ignore the system, but it is doubtful whether this was more significant than the minor subterfuges that can be used in many bureaucracies. 'Non-Japanese managers are at a great disadvantage in the politics of the home headquarters' (Thurley *et al.*, 1981, p. 53)—and in the branches, too.

The nature and applicability of routine procedures were laid down in company manuals and were not particularly 'Japanese'; they reflect a standard bureaucratic pattern.

Delegation to specific managers was rare and limited to cases where speed was essential: commodity trading, for instance, and buying and selling ships. In the latter example the British assistant manager was expected to conduct the negotiations on the basis of his own expertise, but he had to consult his expatriate superior on the amount and timing of the final price.

This might appear to be a 'culture-free' type of business, but there are occupational differences. A British commodity trader sees himself as a specialist playing the market. He will not do the accounting work that an expatriate would accept as belonging to the task. In one case a British 'specialist' was replaced by an expatriate 'generalist', in order to control the results.

Sometimes *de facto*, but not *de jure*, delegation is possible in Tanaka, which provides a degree of flexibility. 'Tanaka is bureaucratic but one must know Japanese psychology in order to reach a *modus vivendi*', was one local comment. The major frustration is the constant movement of expatriate managers, which makes the building of good working relationships difficult and destroys those which have been achieved. On the expatriate side, the possibility of job changing implies a lack of trust, and one British graduate said that for a person in his position there would be an unofficial probation period of two years before he would be trusted.

Informal systems frequently outweigh formal sytems in importance in Japanese companies, and operationally the *nemawashi* processes at Tanaka are more significant than the 'rational' explanation of *ringi* in Tanaka's official description. The latter is expressed in logical terms that local staff might be expected to react to positively, while the informal systems might appear 'irrational' or morally objectionable. An experienced British manager, 'go-between' at the Moriguchi Bank, sees *nemawashi* as time-wasting and irrelevant because he considers that managers should concentrate on objective business decisions. Such views reflect 'a common idea of organisation among [British] managers, which is partly due to economic theory and partly due to the theory of formal organisations, that describes organisation in terms of activities rationally assigned and coordinated to make possible the achievement of an economic objective, which is itself a rational response to market forces' (Lupton, 1971, p. 118), i.e. it is value-laden. Ideally 'the unique right solution should be obtainable by pure rational analysis . . . which will divulge the same right answer to every disinterested inquirer' (Howard and Teramoto, 1981, p. 11). In *nemawashi* socially-based Japanese ethics and political processes collide with (puritanical) British transcendentally based ethics. In an Anglo-American context those who are not 'disinterested' are corrupt. Weberian 'expediency' and 'value rationality', or values, become entwined in confusion, with the practical consequence that expatriates and local staff have little understanding of each other's conception of decision making.

Because the formal description of decision making in organizations like Tanaka is totally inadequate for a discussion of how the system, or systems, work in practice, it is necessary to turn to the analysis of the informal processes.[21]

Informal processes

The support department manager already quoted stated that a written *ringi* proposal normally took two days to secure approval in the London branch. If urgent, a meeting could be called to save the time taken in circulating the proposal. The process was quicker in London than in the head office because fewer people were involved. This apparent speed might seem to contradict the assertion of many Japanese interviewees that '*ringi* is a slow method of decision making'. The discrepancy is due to the *nemawashi* processes, the extent of which was noted by many local staff. To one it was 'people streaming in and out of the departments all the time'; to another it was 'manipulation, office politics and reading between the lines before the comments appear'—the latter an apposite remark. Formal approval is the tip of the iceberg and in a company like Tanaka, which carries out such a variety of transactions, there would be no point in trying to establish the average time taken to make a decision.

'To join in the *nemawashi* of an organisation is regarded as a privilege, a proud badge of membership' (Howard and Teramoto, 1981, p. 11) and a Japanese manager 'needs to be almost diseasedly sensitive to his relationships with peers and seniors' (Plath, 1964, p. 38). A long-serving British manager at Tanaka commented that 'a proposal can be pushed by seeing the people personally; but this *must* be done by a Japanese'. 'Making the *ringi* paper is the least stage', as another put it.

Office politics are not unique to Japanese society (cf. Pascale, 1978, p. 153) and British managers also practice lobbying and persuasion, but the qualitative difference in interpersonal relations and obligations, and in *nemawashi* as a whole, virtually excludes local staff. Japanese group cohesiveness and local staff's lack of a meaningful point of contact with *nemawashi* make it an exclusive process, not to be changed by an improvement in the social skills of local staff.

One senior Tanaka manager stated that '*Nemawashi* is the most important and most time- and energy-consuming part of the job, especially at this company, because of individualism.' This (Japanese) use of 'individualism' refers to the expertise of traders and not to 'individualism' in the British sense, which many local staff felt to be crushed by 'the system'.

In this manager's view, the quality of the relationships established by the proposer are crucial in *nemawashi*. 'These relationships have to be cultivated earlier, through being from the same university, or in the same grade as new entrants to the company, through relations, or through being friends at golf. At a higher rank more importance should be put on relationships in *nemawashi*, including relationships with people in overseas branches etc. *The value of a manager depends on how many relationships he has built up during his years in the company*.' The same point was made by an experienced manager at Mitsui who stated that

Your real position which makes your strength in the company is based very much on how many and how well you know people inside and outside the company. Those personal relationships which I accumulated in my career in Mitsui are probably the most important asset for me to be successful in the company. . . . One of the purposes of a job rotation system is to give staff members the chance to accumulate and enlarge such personal relationships in and outside the company. [Funaki, 1981].

It is difficult for local staff to do this.

To culture-bound theorists, this obstacle would arise from the self-evident differences between British and Japanese values and social organization. To economic rationalists, it would be due to the business needs (as defined by whom?) of a centralized firm, although it can be objected that local staff would be more effective in the local environment and in traditional British overseas markets. An extreme functionalist view might be that the head office strategy is the only correct one but this could be another self-fulfilling prophecy. To a political analyst, the strategy would be ascribed to a managerial policy of preserving power in expatriate hands, and of furthering expatriate careers. The question is why this strategy, and not a multinational strategy on the lines of Philips, Ford, Shell, etc., is being followed.

It is possible that there is no single adequate explanation for the use of managerial systems such as *nemawashi* in the London branches of firms like Tanaka. They may well be determined by a head office decision, which it considers rational in business and personnel terms. Given the long-term employment pattern for expatriates in the company, the two aspects cannot empirically be separated. *Nemawashi* fits Japanese values, as inculcated by socialization processes, and is consistent with Japanese social organization. The rationality of the head office's business policy, which affects the nature and exclusiveness of *nemawashi* in London, is linked with the pursuit of national economic goals, based on the interests and ideology of the national groups, and excluding outsiders. The descriptions of *nemawashi* given earlier by the Japanese managers distinguish between a particularistic informal process, which is traditional in the Weberian sense, and a universalistic legal–rational theory of decision making that would be the ideal of local staff.

The senior Japanese manager quoted also contrasted the Japanese concept of relationships with the Western concept of 'diplomacy'. In his view an example of the latter would be 'knowing whom to disregard because he is unimportant'. He stated that although *ringi* was theoretically a bottom up process, a senior manager 'could suggest to his subordinates that they study a certain matter', implanting his own ideas in their minds and making them feel that they had produced the ideas themselves.[22]

This planting of ideas, which also serves to convince Japanese staff that they are making a contribution to the organization, is a camouflaged top down decision, well in accord with expatriate notions of *omote* ('external appearance') and *honne* ('real aim'). It shows that Japanese managers are quite capable of taking decisions individually, if it were the norm to do so, instead of seeking consensus etc. Whether the norm is functional or dysfunctional will be discussed later. A Sony executive stated that

> To be truthful, probably 60 per cent of the decisions I make are mine. But I keep my intentions secret. In discussions with subordinates I ask questions, pursue facts, and try to nudge them in my direction. . . . Sometimes I end up changing my position as the result of the dialogue. But whatever the outcome, they feel a part of the discussion. [It] also increases their experience as managers. [Quoted in Pascale, 1978, p. 154.]

Local staff in London generally do not 'feel a part of the decision'.

Many expatriate informants commented on the rationale of group involvement in *nemawashi*. One stated that individual decision making presupposed personal answerability, including the possibility of dismissal, but that Tanaka did not have this type of employment system. Individual decision making would not therefore be congruent. The assertion supports the concept of the interlocking connections between the different aspects of employment systems, and the difficulty of changing one part without unintended consequences for others.

Japanese managers continually stressed the need for *ringi* and *nemawashi* in both business and interpersonal relations terms. They argued that the size and complexity of Tanaka's operations made it necessary; but also that it was due to the company's 'traditional' caution and long-term view. One commodity market, for instance, had been studied 'for years' before the company ventured into it.

It was asserted to be essential for (expatriate) interpersonal relations that everyone should be consulted, and be known to have been consulted. Anyone left out would feel a potential threat to his career, as well as 'wet' feelings of unhappiness at his exclusion from the group. This could make him uncooperative or revengeful.

One internationalist expatriate indeed criticized *ringi* on the grounds that it was too 'therapeutic' and not a sufficiently 'rational' way of reaching decisions. He saw it as a restriction on the initiative of competent managers, but among expatriate interviewees this was a minority view.

A British manager believed that the rationale of *ringi* was 'to be slow but sure', although he mentioned the loss of an African contract as a result of delay. He saw the lack of speed as a consequence of the size and scope of operations, and considered that the company was willing to pay a certain price in order to maintain its traditional system; the maintenance of organizational cohesion was worth the occasional loss of business, especially in non-Japanese environments.

Other British views were that '*ringi* is not always necessary but it is part of the system and must be accepted'; that 'objective views on a project are needed, but people who are uninvolved in the business also comment. . . . Technical advice is important but so are status levels.' These perceptions refer to the whole process of *nemawashi* and to the formal system by the undifferentiated term '*ringi*', as did many local interviewees.

The above data show that the informal processes that would be found as integral parts of decision making in corporations in Japan were functioning among expatriates in London, but that local staff, on positional and other grounds, were largely excluded from the processes and felt excluded from them.

Interpretations

One expatriate manager argued that consensual processes stimulated managers to develop their ideas because they were not personally answerable. Japanese managers felt supported by the agreement or advice of colleagues and especially by the 'blessing' of top management. The diffusion of responsibility was functional in the Japanese case because of the embarrassing 'loss of face' that failure would cause if it could be unambiguously laid at one person's door.

Against this view was the assertion of a British manager that 'the Japanese don't like making decisions on their own'. The deviant among the expatriate interviewees was outspoken in expressing the view that Japanese managers were not managers at all because they did not have sufficient detailed knowledge of what they were supposed to be deciding, and did not make decisions themselves. He contrasted them with British managers, whom he saw as having 'real' expertise and being 'real' decision makers. This was almost an ideal typical comparison between generalists and specialists, and between consensus and delegated authority.

A senior British adviser, with experience in Japan, believed that although *ringi* might be slow, it was designed so that no one could complain afterwards and 'to cater for harmony',[23] thus obliging everyone to try to make it work—the alternative being the risk of factionalism and power struggles. '*Ringi* is a bit of both—business and social.'

He believed that 'the qualities of *ringi* are all negative. . . . Cliques in Japanese companies undermine each other and harm the business; and *ringi* inhibits this. Each clique has its pretender to the [presidential] throne.' He then drew an analogy with Japanese politics, where the greatest danger to the prime minister is from the leaders of the rival cliques in his own party who will 'stab him in the back' if they can.[24] The analogy is not exact because Japanese politics function on a patron–client rather than on a long-term employment model, but the problem of how to prevent factionalism is genuine. Japanese socially based ethics are effective in, for example, preventing crime (Vogel, 1980, pp. 204–22), but in a competitive situation there is no transcendental ethic to restrain the competitors. 'The Japanese tend to regard the phenomenal world itself as the Absolute and to reject the idea of an Absolute existing over and above the phenomenal world' (Nakamura, 1971, p. 527). Mechanisms such as *ringi* therefore become significant methods of social control. The relation between employer and employee in Japan is diffuse and the social relations of employees, both in the office and outside, are determined to a high degree by their employment in the company (Clark, 1972). To judge *ringi* in instrumental terms, without considering the social context alluded to by the adviser, would be a sociological error.

Several expatriates claimed that an advantage of *ringi* was that everyone could have his say, but the comments of three Japanese managers showed that this is problematical in the Anglo-American sense because of Japanese social conventions. 'Individuals can't speak out at a conference and can't ignore the links in the chain to the general manager.' 'There can be no sharp refusals at a discussion meeting.' 'A qualified "yes" is not a clear "yes"; there is no sharp contrast of "yes" and "no".'[25] Pascale and Athos (1981), pp. 132-3 contrast Anglo-Saxon concepts of the 'virtues' of speaking out with Japanese concepts of it as socially undesirable.

Some local staff comments showed awareness of these points. 'The aim of *ringi* is consensus. Objectives should be ironed out by negotiations but should one go along with the crowd or make oneself heard? . . . *Ringi* is a safety device.' 'The little man has his say . . . but no one says no.' The last remark referred to the momentum of a project and the difficulty of stopping one that had obtained a fair measure of support. The prestige of managers involved would make turning back hard, and people should know from implicit cues when this point had been reached—another difficulty for local staff, unfamiliar with Japanese behavioural norms.

A senior Japanese credit manager stated that he would give a clear 'no' at the outset to unsound proposals, but this was exceptional. His colleagues stressed the maintenance of good relations inside the *uchi* (house) and the discrepancies between what people might say in public and their real opinions. It can indeed be claimed that the *ringi* system is designed to prevent people from damaging harmony by speaking out, just as the recruitment system weeds out potential deviants. Open opposition is seldom the best tactic in Japanese society, and the political skills of its members are often impressive. Speaking out can harm a person's career, and he is likely to achieve more by the persuasion and negotiating sanctioned by *nemawashi*.

A British manager commented that 'the rigid company code at Tanaka is written into the regulations, concerning promotion at a given age for example,[26] so the more aggressive younger people must defer. The individual can't further his own ends because the company structure is different from Japanese politics.' The last point contrasts with the assertion of the adviser given earlier. This manager sees *ringi* as fostering interdepartmental cooperation and the important long-term relations of trust with manufacturers: so that Tanaka does not suddenly upset them by e.g. dealing with a foreign source of supply that one department has contacted, not knowing that there is already an established supplier. This example, given by a Japanese manager, shows that it is not simply a question of profit maximization, because Tanaka may lose some opportunities, but it is rational if the ultimate aim has a national dimension.

Another Japanese manager contrasted Western concepts of profit maximization with Japanese concepts of diffuse business relationships that involve some reciprocity. To disappoint a Japanese supplier, in order to gain a profitable foreign contact, would result in the loss of all future business with that supplier. In the Japanese context it is therefore rational for Tanaka to forego the profit on the foreign contract for the sake of continued business with the domestic supplier, although the principle would not be rational in a Western industrial context. This explains the necessity for the broad consultation inherent in *ringi*.

The example suggests why ideal typical Anglo-American business rationality is not an adequate analytical tool for evaluating decision making in Tanaka and comparable Japanese firms. This is *not* some diffuse 'cultural' theory, stressing the 'feeling'[27] involved in inter-company relations for example. It is an assertion based on the evidence of the relations within and among major Japanese industrial groups, including cross shareholdings. These are the relations of the control of the smaller firms by the large (e.g. Dodwell, 1978; Japan Company Handbook, 1980), comparable to management control of employees within the firm. One writer describes these hierarchical power relationships as 'the society of industry' (Clark, 1979).

Some might argue that the perception of national economic goals is itself cultural, but it seems preferable to relate them to the power structure and to the political and business elites (Dimock, 1968). Although new groups, such as the environmentalists (McKean, 1981) have emerged, these elites have continued policies analogous to those of the Meiji elite after 1868 (cf. Livingston *et al.*, 1976, Vol. 1; Reischauer *et al.*, 1962, Vol. 2). The example at Tanaka is consistent with this approach.

The criticism that *ringi* tends to be reactive[28] appears to have some justification in the London branch. Committees of senior managers deal with the more strategic decisions, while proposals that come up from section level deal with matters case by case. This arrangement frustrates one British manager who claims that steps are not taken in time and that cases for which there is already a precedent are treated as unique events requiring full discussion. He also complains that in the business departments 'there is very little speculation. Everything is laid down by the book. British firms reward individuals, but reward in Tanaka is for toeing the line, for not being an individual. The London office is a branch of Tokyo, or an extension—part of an empire.' He thus makes head office control over the (limited) decision making in the branch explicit.

Local staff personnel decisions are taken in London, but not business decisions. Among expatriates there was said to be a 'double allegiance': to the head office and to the London manager, in that order. The outspoken expatriate critic already quoted doubted whether there was 'real' leadership or an overall policy in the company. His view was to some extent supported by a fellow-expatriate who admired American functional managers, instead of generalists, and asserted that 'ringi is a soft bed for managers who are not real leaders', but he was less critical of the company in other respects.

A Japanese manager, in the sales company, with considerable entrepreneurial success and an evident ability to negotiate the system, considered that

People can leap on a bandwagon, though one must treat everyone fair and square and keep them in the picture. *Ringi* relieves individual responsibility and is a form of self-defence. Democracy and a reasonable level of education are necessary to make it work and to achieve consensus. Japan has homogeneous education to a reasonable standard.

This 'homogeneity' is part of the problem in a non-Japanese context.

Speaking of decision making and promotion, one British manager asserted that if graduates wanted promotion they would have to be 'brainwashed into accepting the consensus system, which ignores and kills the entrepreneurial spirit. It is a peaceful business sytem which prevent individuals from making blunders.' In his view the old clerical staff had 'had the initiative knocked out of them'.

The question of where responsibility in a consensual type of decision making like *ringi* lies has often been discussed. The entrepreneurial Japanese manager asserted that it could be 'an easy-going way to avoid responsibility—no questions are asked when we are making a profit.' This echoes a British employee's view that 'when things go right no one says anything; but all hell breaks loose when they go wrong'. Tanaka has assessment systems designed to monitor the business department's performance, but no one mentioned a system for monitoring implementation of *ringi* decisions. The same Japanese manager asserted that 'no one raises questions over any unfulfilled conditions of *ringi*', and a British colleague stated that comments or restrictions on the proposal would be overlooked.

If implementation is successful the details may be ignored, but if it is a failure managers associated with the proposal will lose credibility, even if there is no formal allocation of responsibility. One Japanese view was that 'responsibility is first mainly the president's—and then the particular department's, although it is not very clear and people may try and avoid responsibility if things go badly'. A British adviser agrees that 'almost all activities in Japanese companies are bottom up; but the management take responsibility so they must know what is going on'. Because the directors are in Tokyo, some responsibility devolves on the general manager in the branch.[29]

A contrasting expatriate view is that the *kiansha* (initiator) who first thought of the proposal and promoted it, would in practice be held responsible. Another said that although the general manager was formally responsible, the amount of blame attached to a department manager would depend on the case. A young Japanese manager asked 'Is *ringi* responsibility too vague? But if it was too clear no one would take decisions—it would be too dangerous!' A British colleague also believed that the prestige and career of a manager who made a mistake would suffer. Two expatriates disagreed with this standpoint, claiming that 'the weak point of the *ringi* system is that no one is really responsible' and that it was 'a system of common irresponsibility'.[30]

From these comments, it appears that because the general manager stamps the paper and gives his 'blessing', he is formally responsible. But because he cannot be familiar in sufficient depth with the details of so many specific cases, responsibility would pragmatically and informally be laid at the door of those identified as being most closely involved. This of course involves the power relations within the organization and, as in the British case, need be no more than a partially rational allocation of blame. The formal appearance of collective irresponsibility is likely to dissolve in the face of the stronger pressures of career competitiveness. It seems characteristic of Japanese managerial systems that, although there is a generally accepted informal

process, it is impossible to equate this with a formal system because pragmatism and power relations determine the workings
of the process in each specific case. It also needs to be remembered that, because of the comparative absence of job mobility
at the level of large Japanese corporations, being passed over for
promotion is a more serious career setback than in the British
case. British managers, such as industrial relations specialists
dismissed for 'failing to solve the problem' (Thurley, personal
communication), do not carry the stigma that would be the case
in Japan, where the degree of company control implies that it
must be the manager's own failings that are to blame, and where
dismissal means that a most serious, perhaps even criminal, of-
fence has been committed.

During the Tanaka case study a Japanese manager kindly
provided a copy of an article in the *Financial Times*, discussing
the Ataka case of 1975 entitled 'How a Japanese company
turned decision-making tradition upside down'. The data given
do not suggest a convergence between Japanese and local styles
of decision making, but it was necessary to investigate the possibility of change further.

In 1975 Ataka, 'number ten'[31] among the trading companies,
had got into difficulties over a Canadian oil contract and had
asked its main banker, the Sumitomo Bank, for help. The bank,
concluding that a merger was the only hope, approached its
sister company, Sumitomo Trading (now Sumitomo Corporation).

The approach was made on New Year's Eve (equivalent to
Christmas Eve in the UK and USA) and the trading company
replied that it would take months to reach such an important
decision. The bank then approached a rival, but financially connected, trading firm, C. Itoh, which almost immediately agreed
to absorb Ataka. This quick decision, due to 'an elite decision-
making team' (Charles Smith, *Financial Times* correspondent),
averted a disaster, raised C. Itoh to 'number three' and left
Sumitomo at 'number five' in the ranking order.

According to Smith, Sumitomo had been hamstrung by the
'unwieldy' *ringi* system, while C. Itoh could move quickly because of the 'Sejima Organization'. This was a strategic planning
group in the company, named after its founder, a former army
staff officer, who had initiated methods for reaching decisions
quickly similar to those he had used during the war. Smith's

interpretation is, however, open to question. Ataka was 'on the verge of bankruptcy' and the Sumitomo Bank would hardly have arranged the merger with a competitor against the wishes of its sister company (cf. Dodwell, 1978, pp. 448–50). Sumitomo Trading's public answer can therefore be taken as a polite evasion; it would not have missed a good opportunity even during the New Year holiday. Subsequently, the Sejima Organization was dissolved and C. Itoh returned to more standard forms of decision making (Sasaki, 1981, pp. 76–9).

Some Japanese managers at Tanaka suspected that Sejima had been 'kicked upstairs' in order to curb his power and to get rid of his organization. It is easy to see why his rivals should seek to do so and why his organization might have had a disruptive effect on company cohesiveness because of the separation of the elite from the rest. 'One individual should not be allowed to get ahead and make the others unhappy' was one Tanaka comment. This does not imply that cohesiveness and competition did not coexist at Tanaka, but that the situation at C. Itoh had been less balanced, with the threat of factional struggles described by the British adviser above.

Some expatriates agreed that a Sejima-type organization could make correct decisions quickly, but they argued that this advantage would be outweighed by the danger of inadequate consultation, 'leading to a disaster'. How far this was a genuine objection and how far it reflected career anxieties is hard to judge.

Others saw the Sejima Organization's effectiveness or desirability as depending on who was in control. One (euphemistic or naive?) comment was that the company had evidently been unable to find a replacement for Sejima, but in 1981 he occupied one of the senior positions in the company—that of vice-president (pp. 48–9 above; Sasaki, 1981, p. 76).

The breaking up of the Sejima Organization could be seen as a victory of traditionalists over modernists. Both of these tendencies can be observed in Tanaka, but a long-serving local staff member referred to 'empire builders in the support departments who are after power, influence and prestige'. One expatriate manager claimed to have promoted greater use of the *ringi* system, with the assistance of colleagues in other departments, after losses supposedly due to inadequate consultation. This had been justified by the principle that 'top-down decision is not the tradition of this company'. For some managers, that is all that needs to be said.

In 1977 the new president of Sumitomo Trading established a *kambukai* of five senior executives to deal with major business decisions and senior appointments. Smith asks whether this will lead to a new combination of the 'traditional slow but sure consensus-seeking system' with top-down decision making for urgent and important matters. The question is perhaps misconceived, in the sense that the use of informal top-down decision making for major strategic policy issues and for urgent cases is already well established. That it should be made explicit is another matter. If Smith's description of the functions of the *kambukai* is correct, there is no evidence in Tanaka's London branch to suggest a new synthesis between top-down processes and *ringi*; least of all if Smith is claiming that top down is Western and that this points to a new synthesis with Anglo-American managerial systems.

The Ataka case was well known to Tanaka and other trading company staff, and since the Sejima affair raised many of the major questions relating to decision making in a comparable organization, it was a useful focal point in discussion. In general, Tanaka staff found it hard to imagine a similar organization in their own company, even if some regretted this. '*Ringi* is there and will stay' was a typical comment. British views were that 'local staff must learn to live with the system' and that 'local staff have little say in what is fundamentally a Japanese organisation'. Even a 'loyal' long-serving employee commented, 'the Japanese make the real decisions, although there are nice titles'.

Given the dynamic expansion of firms like Tanaka and their competitive organizational climate, it is hard to credit the persistence of *ringi* to organizational inertia. Particularly in view of the informal types of top-down decision making, it can be argued that it is a conscious managerial choice. How this choice affects local staff is discussed in the following section.

The problem of localization

'*Ringi* isn't really working in London but how can this be modified? I am disappointed by the apathy of the local staff and their unwillingness to speak out' was the comment of one expatriate manager. 'Speaking out' refers here to putting forward ideas, as he was able to motivate or, in another view, manipulate his Japanese subordinates to do. He and other expatriates saw British decision making as more authoritarian and less motivational.

In this view, the subordinate has the potential, which the skilled superior knows how to draw out.[32] In Japanese society the concept is based on the ultimate goodness or moral sense of man, which is always there even if it is obscured by 'an adverse environment' (Reischauer *et al.*, 1962, Vol. 1, pp. 80-1). The concept of the moral sense of man dates from the fourth-century BC Chinese philosopher Mencius (Liu, 1955, Ch. V) and its adoption explains why Japanese managers and others in authority can often make effective moral appeals to their subordinates to 'reflect upon their conduct', their obligations, etc. In 1953 a survey showed that a fair proportion (30.7 per cent) of the Japanese population believed in the basic goodness of man.[33] This had led one Japanese–American social scientist to argue that the concept of the Protestant Ethic as a motivational force does not apply in the Japanese context, because the concept of 'original evil' is lacking (Befu, 1971, pp. 170-1). The nearest Western managerial equivalent to the belief in goodness would be McGregor's (1960) Y Theory.

Japanese managers who are convinced of the motivational (or control) benefits of the *ringi* system therefore face a difficult task in changing local staff to Japanese ways, when the latter have been socialized into accepting the authority and ideology inherent in the X Theory, with its roots in the puritanical tradition of the 'sinfulness' of man.

Some Japanese managers were aware that they had been trained to use the *ringi* system, i.e. it could not be taken as given, but there was a perception that it was the normal system and that top-down management was only for recently established or small companies in Japan. One manager wondered whether younger expatriates who wanted to leave the office each day at the same time as the local staff were also 'Westernized' enough to accept top-down management. He concluded that 'the Japanese system of decision making won't be changed. Top down management won't work well with the Japanese community.'

Some expatriates were prepared to discuss *ringi* in critical terms, but there was no evidence they were attempting to defy it; others stressed that there were no plans to replace it under consideration. As one experienced manager put it, '*Ringi* is our company's sytem and we must follow it.'

One younger manager, on his third overseas assignment, had put up a proposal for a Sejima-type organization 'of bright people open to the top management, to promote new business, accessible to all', but it was rejected. He discussed the problem of local staff promotion, which is known to the head office personnel department (personnel manager, personal communication), but to date this has not resulted in significant moves towards the 'multinationalization' of personnel. Local staff criticize 'cosmetic' changes and 'nice titles' when these are not matched by increased involvement in the decision-making process. It is easy for management to maintain its traditional control, and perhaps to make formal concessions, when it is the informal mechanisms that are crucial and frequently beyond the experience or understanding of local staff.

It can be argued that for Japanese business it is functionally necessary that decision making should remain in expatriate hands, *as long as Japanese business retains its present structure*, but can this apply to the entire business of a London branch, or is it a self-fulfilling prophecy? As in the case of the policy of not recruiting graduates in the City or graduate engineers in manufacturing, managerial choice modifies the notion of functional necessity. The latter easily becomes an ideology for retaining power and life chances, which decision making reflects, in the hands of home country personnel. The situation, particularly in the City firms, contrasts with that in multinationals of the Nestlé or Philips type.

Enterprises . . . with a global view, do wish to control their marketing efforts in as many countries as possible; they want to promote their . . . visual images on a global basis. Their aim is not to be looked upon as American, Dutch etc. but as worldwide. (The Japanese firms in this respect seem to differ from other nationalities. They are thoroughly Japanese and apparently want to stay that way.) [L. G. Johnson, in Sethi and Holton, 1974, p. 239.]

Following Teramoto (p. 137), it is important to bear in mind that bottom up and top down are ideal types of decision making —confirmed empirically in Tanaka's London office. Researchers need to treat normative statements made by expatriates with caution because they may be describing the system as it should work rather than as it does. It is also unlikely that a section

chief will know by experience how a decision by top management was reached. Some writers confuse levels and types of
decision making, even if a form of consensus seeking is the
normative process. The question is, at what level are managers
included in it?

According to a Japanese consultants' report, the purer forms
of *ringi* often apply to lower level daily operations, rather than
to significant strategic decision making, once again suggesting
the isolation of local staff. The varieties of decision making in
four case studies are referred to (Technova, 1980, Vol. 1, pp.
29–38).

The consultants conclude with advice to those wishing to
attract Japanese investment to the UK: 'Identify the person
and the organizational unit who are responsible for advancement.' This conclusion points to the controlling members of the
firm, rather than to a single model of business rationality, as
determining the type of decision making. An analysis of twenty-
one firms which had advanced into foreign investment could
find no standard model of decision making, which supports
Teramoto's contention.

The discussion of staffing showed that British managers in
sales and manufacturing enjoyed greater autonomy, and better
prospects and conditions, than those in commercial firms. But
it was also argued that the difference was one of degree, rather
than a sharp dichotomy, and the organization charts of electronics and engineering firms showed expatriates in the senior
decision-making positions.

It is the Japanese manager of Daitoku, rather than British
managers, who enjoys a degree of autonomy, but he must
remain in touch with the UK headquarters and the head office
in Japan. At another electronics company the expatriate general
manager also reports to the UK headquarters (Bennett *et al.*,
1979, pp. 17, 21). Sono Engineering, Okasa Engineering, Minami
Chemical Co., Higashi Chemical Co. etc. are all either under the
control of a regional expatriate director or an expatriate director
on site answerable to the head office.

Decision making in manufacturing subsidiaries in the UK is
not radically different from that at Tanaka in the City. Proposals originate and are approved by top management in Japan.
They are discussed by Japanese managers in the UK, but 'the
UK managers are surprised and confused over new orders from

the parent firm which arrive "out of the blue" ' (Kidd and Tera-moto, 1981, p. 45).

A well-known Japanese professor, writing anonymously, states that Japanese managers abroad are seldom trained to take inde-pendent action and that head offices are seldom prepared to grant branch autonomy. Requests from Japanese managers over-seas are dealt with according to the 'implied credit' established when they were in Japan. Middle managers remain in touch with colleagues in Japan and, as in the above cases, locals are effectively excluded. There is no suggestion that the situation in manufacturing is very different from that in commercial firms.

In Takamiya's electronics study the 'meticulous reporting system, similar to the *ringi* system in Japan, in which every single requisition form has to be signed by managers in various departments', is described as being more 'for information' and 'of rather primitive nature' in decision-making terms (Takamiya, 1979, p. 12).

A supervisor at Sono Engineering complained that 'the com-pany encourages you to put forward suggestions, but then noth-ing can be changed because the methods are worked out in Japan'. At the Irish electronics factory it was stated that no modification of technology was possible because of head office regulations. The use of Japanese machinery sometimes caused servicing problems, although European machines of the same type were available for which servicing was more accessible.

The 'inbreeding' of top managers in Japan, who have spent their working lives in the same company, makes them exclusive in Japan, and therefore exclusive overseas. 'Companies often tend to be moved ahead by an undefined consensus of top manage-ment and general staff' (Hirschmeier and Yui, 1975, p. 282), thereby excluding local staff participation in the branches. The 'undefined' character of the consensus reflects the informal systems. These are both empirically hard for local staff to grasp and conceptually difficult for theorists who search for an intel-lectual framework which is lacking.

In a study of decision making in Japanese production sub-sidiaries in the UK, it is asserted that 'Even if the UK managers find they can obtain a close dynamic relationship with their Japanese colleagues, inevitably the UK persons will eventually learn that they are excluded from the *nemawashi* dynamics. They will thus be excluded from a most important aspect of

managerial decision making' (Kidd and Teramoto, 1981, p. 54).
Implicit communication used by Japanese managers, similar to
that which broadly characterizes communication in Japanese
society, resembles a restrictive code known only to group members or initiaties. It acts as a means of exclusion and control
(Bernstein, 1973).

Teramoto argues that the information and power-processing
mechanisms in Japanese companies are closely integrated and
mutually reinforcing—an observation consistent with Bernstein's hypothesis. Unlike cultural analysts, Teramoto sees the
systems as not only 'a result of historical, cultural and socio-
economic settings in Japan [but also as] a result of conscious
efforts to combine them properly' (op. cit., p. 69). That is why,
in his view, it is difficult to transfer this particular combination
to a non-Japanese environment, although 'if the essence of
management is to be transferable across boundaries, an effective
combination of the two mechanisms (of information and power
processing) must be created to cope with all conditions'. The
'conscious efforts' refer to management and its control strategy.
They are of great significancc for managers elsewhere who want
to understand the effectiveness of Japanese management. Teramoto makes it clear that these efforts have been made in a concrete social context, i.e. managers should not chase after
textbook abstractions but should find hov to make new or
improved systems work in their own societies and organizations.

At the empirical level, managerial control over decision making
in the UK is partly vested in the head office and partly in the
general manager and expatriate managers in the branch. The
local staff are totally isolated from the former upstream part of
the process; while at the downstream end they are isolated from
nemawashi, credit control, and most of the significant decisions.
Given the connection between decision making and position,
this is consistent with the earlier analysis of staffing and the
types of local staff recruited, and it goes far to explain the situation regarding training and promotion. The problem was included
under the definition of the 'ceiling on promotion'.

This was recognized by the consultants engaged by the Department of Industry in the UK when they reported that 'although
Japanese firms unquestionably possess management skills in
decision making and planning . . . the firms' policy to centralize
such functions makes it unlikely that direct investment alone

will be sufficient to induce a transfer of this knowledge to the UK' (Technova, 1980, Vol. 3, p. 34). Significantly, this was written about manufacturing industry, rather than about the commercial firms such as Tanaka, where local staff job satisfaction is lower. The situation does not appear likely to change in the near future because of the policy of centralization.

4.5 Employee relations and communication

Unions and staff associations

Industrial relations in Japanese firms in the UK have attracted some journalistic attention, on account of the 'enterprise union' concept, but there have been few disputes. Interest has focused on the manufacturing firms rather than on the City. Factors in the relative absence of disputes have been the conclusion of single union agreements by new firms on green field sites, the small size of most firms, and the caution of Japanese managers.

Many firms accept shop stewards, who represent a plant level movement without a Japanese equivalent, but make efforts to get them to see management's point of view (Thurley, 1981, p. 53). Despite this absence of problems by local standards, Table 40 shows that Japanese management has the lowest opinion of labour relations in UK subsidiaries (well below the average).

Table 40. Foreign management's perceptions of UK labour relations in their companies

	All %	US %	German %	Swedish %	Dutch %	Japanese %	Miscellaneous %
Good	45.7	46.6	53.3	45.6	28.6	9.1	58.4
Fair	35.7	43.8	25.6	42.1	28.6	54.5	20.8
Poor	16.8	9.6	18.9	8.8	35.7	36.4	20.8
N/A	1.8	—	2.2	3.5	7.1	—	—

Source: Business Location File, 1980, p. 11.

Japanese consultants reported to the UK Department of Industry that 'management–labour relations are what Japanese firms are most critical about in examining the labour situation in the UK. More than half of the firms polled said that they think the UK is marred by strikes and other forms of dispute, whereas only 4.2% said otherwise' (Technova, 1980, Vol. 1, p. 88). Workers were favourably evaluated for their skills but not for their efficiency. In Japan perceptions of British industry are poor, but better among companies operating in the UK, who felt that 'the problem of strikes is not as bad as originally feared'. Many of these firms have fairly stable labour relations, because they are 'small in operational size and continuously handle labour issues' (ibid., p. 89).[34]

Japanese interviewees in the UK and Ireland showed anxiety not only over union activity and demarcation but over the 'voluntarist' system of industrial relations as a whole. They evidently find it easier to grasp the 'legalist' continental conception, and are careful to comply with legal requirements regarding such matters as works committees or the disclosure of information (Thurley *et al.*, 1981, pp. 28, 48), but in Germany they sometimes follow the strategy of keeping the operation small in order to avoid the statutory works committee.

Multi-union representation and the possibility of inter-union disputes are deeply worrying.[35] Most managers appear to have virtually no knowledge of the history of British trade unionism (Pelling, 1976); the development of the role of the shop steward (Goodman and Whittingham, 1973), or the formal and informal problems dealt with by the Donovan Report on Trade Unions and Employers' Organizations, but they are aware of the desirability of making an agreement with a single union.

At Okasa Engineering the plant manager stated publicly that the company had no objection to a union, if that was what the employees wanted, provided they were all in one union. The workforce were initially divided among themselves, but after a majority vote in favour, and recommendations from the Advisory Conciliation and Arbitration Service (ACAS) and even the factory inspectors, a single-union agreement was negotiated. There is a tacit agreement on flexible working practices. It is hard to determine how far this 'paternalistic' company, in a militant area, had endeavoured to create a *'Gemeinschaft* [community] type spirit' (cf. Kidd and Teramoto, 1981, p. 61) among its approximately 200 employees as a substitute for unionization. The British personnel manager stated that the original 'family atmosphere [had] been eroded'.

In his view 'the Japanese regard the union as an unnecessary evil'. They had also resisted appointing a qualified personnel manager until this was recommended by ACAS (and the union!). The manager was then able to use union pressure to overcome expatriate reluctance to employ qualified on-the-job instructors and to establish defined training standards—a move which upgraded his own function.

During the second (interview) stage of the ICERD study it became apparent that many Japanese managers preferred to run their branches without a union, but were prepared to accept unionization if the majority of employees were in favour. Management's ideal appeared to be a 'quasi *Gemeinschaft*' of *insiders* on the holistic model (Ouchi, 1981), rather than the company as a place of work with a legitimate role for union area official *outsiders*, thus reflecting the traditional pattern of control at management's disposal in Japan.

Unionization in Japanese firms in the UK is currently limited to those with at least fifty employees in manufacturing (television, engineering, chemicals), one major distribution firm, one large bank, and one shipping office. The City firms are generally not unionized, like many British firms there, but some firms have an informal staff association or communication structure.[36]

Strategy on unionization varies between firms, based on a pragmatic assessment of whether it is inevitable and on company policies. Minami Chemical Co. adopted the opposite strategy from that of Okasa Engineering by inviting union officials to organize the workforce. This was the decision of the British general manager, who stated that 'you've got to have it. This is a militant area.' He obtained a single-union agreement with the AUEW, and pays a small premium for flexibility and a larger one for no formal tea-breaks. The aim was to forestall trouble and the company, not being a member of the Engineering Employers Federation (EEF), did not suffer from the AUEW engineers' strike of 1980. Three craftsmen belong to another union, and white-collar staff are excluded, but the AUEW has sole bargaining rights. This is partly designed to keep the continuous process running smoothly. The company has fifty employees, showing the necessity for unionization even at small establishments. The plant manager doubts whether a Japanese-style enterprise union would be acceptable, and the normal pattern of relations with stewards and external officials is followed.

In most cases unions apply to the company for recognition.

Three applied to Sono Engineering, which has a workforce of slightly over two hundred, and a single-union agreement with flexibility was negotiated.

Reflecting the low average age of Sono employees, the shop stewards were said to be inexperienced, compounding the difficulty when the company made its 'final' offer at the first negotiating stage. The stewards had been instructed to settle for a higher figure. An area union official was called in who saw that the company would not increase their offer, and the stewards accepted it when they understood that the union would not back their claim further.

Sono stipulates the wearing of uniform in the contract of employment, and is characterized generally by a more Japanese management style than most. One reason why the uniform has not created problems has been its introduction from the beginning. In contrast, the British personnel manager at Okasa Engineering thought that the company missed the opportunity of bringing in its employee savings scheme because it had hesitated.[37] The stage of development of a company and timing are important factors in an analysis of unionization.

At Higashi Chemical Co. (also fifty employees) a single-union agreement was signed after opening. The expatriate managers were said to be 'very worried' (British director), but there have been no problems. The British director is responsible for union relations. There is a tacit agreement on flexibility but, as at Osaka, not in writing. Nine employees belong to another union, but this has not affected sole bargaining rights.

At Daito Engineering, a firm in the South East with fifty employees, there is no union. The two chemical companies above have predominantly male, full-time workforces, but Daito employs mainly part-time workers, housewives from a nearby council estate: a situation that explains non-unionization. The area is not militant and has no traditional heavy industries. Employees who successfully introduce a new shopfloor part-timer are rewarded with a premium.

The expatriate managing director stated that 'if a union organizer came here and the workforce felt that they should become members of a union, then so be it; we would accept their wishes. But it has never happened.' This remark, and its unenthusiastic tone, was typical of many.[38] The sales manager asserted 'there is a family atmosphere here, although we tend to

run along British lines. I am sure everyone feels they are working
for something different from a conventional British company.'
The company is a small firm that might be described as approaching a quasi *Gemeinschaft* organization, but it is not clear how
far this is due to expatriate influence. The British administration manager, who is not anti-union, plays an important role in
employee relations and in creating the climate. He is a retired
Army NCO and responsible for all personnel matters.

Relations were different at one sales and service organization.
Having chosen a location in a militant area, the company was
faced with a union recognition dispute led by activists, described
by the seasoned British personnel manager as 'moles'. The dispute lasted five weeks, during which male employees staged a
sit-in and barricaded the warehouse for thirty-six hours. The
company then recognized the union, but dismissed the entire
workforce, a step facilitated under UK labour law by their short
period of employment. The expatriate general manager was said
to have been officially reprimanded, indicating how seriously
the activities of Japanese firms in Europe are taken from the
viewpoint of the national image.

This dispute, which was leftist rather than anti-Japanese in
origin, produced two decisions: the first was to abandon plans
for a manufacturing operation in the UK; the second was to
move to a non-militant area, where the company now operates
successfully with an expanded workforce. There has been no
fresh demand for unionization.

Another sales and service organization, in the electronics
field, has encountered difficulties over unionization, but unlike
the company above it has a multi-site operation. Transport staff
became the source of disquieting rumours.

The first personnel managers were not specialists, but the
company decided to employ an IPM qualified professional, with
experience of multi-union environments. To deal with the situation that had arisen, the new personnel manager established a
consultative scheme, covering all sites. Some staff approached
ACAS, but the company countered this move with the argument
that it had uniform bargaining for all its sites, not local bargaining. ACAS recommended recognition for collective bargaining
for certain categories of personnel at the main depot and the
company reluctantly accepted. Union representatives now
attend the meetings of Daitoku's national consultative council.

The consultative scheme, unique among Japanese companies in the UK, was set up with the assistance of a local technical college. Elected representatives from each site meet management monthly on a regional basis and produce an agenda for national meetings, which are held every three months. The regional representatives elect the national representatives. The personnel department runs combined courses for managers and representatives on how to conduct meetings. British managers had to be convinced that the scheme was necessary, in spite of the unionization problems. 'They like to be kings of their own domain but instead of an external union it is better to develop an internal consultation mechanism into a type of internal union' was one local manager's view.

When the scheme came into operation the company had five hundred employees. An explanatory document stated that a typical regional council meeting consisted of: reports on the region's monthly performance; a report from the national representative on the last national meeting; proposals on cost efficiency, improved working methods, housekeeping improvements, safety, etc. It was claimed that the scheme had improved communication and provided more feedback and ideas from staff. Several of the items reportedly discussed at the regional council meetings are clearly of great interest to management in the furtherance of its business aims. In 1980–1 the national council began to conduct wage negotiations. Using the London Business School economic forecast, management makes a presentation, with an indication of its ability to pay. The council has a full-time coordinator. The main initiative for its formation appears to have come from the British personnel manager, and it remains to be seen how far this type of internal union can develop.

One shipping line, Ueda Transport Co., with forty employees, has been unionized since 1975. In order to discuss a pay claim, local staff invited a union in, and the company agreed to recognition if there was at least a 50 per cent vote.[39] According to the senior British manager, membership is now nearer 40 per cent and limited to younger staff. He, or another senior British manager, with over twenty-five years' service in the company, frequently meets two elected representatives, with whom memoranda on wages and conditions are exchanged. Another topic was the replacement of instant dismissal by suspension, described by the manager as 'like removing all management's teeth'. In his view 'this is a family concern and treatment is good. . . . Management will agree if possible', a view perhaps contradicted by the approach to the union. In the three and a half years between unionization and the research interview, there had been an average of less than one meeting a year with an external official. One meeting had, again, concerned a wage claim, leading to a compromise sanctioned by the head office. The manager did not see the union as a positive channel of communication for management.

When P. & O. and Ellerman lines were being organized there were talks at Oka Transport Co., another shipping line, with the Association of Scientific, Technical and Managerial Staffs (ASTMS), but the staff voted a proposal down. The senior British manager commented 'The Japanese would be worried about a union.' Department managers saw it as their responsibility to meet individuals and to make recommendations to the senior management if necessary.

At Nippon Transport Co., a larger firm than either of the above, there have been several approaches by ASTMS, and in 1977 there was a movement that 'either petered out or got trodden on—a pity, since it might have put off the union'. The British personnel manager thought that a staff association at a future date was possible, but 'management don't want a union because they like to believe they are satisfying the staff—though the latter don't think so'. It is significant that this personnel manager, under a Japanese superior, was not certain what had happened to the movement in favour of unionization.

There were said to be some employees in favour of a union at Nishi Trading Co., but not enough to constitute a guaranteed membership. In the late 1970s a staff association was formed, with a committee of fifteen and four representatives to meet management every two months to discuss pay and conditions, although it has no formal negotiating rights. It brings pressure to bear and, according to one British manager, unions 'are a potential threat to the Japanese'.

In another instance of dissatisfaction with pay, three self-appointed local staff representatives approached the management at Sanno Trading Co. in the late 1970s, and it was agreed to hold semi-official monthly meetings. Four representatives, regularly elected by the local staff, meet the administration manager over coffee and sandwiches, but this is not officially recognized bargaining. The manager described the meetings as 'useful for communication', and the representatives as 'reasonable—not a union'. This is a pragmatic response to pressure and an attempt to use the informal association to management's advantage. Such a staff association may represent an intermediate state between unionization and no organized consultative structure at all, but from management's viewpoint this may already be the thin end of the wedge.

Proposals for unionization at Ebisu Trading Co. failed to attract sufficient support, and instead bi-monthly meetings for local staff departmental representatives are held. The latter are generally older long-serving staff, who presumably identify more with the company, and the structure is described as 'replacing' a staff association.

The only City firm with a fairly active union is one of the banks, where the National Union of Bank Employees (NUBE) was recognized in 1974, again in a move over pay. The union is now the Banking, Insurance and Finance Union (BIFU). One British manager admitted that pay had slipped behind—although it was more than made up by backdated increases—and alleged that impatient 'agitators' had brought about unionization. He estimated that 56–8 per cent had been in favour then, with a smaller current figure, and claimed that because communication had been poor, the union had been able to take the credit for loan schemes etc. introduced by the management. He asserted that several staff in one department had left the union over its alleged failure to support their pay claim, but another manager accused the union of promoting excessive demands. It was said that the original union supporters had left the bank anyway and, given the turnover in the City, this appears likely. Japanese staff recruited locally are invited to join the union.

Union negotiations concern pay and working conditions but not promotion. The chairman and secretary of the union are among the older long-serving staff. The BIFU official responsible for all foreign banks in London is the external official with whom negotiations over the annual wage settlement are held, and over other matters as they arise. One British manager sees an advantage for the bank in being able to learn from the BIFU negotiator what settlements others have made, and these can then be relayed to Japan.

On his side, the BIFU official is not concerned that other

Japanese banks are not unionized. He is aware that, because of the harmonization of conditions among Japanese City companies, others will probably follow the types of agreement that he can achieve. In such matters there is considerable lateral communication between firms, and trading and other companies in the City will telephone to inquire what policy the bank is adopting on a particular issue of pay and conditions.

At Moriguchi Bank three potential unionists were turned away at the recruiting stage, and it was alleged at another bank that

The bank does not respect the right of their employees to be represented by trade unions. Management in the UK claim that they do not have the authority to take decisions and use delaying tactics when dealing with trade unions.[40] Promotion for local staff is generally not available, with vacancies being filled with staff brought from Japan. [FIET, 1978, p. 23.]

This refers both to managerial prerogatives and to the policy on staffing, particularly the deployment and training of expatriate staff that were discussed above.

These data show the reluctance of expatriate management to become involved with local unions more than necessary. A variety of strategies is employed in order to reach a pragmatic accommodation. Union relations are typically left to British managers, as expatriates are not trained to handle them. Unionization in the larger industrial enterprises is almost inevitable, but in the special conditions of the City firms unionization, or the formation of staff associations, has generally been prompted by dissatisfaction over pay. In spite of management anxiety, there seem to be few outstanding problems.

Communication

The concept of communication is a broad one. It covers areas such as head office–branch relations, interdepartmental and interpersonal relations, the social integration of company personnel into the organization both in working hours and outside, the structures of communication committees, sports and social clubs, Quality Circles[41] etc. and, in the Japanese case, wives' associations. Given the variations in size, type, personnel, and stage of development of firms, it is only possible to make some general conclusions after detailed cases have been examined. Reference has already been made to firms with a more 'family-like' atmosphere, in contrast to the larger, more formally or bureaucratically organized corporations, and this comparison will be borne in mind below.

Sono Engineering, with its Japanese management style and work organization, has one of the most developed systems of meetings. An overlap of ten minutes allows outgoing shifts to brief incoming shifts. Chargehands meet weekly and there are monthly production, planning, engineering, and 'expenditure curtailment' meetings. Employees appeared aware of the significance of the daily briefing groups, and to be highly quality conscious. As part of the new approach to quality control, operatives do their own quality checks.

The departmental briefing groups were established with assistance from the Industrial Society, and aim at high quality performance and commitment. The consistency of the effort to ensure full communication is functional, but it rests on managerial policy and managerial competence. This also applies to the company's policy of social 'egalitarianism', to be discussed below. Several informants mentioned that at the annual shutdown the Japanese plant manager had personally wished employees a pleasant holiday as they left the factory, which, they said, 'British managers would never do'. This combination of 'human relations' with task-oriented competence had produced an impression that should not be underestimated.

At Higashi Chemical Co. 'the Japanese managerial practice of involving everyone' (British director), has led to the introduction of shopfloor meetings every morning, attended by managers and supervisors, but otherwise the firm follows local custom and practice. The meetings are said to be effective.

Like Higashi Chemical Co., Daito Engineering is almost entirely run by local staff, but the development of the company has been along different lines. Before the localization of staff already referred to, a 'dictatorial, hard-line' managing director had evidently tried to impose unilateral control and there had been tension between expatriate and local managers. The latter had been 'enthusiastic and did overtime but were equally determined not to be done down'. The problem was resolved with the arrival of the new internationalist managing director, and the withdrawal of all but two of the expatriates.

In communication, the personality of individual managers may be crucial. In Daito's case the administration manager 'believes in telling people what is going on', and has introduced a communication committee despite the opposition of the (British) plant manager. He also believes that the basis of good employment relations is to have clearly laid down policies, and the company handbook gives formal job descriptions.[42]

Under his influence work stations have been arranged so that staff can talk to each other to alleviate the monotony of assembly work, which is 'inevitably repetitive and boring' (his phrase). This contrasts with the rules at television makers such as Daitoku and Kansai against talking on the job. Daito, like many firms, has an annual dinner dance, but a special feature is that every month employees whose birthdays fall in that month have lunch with the administration manager, when they can discuss problems and ideas. This closeness of communication can be achieved in a small company but other examples, such as Minami Chemical Co., show that very different situations are possible. In both companies the personnel function is exercised by British managers.

Employees at Miki Precision Products receive a staff handbook, setting out promotion policies and procedures and rules, drafted by the experienced British personnel manager. There is no consultative structure, but the assistant managers are briefed on management meetings and are responsible for the dissemination of information to staff. British managers meet fortnightly, under the personnel manager or the general affairs manager, and may ask a Japanese manager to attend for a specific reason. The Japanese general manager attends twice a year 'for a frank talk, without minutes'. 'The company is mostly run by local managers, with an injection of Japanese philosophy' (personnel manager); an almost identical comment was made by his equivalent at Daitoku Distribution. But 'more financial information than before is sent to Japan'; i.e., head office control of business operations has been tightened, and manpower plans are sent annually to Tokyo where, unlike some companies, the head office modify them. The personnel manager had been impressed by the company allocating £500 to the sports and social club when he had requested £200, and for granting more generous awards for staff with three, five, and ten years' service than he had proposed. This concern with 'human relations' and conditions of work may have been partly a reaction to earlier difficulties, and therefore, a deliberate policy to improve communication and rewards. The company has a pension scheme, not differentiated by status, for all employees.

Daitoku Distribution is also an 'equal status company', described as 'very employee oriented. The company's main asset is its people' (British personnel manager). As at Daito, management has changed from largely expatriate to mainly British, with a British managing director, and there is considerable emphasis on sports (including Sunday golf and tennis for all grades of employees) and disco parties, etc. But the personnel manager is critical of Japanese 'preoccupation with status, indecision and the fear of mistakes'.[43] He notes a reluctance of Japanese managers to face the embarrassment of dismissals, and their use of indirect communication. In one case, an expatriate manager would attend job interviews but would only speak afterwards. In another, expatriates who disagreed with the actions of a local marketing manager spoke to the personnel manager instead, evidently expecting him to pick up the cue as a 'go-between'.

'To throw them more together', the personnel manager put all the senior expatriate and local managers on a yacht to sail to Cherbourg one weekend. As in the case of the administration manager at Daito, this was his own idea, and it provides an interesting comment on what some managers in Japanese firms are able to do. Such actions cannot be easily explained by some type of 'catch-all' economic or technological argument.

In companies with mixed personnel it is to be expected that social and linguistic differences will create communication difficulties, but it would be facile to suggest, as some expatriates appear to do, that an improvement at this level will solve all communication problems. 'Previously Japanese managers [at Daitoku Distribution] wanted to return home to a hero's welcome for having achieved the same per cent increase in turnover as their predecessors, but now the British managing director wants an increase in profit' (personnel manager). Like the competition for managerial positions referred to above by Kagami, this is a conflict of interest that cultural mystification cannot hide. It is hard to see how communication between two rival groups in such a situation can be close.

Mixed organizations also face the problem that measures designed to improve communication may worsen it because of differences in expectations, based on specific behavioural norms.

Toho-Morita Distribution, for example, holds monthly staff meetings of departmental representatives and directors; these appeared to be an advance on the previous suggestions scheme. In practice,

The meetings are all one way. The representatives speak but the Japanese keep quiet. This makes the representatives aggressive. They wonder what the Japanese are thinking. The Japanese wonder why the representatives are aggressive, when all they want to do is to be friendly . . . locals feel kept in the dark, while Japanese wonder why their ideas aren't getting across. [British administration manager.]

This is almost an ideal typical example, reflecting many similar comments on communication. An approach by a white-collar union in 1978 was voted down by local staff, but relations are strained. It was asserted that 'previously there was a family feeling but now the company is bigger'——but its growth to approximately three hundred is evidently not the only factor.

Some managers consider that *ad hoc* compromises are largely to blame. The British coordination manager at Oka Transport, responsible for communication (another former military man), said that 'we tend to fall between two stools. It would have been better to have had a fully Japanese office, without a layer of European management——or else a fully British office. There would have been two ways to run it; instead of making a poor compromise.'

'Trust' is a major issue, even in small organizations. At Mori-guchi Bank, with no more than twenty personnel, there is a high level of informal communication in the branch, with a high level of head office control. The senior British manager, and 'go-between', observes that there is a 'suspicion of new *gaijin*' (foreigners, i.e. British staff in Britain), and that it takes three years to gain management's trust. 'You have joined the family from the Japanese point of view——but not from the British. . . . There is *esprit de corps* among the Japanese but local staff are not aware of it.' Trust, the closed group, and the language prob-lem, affect communication.

This manager sees different concepts of authority underlying different styles of communication. 'When a girl is just ordered to do something by a Japanese manager, she gets upset and cries and tells me she wants to leave.' In such cases the function of the go-between is to act as a shock absorber, and to deal with the problem caused by mutual unfamiliarity. A manager at

Sodo Bank stated that 'we are not good at presenting the way of doing things', explicitly, as in job descriptions. He also considered that although there were the usual circulars in use and departmental managers were responsible for briefing their British assistant managers informally over lunch, 'most people don't know what is going on'.

Similar difficulties were reported at Nippon Investment Bank, an organization with forty-five staff. The expatriate administration manager asserted that head office control, as well as linguistic and social difficulties, made communication hard and that the lack of training meant that another opportunity for communication was lost. This was specifically mentioned in the context of trying to wean local staff away from the 'it's not my job' type of demarcation, which expatriates find frustrating and difficult to deal with.

Managers at this bank, at Sodo Bank, and Kiku Bank, all asserted that current and future expansion would lead to greater head office control, which might be expected to have negative implications for communication in the branch. Language was stated to be 'a severe problem' at Kiku Bank. At management meetings, either an expatriate would have to translate or the meeting would have to be held in English; either way this would take too much time in an organization that was under continual pressure.

How far even good communication is effective is debatable. The British go-between at Tanabe Bank explained that written circulars were in use and that hand-picked individuals were informed verbally about business activities, so that they could pass the information on to others, but he commented that 'it would be a waste of time to tell everybody, including those who are not interested'.

This bank is seen by local staff as very 'foreign' or 'different'. Considerable attention is paid to 'human relations', using the informal means of parties, raffles, etc.; and the accessibility of managers in the open-plan office was favourably compared with the remoteness, in (smaller) branches of British banks, of British managers. 'Management mixes well with staff', was one comment, comparable with the perception of social 'egalitarianism' at Sono referred to earlier.

At the securities companies, on the other hand, communication seemed poor, although two companies each had forty employees and the third had eighty. Senior local staff complained that 'local staff resent being totally uninformed on all matters of policy'. This practice may be traced to the business itself being even more 'Japan-oriented' than the trading companies, and to the expertise being effectively an expatriate monopoly.

Companies such as Nishi Trading have separate management meetings for expatriate and local managers, while at the more internationalist Ota bank there are joint meetings, in English. At Maruyama Trading Co. an expatriate manager regretted the absence of such meetings, but finds that communication with local staff 'is not family to family and some local staff are apathetic in any case'.

At Maruyama, Nishi, and Tanaka trading companies, the departments were said to be largely isolated, particularly when located on different floors, and a British manager at Nishi asserted that 'most staff's picture of Japanese management comes from a particular department manager'. This argues poor interdepartmental or intracompany communication, and shows the risk of generalizing from a particular experience.

In Japanese companies communication is not restricted either to working hours or formal systems. ' "After hours man" resents undue intrusion on his free time but he depends on the organization and must submit' (Plath, 1964, p. 183). British staff typically leave work punctually, while expatriates stay and utilize the opportunity for informal communication both at the office and very often outside it later. Local staff, not integrated into the organization, often see this as tantamount to neglect of the family, and as an example of 'living to work' instead of 'working to live'.

Since so much is discussed or communicated informally in Japanese organizations, either in the office or in bars, restaurants etc., this accusation represents a serious cleavage. Japanese managers have the right and the duty to communicate according to a diffuse role conception, while in the UK work and leisure and their accompanying roles are clearly differentiated. A young British manager at Tanaka Trading Co. explained that he was willing to join his Japanese colleagues after work for a drink and a mixture of business and social conversation before getting married, but not afterwards.

In London the wives of Japanese company employees automatically belong to the company *Fujinkai* ('wives association') and must attend its meetings. This system aims at company-related communication, but is 'an invasion of privacy' in local terminology.

It seems probable that the term 'communication' itself has such different connotations to British and Japanese personnel that its usefulness is limited. A department manager at Tanaka, for example, stated that

The lifetime philosophy continues even with the young. Therefore each individual belongs to someone or something, such as parents, family, place, prefecture or organization. We tend to stick to relationships with the family, old school friends, teachers etc. We can't be individuals like you. These are *not* cool relationships. We trust and rely on each other. I think of my community or family, parents, company or group, before speaking to outsiders and I will stop speaking out if it may harm my group, even if I know it is true.

This unusually clear statement combines the elements of group exclusiveness and socially based ethics referred to above. It characterizes the types of informal communication that group members know how to use and to understand and Dore's concept of 'the enterprise as community' (Dore, 1973, pp. 206–21).

It is methodologically unsound to impute concepts to actors, especially when they belong to a different social context, but statements by the actors themselves may be revealing and may provide qualitative data that bring sociological concepts to life. The Japanese manager at Tanaka Trading Co., who criticized Japanese managers for not being 'real decision makers', insisted that 'they don't like being alone. They are at a loss when isolated and with free time. So they like golf for its "togetherness",[44] but it's pointless to take this or anything else up unless one is genuinely interested oneself. They will take up something—or anything—if it's done with other people but they won't do it by themselves.'

This is an ideal typical, or 'perfect', confirmation of the 'individual/groupishness dimension' identified by Dore, and suggests why terms like 'communication' mean such different things to different social groups. It is not implied that the above is a unique Japanese pattern of culture—because it is the result of socialization (cf. De Vos, 1973) and social interaction in a given social context—just as much as the contrasting individualistic values in British societies are, which the above manager has to some extent adopted in his attitude to groupishness. The implications of group social dynamics for communication, and for the exclusion of those who do not belong to the group, are relevant to the situation in the UK. The manager's remarks additionally support the view of his colleague, who criticized the 'therapeutic' aspect of *ringi* for expatriates.

Contrary to expatriate expectations, communication has been generally more successful with blue-collar workers than with white-collar employees and managers. This result is consistent with expatriate expectations regarding the different types of local staff in the industrial context, especially the anxieties over blue-collar unions. It can be explained both by the success of the Japanese approach to the shop floor and by the receptivity, i.e. the attitudes and interests, of the shopfloor itself. This harmony contrasts with the conflicting interests of expatriate managers *vis-à-vis* local managerial and white-collar personnel in white-collar firms.

The Japanese management style, recruitment policy, and development of briefing groups at Sono Engineering, have been referred to earlier. Local staff appreciated the care spent by management on the individual, in terms of flowers for the birth of a child, a wreath for a funeral, etc., comparable to practice in Japan.

The main ideas that had been communicated were quality, flexibility, and an egalitarian identity of interest. The high degree of employee awareness of the importance of quality was fostered by the briefing groups, the shift handover procedures, and by operator responsibility for quality checks. Flexibility was built into the understanding reached with the union and was exemplified by the frequent presence of Japanese managers on the shop floor, willing and able to help with different tasks. Egalitarianism was expressed by the wearing of uniform by *all* managers, white-collar and blue-collar employees, by the single-status canteen, the absence of overt status symbols like reserved parking spaces, etc. Interview comments showed that this was important to the shop floor and that, together with the other factors mentioned, it encouraged greater commitment than the prevailing situation in other firms described by them.

The essence of these policies can be summed up as a combination of task orientation, managerial competence, flexibility, and human relations. The latter is not a starry-eyed ideal but a pragmatic recognition that the operation of the enterprise as far as possible as a 'community' (Dore) is the best way to achieve management's aims. It should be stressed that Sono is strict regarding timekeeping, absence, mistakes, and, above all, the quality of work. The appeal of symbolic egalitarianism, combined with the professionalism[45] of Japanese managers, was clear from interviews with British staff.

Further evidence of expatriate success was provided by the case study at Minami Chemical Co. At the start-up there had been considerable Japanese influence but, after the expatriate managers and trainers were withdrawn, it was alleged that the company was slipping away from Japanese egalitarianism back into 'bad old' local ways. The British plant manager had stated his readiness to hold shopfloor meetings, but when actually requested to do so, replied that there was no time. Relations in the plant were on a first name basis, including the plant manager, and he was neither personally unapproachable nor 'old school', but he evidently failed to identify the cause of frustration. It was claimed that, in this firm of fifty, there was a clique of people recruited from another local firm that had been characterized by poor labour relations and the functional division of tasks etc. This was said to be why the 'bad old' practices were tending to seep back.

These data underline the importance of not assuming that communication is automatically better in small firms, and of recognizing that companies are not static organizations. They are subject to the dynamics of change, and it was evident in this case that the tendency to move from a more Japanese to a less Japanese type of organization was not constructive in the eyes of the workforce. Even at Sono, some pessimists argued that the company could 'go downhill' under the influence of local management and end up with the same problems as other local firms; although this eventuality appeared to apply more closely to Minami Chemical. The dissatisfaction at the latter was the mirror image of the satisfaction of shop floor workers at Sono, particularly in regard to the alleged status consciousness etc. of British managers. The problem was that the shop floor had felt 'equal' when Japanese managers were in charge. Manager–shop floor and white-collar–blue-collar distinctions had been played down, but as Japanese influence increasingly receded, they felt that British management was trying to put the clock back.

Partly because of stereotyped fears of 'militancy', some

Japanese managers appear unaware of the fund of potential goodwill and the positive expectations that they can tap at British blue-collar worker level.

In the Minami case it should be stressed that the plant manager was from the local community, that he did wear company uniform all the time, and that, despite the tone of some comments, he did not put overt status barriers between himself and the workforce. He did not have a grand office, but spent a considerable amount of time moving around the plant and made no difficulties about interviews with shop stewards.

The British managers did not wear uniform, and an event occurred during the study which appeared to sum up shopfloor remarks about communication and status. The Japanese managing director from the regional headquarters was expected for a day's visit. Before his arrival, British managers took off their suit jackets and changed into company uniform for his benefit. This was greeted with knowing looks and comments that 'this is the only time they wear uniform'. Office staff do not wear uniform at all, in contrast to the practice at Sono.

At Higashi Chemical Co. there are expatriates in several senior managerial positions, unlike at the Minami plant. Working practices and organization are more British, although there are the morning meetings already referred to. Unlike at Sono and Minami, where shopfloor workers are responsible for quality checks, there is a functional division between quality inspection and line operation, with a separate laboratory. Yet Higashi and Minami have workforces from the same part of the country.

Higashi has no plans to introduce Quality Circles. Minami claims to have a Quality Circle, but since it consists of managers and supervisors this is inaccurate (cf. Hutchins, 1980; JETRO, 1981; Takeda, 1981, etc.). Circles are based on the concept of quality as the responsibility of *all* levels of employees and on a concept of communication, or participation.

Quality Circles in Japan have been established by management, not employees (Kidd and Teramoto, 1981, p. 67). In some Japanese companies in the UK the impetus for change has come from British managers. Two firms have set up 'powerful employee representative committees' (Thurley, 1981, p. 53), with union support, one of which resembles the constitutional scheme introduced by Brown at the Glacier Metal Co. in the late 1940s (cf. Brown, 1960; Kelly, 1968).

Communication and industrial relations have been considered under the same heading because of their interconnection. Examples such as Sono suggest that egalitarian communication, combined with managerial competence and close supervision, can go a long way to solving industrial relations problems, instead of 'attacking' them directly.

The Toshiba case (*Financial Times*, 3 April 1981) exemplifies this approach. All 300 employees enjoy the same holidays, sick pay, redundancy entitlement, canteen etc.; in other words this is a single-status company. There is an advisory board elected by the entire workforce, from ten functional constituencies, with access to all company information; there is a single-union agreement. R. Sanderson of the Electricians'' Union (EEPTU) stated that the system represented a total concept. 'You can't have bits of it, like reduced manning. It hangs together as a package.' The scheme is described as 'the most radical' to date (Thurley, personal communication). This type of representative system has not been introduced by other Japanese TV makers in the UK, which shows the danger of relying too much on technology in attempting to explain company organization.

In Japan Quality Circles are found in the service sector, in, for example, the Sanwa Bank (*Financial Times*, 13 August 1980), but communication in Japanese firms in the UK varies both between and within the manufacturing and commercial sectors. It is generally more developed in the former, as the above examples show. This reflects the interests and aims of Japanese management, which are functional or instrumental factors.

The difference in the mode of communication and its dynamics refer to the social context, covering such points as the values implicit in Japanese informal organization and behavioural norms. These are 'expressive', or in Weberian terms, 'affective', aspects of communication, specific to Japanese society and organization, that concern feeling, climate, and perception. Together with such expected problems as language itself and the connotation of words,[46] they form the other component of communication that differentiates local staff and expatriates.

The case studies at Sono and Minami in particular showed that expatriates, contrary to their expectations, can often communicate better with British blue-collar workforces than with their white-collar[47] and managerial staff. This was argued to be related to the different interests of these categories *vis-à-vis* expatriate management. In addition, the solidaristic orientation of blue-collar workers is more compatible with Japanese single-status group organization and ethics, while the individualism and careerism of British managers and white-collar employees lead to a divergence of outlook and considerable difficulties in communication. The job mobility of white-collar and managerial staff makes it difficult for Japanese management to control them as it would be able to in Japan; consequently it has no precedent in the home society that would help it to find more effective means of communication. But it was argued earlier that the conflict of interest, involving the exclusion of local staff from more than limited decision making and substantive authority, is the more intractable problem, and that as long as this remains the case, communication will be unsatisfactory. This state of affairs is the fundamental explanation of Japanese management's 'deviation' (Inhohara, in Thurley *et al.*, 1981, p. 29) from its home policies and practices.

Notes

1. As a joint venture, Rank-Toshiba's annual production target was 350,000 TV sets. Actual production was 270,000. In December 1980 Toshiba assumed full control, rationalizing managerial and production systems (see below). Politically, joint ventures may be seen as more acceptable in the UK but wholly-owned subsidiaries are generally more successful in terms of innovation of new production and management systems. Rank-Toshiba is not the only joint venture to have changed to wholly-owned Japanese control.
2. The Department of Industry commissioned the Technova report as part of its campaign to attract Japanese investment.
3. 'Lower growth' in Japan still means, for example, the annual rates of over 5 or 6 per cent between 1976 and 1980, increased technology exports, and energy saving. See 'Prospects for the Long Range Economy of Japan' by the Research Institute of the National Economy (*The Times*, 14 August 1980).
4. Reports of disagreement between top Nissan executives have provoked scepticism. Nissan is the unwitting victim of the idealized images of unbroken consensus put about by those who oversell harmony. It is also said that the Nissan union is stronger than Toyota's and that its leaders are worried about 'exporting jobs'. Sluggish demand during a recession makes investment in extra capacity unattractive.
5. In the 1980s one of the major trading companies in Tokyo changed its

     sections into 'teams', to provide more titles for members of the large intakes recruited during the more expansive 1960s (personnel manager, personal communication).

6. Control of business and personnel is centralized in the head office. Ford, Pfizer, IBM, and other mature American multinationals have varying numbers of local nationals in senior positions outside their own countries, but images of the homogeneity of multinational managers may be overdrawn (cf. Sampson, 1974, pp. 15–21).

7. Other reported cases of British directors are at a sales company associated with Tanaka Trading Co. and, since 1981, at Nishi Electric Co. They are rare examples.

8. HNC stands for Higher National Certificate, HND, Higher National Diploma. Two-year work-related courses in business, technical subjects, etc. taken by school leavers at age 16, those already in work (as part-time/sandwich courses, etc.), at polytechnics, colleges of further education, etc. A (Advanced) Level of the General Certificate of Education (GCE), taken at age 18, normally in three subjects, is also required for university entrance. The GCE O (Ordinary) Level, is usually taken at school leaving age (16), the number of subjects depending on ability. Most shop floor operatives at Minami Chemical Co. had no 'O' Levels at all and in terms of exams passed, educational standards in Britain are poor. Education in Britain is accorded less attention and status than in Japan, where its importance in the national recruitment system is crucial.

9. Technology transfer is not the major focus here, but it has been an issue, together with the development of local personnel, in the Nissan negotiations.

10. British managers rarely have an expatriate subordinate. 'Japanese of lower rank will be carefully kept apart from British managers' (Isherwood, 1982). This is seldom discussed.

11. But Tanaka is generally regarded as more 'progressive' than some of its competitors.

12. The issue is, how is 'competence' defined?

13. The prevalence of overtime in Japan, whether necessary in business terms or not, has implications for control already referred to. At Tanabe Bank in London, expatriates were said to put in seventy to ninety hours a month, and senior local staff fifty hours. Overtime is less costly than additional staff, has a built-in flexibility, and is useful as a means of motivation and internal selection for promotion.

14. At Sono Engineering the personnel manager had worked for a period on the shop floor and was able to give a good explanation of the production process and quality checks.

15. Small in the UK, but not in Japan. See Japan Company Handbook.

16. A comparative study of British, American, and Japanese electronics companies in the UK found that half the managers and supervisors at one Japanese company had been promoted from the shop floor (Bennett et al., 1979, p. 64). But this does not affect the ceiling on promotion.

17. But Takamiya found that Japanese work organization in the UK fac-

tory produced lower rejection rates than a comparable British company with more sophisticated testing equipment. The Technova report stated that Japanese TV makers in South Wales were producing a small range of less advanced sets only; technology *per se* should not be overestimated.

18. At the same time they must avoid acquiring a reputation as employers of 'cheap labour'.

19. 'Like a colonial situation' (British personnel manager).

20. The criticisms of some expatriates have been included but it is likely that others were reluctant to speak out; it might have seemed like a 'betrayal'.

21. It is not to be inferred that anyone was trying to hide the informal processes or that they were unethical. They are the normatively sanctioned procedures, but because they are informal and shifting they cannot be pinned down by a formal description.

22. In a 'dry' (emotionally cold) or 'logical' British or American setting it could be seen as 'manipulation'.

23. His own word. 'Harmony' (*wa*) is a paramount value of Japanese social organization. It results from the expected performance of allotted roles, without egotism.

24. The reference is to the patrimonial character of factions in Japanese political parties and to factionalism in different types of organization (cf. T. Ishida, 1971, pp. 64–9). Presumably it is the potentially disruptive centripetal tendency towards factionalism that makes the repetition of the ideology of the centrifugal forces of harmony and consensus necessary.

25. It is a common observation that 'yes' frequently means 'I heard what you said', rather than the logical opposite of 'no'. It is frequently repeated during telephone conversations. Cautious people 'never take yes for an answer'.

26. Large companies have a directory, similar to a British Army staff list, listing all managers in ranking order.

27. Although 'feelings' are important in interpersonal relations with clients etc. in other companies, and are stressed in the ideology.

28. But how good is forward planning in British and other firms?

29. In Japan the head of an organization often 'takes responsibility' by resigning after an accident or scandal, although the public are aware his responsibility is symbolic rather than substantive. Following Durkheim, 'harmony' is restored.

30. Managers in large Japanese corporations are generalists (cf. decision making in Japan, Chapter 3). The theoretical possibility of assignment to any task, the absence or unimportance of job descriptions, and the ambiguities of responsibility in *ringi* are functionally related within the long-term employment structure. The generalist concept is not just an 'idea', but an integral part of the company structure.

31. A common expression used about competing organizations, widely understood in Japanese society, and revealing both keen competition and a preoccupation with the ranking order.

32. Cf. the thinking behind Quality Circles: that ordinary employees have

a contribution to make because they know the job by experience (Inagami, 1982; Hutchins, 1980).

33. Cf. Rohlen's example of a bank president warning his staff against falling prey to consumerism and becoming 'a sorry spectacle of decline like Britain' (Rohlen, 1974, p. 51). Moral appeals are more effective in Japanese than British organizations, where they are less socially acceptable. Cf. also the 'self-criticism' etc. practised in China. Confucian influences have been strong in both societies.

34. The international comparisons of working days lost through industrial disputes show Britain's position, yet the 'strike prone' image persists despite other countries with worse records (cf. Hyman, 1972, p. 30).

35. Nissan, for instance, is said to fear rivalry between the AUEW and the TGWU.

36. Japanese staff who would be in the union at home have no union representation in the UK. One younger interviewee complained that this was a factor in delays in salary increases (decided in Japan), which did not allow sufficiently for UK inflation.

37. See 'The Cycle of Goodness' (Appendix). The savings scheme was approved by 10 per cent of local staff; 40 per cent thought it was 'all right for the Japanese'; 50 per cent thought it was 'bull'. At a vote it was backed by 93 per cent of employees but only nine, of whom four were managers, were willing 'to put money on the table'.

38. Some expatriate managers have the impression they *must* recognize a union after a majority vote, but the current powers of ACAS are advisory only—as its name implies.

39. The white-collar union ASTMS.

40. The same allegation was made about a French bank in London.

41. Quality Circles have received attention from, for example, the *Financial Times* (1981). Up to 200 British companies, but no Japanese companies in the UK, have Circles. They are reported from one Japanese electronics firm in Ireland and one assembly operation in Belgium. Other forms of quality control, briefing groups, etc., have been introduced. Some Japanese managers doubt whether local staff can make Circles work, in spite of the American origins of quality control in the work of W. E. Deming and J. M. Juran.

42. This standpoint probably reflects his Army experience; cf. the formal systems put forward by another ex-Army personnel manager and, more generally, the approach of (Colonel) Urwick to formal organization.

43. Cf. previous comments on the alleged reluctance of expatriate managers to make decisions.

44. A concept originating in the United States.

45. 'Professionalism' in the sense of competence and dedication to the task, not in the sense of a narrow occupational or status consciousness, as it frequently means in the UK.

46. Cf. the mutual complaints of American and Japanese executives that the other 'couldn't understand' objectives (Ouchi, 1981, pp. 39–43).

47. Cf. Goldthorpe *et al.*'s (1968) example of right-wing white-collar

employees (draughtsmen) who were as militant as shop floor workers over wages and conditions. Expatriates would generally expect white-collar employees to identify more with the company, or to be more loyal, because this is what they would expect of better educated white-collar staff in Japan. The automatic equation of British white-collar staff with Japanese, in spite of the differences in employment systems, is interesting. It again points to the lack of adequate orientation training.

5 JAPAN'S RELUCTANT MULTINATIONALS

5.1 The host country context

The aspect of management as control and the conscious management choice of strategy, from among a number of different
theoretical possibilities, have already been stressed. It is argued
that they are major determinants of the respective presence or
absence of Japanese managerial systems in the UK, but it would
be wrong in a multinational situation to ignore the constraints
of the host society on the multinational management's strategy.
There is mutual action and reaction between the two. The following therefore outlines aspects of the situation in the host
society which are relevant for Japanese management and which
may to some extent constrain it.

In spite of trade problems, the periodic accusations of the
'dumping' of ball bearings, etc., there are widespread positive
expectations in the UK of Japanese management,[1] and previous
assumptions that British management had nothing to learn are
no longer officially approved.[2] There is thus a fund of potential
goodwill.

It was argued previously that the parts of a society's industrial
structure are interconnected and that they are linked with other
features of the wider society (cf. Dore, 1973, p. 10). These
structures are not rigidly determined: society contains competing groups and individuals who promote new ideas, new technology, and new power arrangements. A society does not exist
in isolation, for otherwise social change would be impossible.
This leaves the problem of 'how far is it impossible to reconcile
Japanese values and assumptions on corporate goals with a
market-based and occupationally-structured society?' (Thurley
et al., 1976, p. 1).

The development of industrial society in Japan itself, based
on the importation of foreign technology and techniques of
production management etc., should put the UK situation into
perspective (cf. Gibbs, 1980, p. viii). Bodies of British managers,

such as the Industrial Participation Association, show an interest in exploring Japanese managerial practices and their possible transferability (Bell, 1981, p. 13). It cannot be assumed *a priori* that Japanese systems 'won't work' in the UK.

In Japan the crisis of 1945 stimulated the modernization of Japanese industry and the evolution of a corporate structure adapted to the situation (cf. Hirschmeier and Yui, 1975, p. 283). To the extent that UK industry and society are ripe for change in the 1980s,[3] the introduction of Japanese managerial practices may help or hinder, but in the Japanese subsidiaries themselves this is likely to be a less important issue than the positions allotted to local staff. The overriding issue remains head office policy.

The Technova report, aimed at providing practical advice for the management of Japanese firms in the UK, concluded that the seniority system[4] and the enterprise union structure were not exportable to the UK because of 'the social structure and employment practices. . . . A forcible implementation of these two systems would create labour disputes.' On the other hand, they believed that long-term, or secure, employment and welfare benefits were desirable possibilities, although it was not clear how companies could implement or afford them. They also believed that 'a delegation of authority to lower-rank employees in initiating issues for decision making is concordant with the principle of . . . participative management in the UK' (Technova, 1980, Vol. 1, pp. 95–9).[5] There was no mention of a delegation of authority to British managers.

Demarcation, occupational structure, and the 'that's not my job' ideology are difficulties for which, in some cases, Japanese management have not been prepared (cf. H. Ishida, 1977, pp. 102–9); but the single-union agreements, with understandings on flexibility, reached by British firms on new industrial estates show that the problem is not insuperable. It could be more serious at management level because of careers and labour market and status concepts.

Takamiya's electronics study showed the successful[6] introduction of 'hard' systems of production management and some 'soft' systems of the 'single-status' company type, but the Technova consultants warned Japanese managers that they should exert themselves to communicate 'the principles of Japanese management systems', or else their adoption 'would never function smoothly' (Technova, 1980, p. 99).

At Sono and Minami the training given by Japanese engineers was warmly appreciated, although their English was not as good as the City managers'. On the other hand, the generally under-developed state of training, contrasting with what is widely believed to be the case in Japan, suggests that few companies are following the consultants' prescriptions. A problem may be the difficulty for Japanese managers as trainers in a non-Japanese society, with a so-called 'rational' intellectual tradition, when Japanese organizations rely heavily on implicit communication and shared values (Pascale and Athos, 1981, pp. 97–102). 'There is a cultural problem for Japanese managers; they just feel that is the way to do it' (Inohara, in Thurley *et al.*, 1981, p. 28). British staff want to have the reasoning explained and are not satisfied by being told it is 'the company way'. The role of Japanese managers as effective trainers in the way recommended by the consultants is, at the time of writing, open to doubt.

It is asserted that in Japan 'power over industry as a whole has passed to a category of professional managers and away from the individual private investor' (Clark, 1979, pp. 85–7). Has this 'managerial revolution' advanced as far in the UK as in Japan?[7] If not, it is a reason additional to the occupational structure problem that makes changes in managerial systems difficult. Similarly, it is reported in France that some firms reorganized by American consultants 'barely conceal the persistence of old French systems of hierarchy and routine' (Ardagh, 1977, pp. 66–7). This was alleged to be the problem at Minami Chemical Co.

On the other hand it is asserted that Swedish firms in the UK have been successful in 'treating Britons as if they were Swedes; as if their attitudes to work and employment were untainted by two hundred years of British industrial history' (Mant, 1979, p. 83). According to Mant, the Swedes were able, after a time, to establish Swedish standards as the norm. Foreign managers in the UK need to be aware that they can often innovate more successfully than British managers, especially if they have the charisma of success of Japanese management.

In practice management makes decisions at a given moment and there is a danger of reification and unreality in taking managerial practices out of their temporal context. At the British Steel Corporation, a group of managers was divided between those who believed that a time of crisis (the McGregor rationalization plan of 1980) was the time to innovate and those who believed that it was a time to 'hang on' and not to attempt to introduce new practices (personal communication). For Japanese management, a time of crisis in British business and industry may be more favourable in terms of gaining acceptance for unfamiliar methods and for meeting employee expectations. The problem then is why the companies have not appeared to be making more use of the opportunity, especially when the economics of the situation are in their favour.[8]

5.2 The home country strategy

Executives of a major electrical company and of an automobile manufacturer at the Tokyo headquarters, when asked why their companies did not introduce more Japanese managerial practices into their UK operations, took this as a criticism, or perhaps a disappointed expectation. They replied that Japanese companies found it difficult to manage in European countries, with their separate legal traditions and 'complicated ways'. They contrasted this with the situation in the USA, which they claimed Japanese companies found less complicated (Thurley, personal communication).

The majority of compromises at present found in the UK are *ad hoc*, and not a purposeful attempt to combine the best of Japanese and local practice. In some companies, such as Oka Transport, this was seen as resulting in a failure to get the benefits of either approach.

All Japanese companies in the UK operate a dual employment system. Recruitment, training, assignments, reward, promotion, bonuses, and fringe benefits, differ between expatriates and local staff. In many firms, such as the major commercial companies, this results in the two employment systems, and therefore the two categories of personnel, being effectively insulated from one another. Given the system of overseas postings found in virtually all companies, resulting in the continual movement of expatriates over the heads of local staff, the effect of the two employment systems is increased by company policy. It is not simply contingent, as if the companies were passive; it is a conscious managerial choice. In this light, it is reasonable to argue that the policy will not change unless the strategic planners at head office decide that the advantages outweigh the risks, particularly in the problem of internationalization.

Despite what cultural analysts might expect, the degree to which Japanese managerial sytems have been introduced into the UK varies considerably. It has been additionally possible to make a broad contrast between the sales and manufacturing operations on the one hand, and the City firms on the other, although it was argued that the contrast should not be over-drawn, bearing in mind that all firms are under the centralized decision making of the head office.

For analytical purposes it may be useful to place companies on a continuum, ranging from 'most Japanese' at one end to 'most British' at the other; the former will show the greatest introduction of Japanese managerial practices as a conscious policy applied to local staff as well as expatriates; and the latter will be the organizations conforming most closely to local custom and practice.

'Most Japanese' firms

Policy of educating local staff. (Possible assumption of universal applicability of Japanese managerial practices.)[9]

1. *Sono Engineering (manufacturing)*. Uniform worn and commitment to overtime in employment contract. Single status, including sick pay. Strong emphasis on quality (Japanese engineers). Stability of employment. Shift handover. Motivational system (frequent appraisal). Developed meeting structure, close communication. Training in Japan (before recession). 'Name' on products. Japanese plant manager and regional MD. British personnel manager enthusiastic supporter of Japanese management style.

2. *Okasa Engineering (manufacturing)*. Confidence in company philosophy, explained to all entrants. Pressure from head office to introduce employee savings scheme. Strong upstream control ('one-man', family controlled firm). Expatriate control of information. Policy to implement Japanese systems but making little headway (problems in training, workforce recruited, militant area). Similar *size* to Sono but different organizational climate; expatriate control at plant higher. President's portrait etc. in reception room. No British personnel manager initially appointed—reluctantly accepted under pressure.

3. *Sanno Trading Co.* Personnel manager and assistant Japa-

nese (no 'go-between' etc. as in other trading firms of same size). Implementation of head office personnel policy. 'Paternalism', e.g. ethical appeals to unsatisfactory staff, not dismissal. Moral exhortation re standards expected, on notice board. Conservative 'philosophy'. Informal staff association, used to explain company policy. No locals above assistant manager (unlike most trading companies).

4. *Daitoku Electronics* and 5. *Kansai Electronics (manufacturing)*. Recruitment and training of (especially female) school leavers. Work group meetings. Discipline and reward systems. Strong emphasis on quality and cleanliness. Japanese production organization (expatriate engineers). Motivational and performance checking/improving systems. Professional British personnel managers implementing expatriate policy.

One electronics company in Ireland, with many similarities to 1, 4, and 5 above, and with a 'traditional attitude', like 3, can be added to the list.

'Most British' firms

Policy of following local custom and practice, or of 'localization'. (Possible assumption of particularistic nature of Japanese, and British, practices.)

1. *Minami Chemical Co. (production)*. British plant manager, attending meetings of company plant managers worldwide. Claims of promoting own expansion, exports, etc. in consultation with Japan and European HQ. Quality Circle with no shop-floor personnel. One (young) expatriate accountant. Alleged re-emergence of British patterns after expatriate withdrawal.

2. *Higashi Chemical Co. (production)*. British director (chemistry graduate) in charge of production, personnel. 'No Japanese philosophy'—except morning meetings. Quality specialists in laboratory. Locally employed Japanese procurement manager.

3. *Daitoku Distribution (sales)*. Expatriate MD replaced by local. IPM qualified personnel manager. Claim of influence on design, selection of products for UK market. 'A British company, with some Japanese influence.' Contrasts with Ishi Sales, where top management are Japanese and low-level personnel secretary, British.

4. *Daitoku Electronics (sales)*. Relatively recently established (1978). Japanese MD but local deputy, largely in charge. IPM

qualified personnel manager. Qualified British company secretary (accountant). New products, expanding market.

5. *Daito Engineering (assembly)*. Official policy, 'This is a British company'. Japanese MD, permanent resident. Expatriate managers (eight) withdrawn. Engineer remains. Mostly part-time workforce.

6. *Daimon Engineering (sales)*. Experienced local manager replaced Japanese MD. Japanese purchasing manager only expatriate influence.

7. *Saiin Engineering (assembly)*. Experienced British manager, unfamiliar with Japan. No expatriates, but half-yearly visits. Regional European control. Wide power of local decision.

The list of 'most British companies' excludes companies where local staff have only 'prestige' titles and those, such as Miki Precision Products and Hito Engineering, where the presence of, for example, British personnel specialists does not affect expatriate control at branch level. Such companies do not have a policy of localization.

The list refers to companies at the time when the study was undertaken and does not attempt to predict trends. Since the study was made one bank has engaged an IPM qualified British personnel manager in an effort to improve productivity. This is an unusual move for a City firm and is perhaps a judgement that, as in several manufacturing and sales companies, the personnel function is best contracted out to a qualified local manager. It is not implied that the companies on the list will necessarily persist in their present organizational form, and the majority of companies, where there is an *ad hoc* compromise, do not appear on it. They are neither 'localized' nor pursuing a conscious policy of training local staff in Japanese methods ('Japanization').

Sono appears to be the company where the greatest attempt is being made to foster a Japanese-type normative organization, and it shows a higher degree of integration between locals and expatriates. This may be assisted by the relatively large number of local managers and by the conscious policy pursued by the Japanese plant manager and the British personnel manager. At the other end of the scale, Daito Engineering is a rare example of a declared policy of localization. At branch level, the pursuit of any consistent policy is constrained by the constant arrival and departure of expatriate managers. This is both the cause and effect of *ad hoc* arrangements and perhaps an indication that many UK operations have a relatively low priority on the head office scale, or are small in size.

Among manufacturing firms, the Japanese character of the two electronics companies compares with the British-inspired 'Glacier-type' system at the reorganized Toshiba plant. They are also dissimilar from the joint-venture organization of GEC–Hitachi. Mitsubishi Electric took over not only the bankrupt Tandberg operation but also its existing workforce. Toshiba rehired a proportion of the previous workforce, while Sono and the two TV makers have relied on young workers and school leavers.

Among distribution firms, the degree of local control, including the personnel function, at the 'most British' companies listed, contrasts with the situation at Kansai Distribution and especially Toho-Morita, where there is a British general affairs manager, rather than an IPM qualified personnel manager. Ishi sales has a lower-status British personnel secretary.

Sanno Trading Co. appears to be the least 'international' of the City firms, although its business activities compare with those of Tanaka and other trading firms. The banks represent different degrees of compromise, and are therefore not included in the list. Claims of 'localization' are rejected unless they are reflected in company structure.

In the light of the generally low level of Japanization in the UK, the extent at Sono of the 'hard' systems, referring to production engineering, quality checks, the orderliness of the plant, etc., and of the 'soft' systems, referring to the egalitarian single-status approach, is noteworthy. It may be contrasted with the situation at the Irish electronics factory, suggesting that functional reasons for such systems are important although the variety that is seen to exist—even, according to Takamiya and others, between the two electronics companies—and the issues of managerial competence and strategic choice show that these reasons should not be conceived of deterministically.

In Sono's case the management had been largely successful, according to interview comments, in inspiring the workforce to follow the new way of working,[10] whereas comments on the firm from those outside it were less favourable with regard to its 'school' uniform and strict discipline. An important factor was the professionalism of Japanese managers who were seen as dedicated to the task and to the company, and to be avoiding the status connotations of professionalism as interpreted by local managers.

Situations in specific companies vary and a factor at Sono was the approachable, friendly character of the Japanese plant manager. He contrasted with a securities company manager, who was clearly less popular and who made little effort to conceal his low opinion of local staff. Particularly in small companies the influence of individuals can be decisive.

A joint venture in Scotland was changed to full expatriate control (like Toshiba after the split with Rank) because management believed that this would result in improved performance; a similar case is reported from Belgium. It is not yet known how this has affected the 'hard' and 'soft' systems in the company but changes appear likely. Tanabe Bank is Japanese in its human relations or classless approach, and in work organization, but its degree of incorporation of local staff into the managerial structure is lower than at the more internationalist Ota Bank.

Problems of local staff promotion are not restricted to the UK. They have been reported from Belgium (Hanami and Dumortier, 1979, pp. 116-18, 171-5, 188-90), from South-East Asia (Sekiguchi, 1979, pp. 144-5), and from overseas operations in general (Nakase, 1980a, pp. 19-21). In the United States a case, opened in 1975 and still running, alleged discrimination under the 1964 Civil Rights Act, concerning promotion at C. Itoh in the USA. Out of thirty top managers at this major trading company, twenty-nine were Japanese (Gladwin and Walter, 1980, p. 408). The Japanese consultants engaged by the Department of Industry in Britain reported that 'life-long employment, paternalism and bottom-up decision making etc. [were] often used as a *rational* [*sic*] not to appoint or promote the nationals of host countries to the management positions in the Japanese foreign subsidiaries' (Technova, 1980, Vol. 1, p. 28). The report underlined the retention by Japanese companies in Europe or in the USA of their usual managerial practices among expatriates.

In the not anti-Japanese view of an American of Japanese ancestry, 'probably no form of organisation is more sexist or racist than the Japanese corporation . . . [which operates] as a culturally homogeneous social system that has very weak explicit or hierarchical monitoring properties and thus can withstand no internal cultural diversity' (Ouchi, 1981, p. 92).

The use of the term 'cultural' may be questioned, on the grounds that the distribution of power and conscious managerial strategy are of major importance. Although the type of cultural (i.e. social and ideological) exclusiveness described by Ouchi exists, it is argued here that his assertion is special pleading because it seems to take as 'given' what is in reality purposive social action. He appears to ignore managerial control at enterprise level and the overall strategic aims at higher levels of decision making. The assertion is 'Japanese' to the extent that it shows organizations as 'natural' or 'organic' phenomena, instead of as human constructions.

Awareness of these problems and of the factors relating to the ability of management in Japan to exercise the type of managerial control already discussed have led some to wonder anxiously whether Japanese management can be as successful overseas as it has been at home. 'Japanese management has been compelled to leave the comfortable sanctuary of a familiar and supportive environment supported by a highly cohesive and homogeneous culture' (Yoshino, in Vogel, 1975, p. 147). Yoshino fears that the policies and practices used so effectively in the home society will be modified abroad and that the companies may lose the qualities that have accounted for their original success.

Leaving aside the stock normative reference to the 'homogeneous culture', the emphasis on the compulsion to operate overseas is significant. It reflects the sub-title of Ozawa's 1979 book, *The Political Economy of Outward Dependency*. 'Compulsion' and 'dependency' both imply an unwelcome constraint. From Japanese management's viewpoint this can easily be understood from Yoshino's assertion of the 'comfort' and 'familiarity' of the home environment, where, with its 'cohesive' organization the companies can enjoy a high degree of control. The inference that they will find this difficult to enjoy overseas is clear.

It is inconceivable that management would willingly give up the advantage of this level of control at home for the difficulties it faces in expansion overseas, especially when it has 'homogeneous', i.e. exclusive, and isolationist tendencies. Yoshino uses the term 'emerging multinationals', but this neutral term may suggest a natural rather than a conscious process of development. This 'emergence' and the generally low profile adopted by Japanese companies in Europe contrasts with the expansive and outward-looking orientation of American multinationals. These have frequently exhibited a belief in the universal applicability of the rational principles of American management, a stance very different from that of Japanese managers, who believe that the special qualities of Japanese management are not exportable.

Lehmann (Thurley *et al.*, 1981, pp. 8-10, 51-3) and others therefore argue that the current slogan of internationalization is largely empty, and that there are no properly thought out means available whereby it can be translated into reality. Assuming that the term 'internationalization' has a standard connotation, it can be argued that Japanese companies operating internationally are not multinationals in the sense of Philips, IBM, Shell, etc. (cf. Behrman, 1969; Kojima, 1978, p. 221; Takamiya, 1979; Vernon, 1977, etc.), and that their hesitancy to leave their 'comfortable sanctuary', to evolve unified managerial practices and to integrate local staff makes it more suitable to describe them as 'reluctant multinationals'.

Their reluctance goes deeper than, for example, the 'transferability' (cf. de Bettignies, 1980, 1981) of Japanese managerial practices to other societies, even though this is an everyday problem in overseas operations. The reluctance has its roots in the home society and in the policies of its business leaders.

The effect of the threat and actual use of force by the Western powers in the opening of Japan was not lost on the ambitious lower *samurai* who became the Meiji ruling elite (Reischauer *et al.*, 1962, Vol. 2, pp. 218-19). In his treatment of Japan's industrialization and labour-management relations, a contemporary scholar refers to 'the pressure from more advanced Western nations to shift from a feudal to a modern society and the fear of being colonised by the Western powers' (Hazama, n.d., p. 2). In 1868 Japan had 'been "dragged out" into the Western type international community where the stronger preyed upon the weaker' (Fukuzawa, one of the modernizers of Meiji Japan, quoted in Aso and Amano, 1972, p. 15). In 1892 Herbert Spencer advised the Japanese prime minister of Japan's position of 'chronic danger' and warned him that the dominant powers should be kept 'at arm's length' (quoted in Hearn, 1955, p. 481). Japan's industrialization was the result of the conscious policy of the Meiji ruling elite, who were able to plan its development with Western experience in mind. It was a purposive decision, based on an appreciation of the political, military, and economic threat from the West, not the type of *ad hoc* process that took place in Britain.

Japan's international situation has changed since 1868, but some attitudes, perceptions, and aims have not radically altered, as the earlier quotation from Ozawa on the 'mercantilist' official policy from the 1950s onwards shows. The threatening image of the Black Ships of 1863 was in evidence in the discussion of the liberalization of capital in the 1960s and the feared foreign 'invasion', or takeover of Japanese companies, which did not in fact materialize. Trade disputes with the EEC, the USA, etc. do nothing to make the environment outside the 'comfortable sanctuary' appear more promising, or more like an area where Japanese management will be able to control the situation. Business strategies are not necessarily determined by popular attitudes but they may be influenced by them, and negative images of non-Japanese are not likely to improve local staff relations.[11]

The reasons for Japanese company investment in Europe and America, such as the protection of markets (Gladwin and Walter, 1980, p. 504), corporate competition, and the advantage of a base within the EEC tariff area, have already been referred to. The threat of sanctions is an incentive to invest but it is external compulsion.

Japanese firms' 'lack of experience in international management' (Sekiguchi, 1979, p. 93) may be authentic, but to claim that this prevents internationalization is a 'chicken and egg' argument; nor does it take Japanese managerial success in difficult environments into account. Matsushita succeeded in reducing an initial rate of absenteeism of 20 per cent at its Welsh plant (Beresford, 1981, p. 156), and the electronics companies have been successful in obtaining components of suitable quality from local makers, even if they are not yet completely satisfied. Arguments such as 'lack of experience' can too easily become self-fulfilling prophecies.

More relevant are the 'long-range domestic trends' (Reischauer *et al.*, 1962, p. 189)—the long-term plans of the government ministries (JETRO, 1979), including MITI and its concept of restructuring the Japanese economy—and the long-range plans of the private corporations, which are often described in the West as major causes of Japan's economic success (Trezise and

Suzuki, in Patrick and Rosovsky, 1976, pp. 757–811; Magaziner and Hout, 1980, pp. 1–44, etc.; Gibbs, 1980, pp. 35–57, etc.).

It was reported that 'all the Japanese car companies have two fears—that European and American markets may be progressively shut off by formal, or informal, import controls, and that the investment of General Motors and Volkswagen etc. is resulting in increased pressure to compete globally' (*Financial Times*, 30 January 1981, 'Nissan's British-made option'). This is consistent with Yoshino's view of the firms being compelled to venture overseas.

'Maxcy suggests that the threat of higher external tariffs is the main factor encouraging the Japanese to produce in Europe and North America, despite the fact that they lose some of the advantages of the economies of scale and access to Japanese labour' (M. Casson, reviewing *The Multinational Motor Industry* by G. Maxcy; *Times Higher Education Supplement*, 31 July 1981). If the companies are to remain competitive in the long term they must move abroad, however unenthusiastically.

The Economist asserted that 'Japan's most conservative businesses are at last accepting the message; avoid protectionism by moving abroad' (7 February 1981). A leading article in the *Financial Times* repeated the theme of the threat of protectionism: 'There are welcome signs that the reluctance of Japanese companies to invest directly in their main markets is being overcome, partly in response to political pressure' (23 February 1981).

But when they do move abroad, Japanese firms maintain separate employment systems and do not, for example, recruit British engineering graduates.

The heavy Japanese expatriate pressure in affiliates around the world, together with often far superior wage and fringe benefits, is sure to create growing problems for Japanese multinationals in the years ahead. The Japanese response is, as in other cases, essentially reactive and although some companies are trying to change their ways to avoid problems down the road . . . most won't change until they are forced to. (Gladwin and Walter, 1980, p. 408.)

Pressure for localization is resisted on functional grounds and others relating more to the types of concept described by Ouchi.

The use of the words 'compel', 'force', 'threat', 'pressure', 'reluctance', in the above quotations, underlines the reluctance to move abroad and the subsequent reluctance to give substantive authority and promotion to local staff. What is involved at both stages is the degree of managerial control; and Lehmann's criticism of the rhetoric of internationalization meets both cases.

Following the approach to the theory and practice of managerial systems above, it is not argued that this 'reluctance' can be explained monocausally. A cultural explanation might point to the insularity of the Japanese ethos.[12] A functional explanation might allude to the problems for Japanese management with British career-path-oriented managers, defective components (cf. Technova, 1980, Vol. 3, p. 70), occupationally-based unions, etc. Both arguments are to some extent relevant and there is no *a priori* reason for them to be incongruent in the Japanese case, because the 'rational' problems of overseas operations fit their images of other societies as inhospitable and organized on different lines from Japanese society.

One television manufacturer is obliged by host country pressure to use British-made tubes (against its will), and in other cases British component makers have declined Japanese contracts because the standards demanded would erode profit margins. The consequent 'reluctance' of Japanese managers, both in a business sense and in a value-laden sense, is understandable. During the research visit to Ireland in 1980, one Japanese manager complained bitterly to a Japanese member of the team of the difficulties involved in overseas manufacturing operations, but expressed resignation because 'the present day world situation demands it'.

In the 1970s 'Japan was induced to embark on a policy of investment in overseas mining, agriculture, and fishing industries in order to gain some measure of security for her supplies of primary products . . . in accordance with . . . the "Development and Import Strategy"'' (Allen, 1981, p. 3). Subsequent Japanese successes in the export markets of Europe and America, producing trade imbalances, then became an inducement to invest directly in these areas (ibid., p. 5).

Such investment can sharpen corporate competition. Funaki points out that Japanese electronics firms in the UK did not invest because they were facing competition from British manufacturers: 'Rather I suspect it was because they have had to face competition from Japanese companies. Because Sony did this, National and Hitachi had to do the same, and because Toyota did this, so did Mazda, and so on' (Funaki, 1981, p. 11). Some

smaller firms, such as Saiin Engineering, may be expanding overseas because of the lack of room at home. This expansion of
companies that are 'immature' by the standards of American
multinationals is a form of domestic competition, compared by
Ozawa to the export of Japan's 'dual economy' of large and
small firms.

Corporate competition does not necessarily make overseas
operations more palatable. The Technova report drew attention
to the non-recruitment of local engineering graduates and to the
fact that the Japanese television makers in the UK were producing a small range of less-sophisticated sets. They provided employment and examples of managerial practices that are of
interest in the UK, but little prospect of technology transfer.
The technical level of these operations can be contrasted with
the increasing use of robots in Japan itself (cf. JETRO, 1981).

From the local point of view these operations, and the concentration of other Japanese companies in Wales, may seem
extremely important, while from the head office perspective
they may appear as fairly small points on a map of the world.
In spite of lower labour costs than Belgium, Germany, etc., and
other advantages previously referred to, the UK has not proved
particularly attractive to Japanese manufacturers. It tends to
have the image of 'an old industrial society suffering from the
problems of stagnation' (Technova, 1980, Vol. 1, pp. 82, 91).

This image is related to the values, perceptions, and reactions
of Japanese managers. The objection to economic determinism
is that it appears to posit a totally rational perceptual and conceptual apparatus, which in any society is impossible. Managers,
who are committed to corporate goals, may see themselves as
'practical', without the time for 'unsubstantiated theories' etc.
In fact, 'managers do not deal with complex reality as a whole.
When they try to theorise and to explain behaviour, they do
what social scientists do: they break up reality into compart-
ments; and when they act, they act from partial theories—as
practical economists, for example, or practical psychologists'
(Lupton, 1971, p. 22). It is not, therefore, clear whether the
criteria Japanese managers have in mind when they evaluate
overseas operations are based on 'objective necessity'.

One experienced plant manager in Ireland complained about
demarcation, without any evident knowledge of its context.
Some expatriates give the impression that they have little interest

in understanding local practices, and the inadequacy of orientation programmes before moving overseas suggests that this understanding is not a company priority.

It was argued that the term 'manage' etymologically and empirically, means 'to control', without which the other aspects of management (Thurley, 1975, pp. 2–3) lose an essential part of their significance. In Japan 'the degree to which the present system reflects conscious managerial policy' (Hill, 1981, p. 54) should not be underestimated.[13] The lower degree of control that Japanese management can hope to exert abroad is the logical conclusion to Yoshino's statement that they are reluctant to leave their 'comfortable sanctuary'. Less control means fewer options and more operating difficulties.

'Few people will deny that "The Japanese System of Management" has substantially contributed to the phenomenal postwar growth' (Hirschmeier and Yui, 1975, p. 282). It is therefore understandable that management should seek to preserve its high degree of control, whether this is always 'objectively' necessary or not. Hirschmeier and Yui trace a connection between Japanese management and the values of the wider society and at a general level it can be argued that the desirability of control, or power, is never exhausted.

In Japanese society competition takes place in the context of expected role performance. This is akin to the Weberian concept of the 'office', according to which the office holder *qua* holder is important, not the individual. But it was shown that the presidents of some Japanese companies that are well known in Japan can wield power to an above average extent. The restraints on factionalism and disruption that operate in Japanese society have been already discussed. In any system there may be a tendency for power holders to seek to maintain, and expand, their power, whether it is necessary in order to fulfil their specific functions or not. At Tanabe Bank, for example, it was alleged that the control system actually led to lower performance because of the creation of unnecessary paperwork. The high degree of managerial control in Japan may be explained as having functional aspects and others (*pace* Hirschmeier and Yui) related to the values of the society; but it can be argued that the real point is that management has achieved it, believes it is necessary, and does not intend to lose it.

The alternative explanation of Japanese managerial systems

as control, is that of 'committed' left-wing writers, such as Nakase (1977, 1980, 1980a) and Halliday and McCormack (1973). They see Japanese overseas expansion, with hindsight, in terms of the coordination of Japanese and American strategies. They do not explain the differences between Japanese and American industrial structures, labour markets and employment systems, the types of relations between major firms and sub-contractors, and managerial practices. To others, the skill with which Japan's own economic interests have been promoted by MITI and the companies has been impressive. So impressive, indeed, that it has led to serious trade disputes at different times with the USA over textiles, steel, cars, etc.—despite the fact that some accuse Japan of economic collusion with the USA.

In the UK the effect of the environment on Japanese managerial systems or thinking seems negligible. 'The UK is good for leisure, but Japan is better for business', was how the plant manager at Sono put it. Young expatriates in London may grumble when they see local staff leaving punctually; individuals like Mr K, an employee of a major corporation, may be reluctant to return to the greater discipline and social conformity of the head office in Tokyo; company wives in London may enjoy their greater social freedom—but none of them have real influence *vis-à-vis* the companies in Japan.

It is plausible to argue that there must be *some* influence from the cumulative effect of the increasing numbers of Japanese who have worked abroad, but it need not be in the direction of increased 'Westernization' or 'individualism', as some in the West appear to expect.[14] One young graduate at Tanaka Trading Co. criticized the 'stupidity' of local staff for lacking commitment or ambition, with what seemed like a feeling of 'Japan as Number One' (Vogel, 1980). A long-serving employee at one of the banks noted that in recent years expatriate managers invited local staff out on fewer occasions, showed less interest in local cultural life in London, and behaved with a new 'cockiness'.

It has often been observed in Japanese society that 'humourless radical students continue to transform themselves in the space of a few months into humourless dedicated company men' (Dore, 1973, p. 213). Dore sees this as a strong defence mechanism against the 'my homeism' that senior Japanese managers worry about.

Changes in Japanese managerial systems since the oil crisis have come primarily from domestic structural causes, and it appears unlikely that they will undergo major modification in the near future. A critical observer of Japanese society believes that the present employment system 'is perhaps the only way of keeping a huge labour force gainfully employed, with minimum friction and maximum security for all concerned' (Kawasaki, 1969, p. 112). Although there was considerable social change under the Occupation, the structures of decision making have remained fundamentally unaltered (Ishida, 1971, pp. 32–3).

Some changes may come because of the slowing down in the rate of economic growth (S. Takamiya, 1979) but, after a two-year study, the Labour Economics Research Sub-group of the Japan Institute of Labour concluded in 1973 that the principal result of discussions being held would be 'a mere shift in the fixed age for retirement from 55 to 60 without any significant change in the compulsory or coercive aspects of the system' (Kaneko, in Nishikawa, 1981, p. 123). The significance of the assertion is that there is little present likelihood of a modification in the pattern of managerial control. From the tone of the remarks, it is clear that Kaneko is a partisan of change.

A 1976 survey of company presidents' views on long-term employment, however, showed that 45.2 per cent were opposed to change but that 54.4 per cent were in favour: 55.7 per cent thought there would be change, compared to 43.9 per cent who believed there would not (quoted in Inohara, 1977, p. 31). 'Change' is an imprecise concept. Raising of the retirement age, the increasing use of contracting out and temporary female labour—to allow management greater elasticity—have been noted in many companies (Yashiro, 1981), if this is what is understood by change; but it seems unlikely that there will be a major break with the long-term employment policy.

Current practice already contains the means whereby management can make adjustments in a particular situation, while continuing to enjoy the associated benefits of control; and commitment to the ideology remains firm. A major break would require the agreement of the unions, and it is not clear what they would be willing to trade as a *quid pro quo*.[15] Inohara concludes that 'the fate of personnel administration, in [its] present form of operation, depends on the fate of "life-

long employment" and the "seniority rule" ' (i.e. system: Inohara, 1977). This view is consistent with the emphasis placed
above on the position of these practices in the Japanese employment system; without them managerial control, work group
cohesion, and the present patterns of decision making could be
jeopardized.

Managers at Tanaka Trading Co. were aware of the interdependence of these systems and some feared the 'unintended
consequences' that might upset one part if others were modified.
What, for example, is the implication for flexibility of assignment or job allocation, and for 'loyalty', if the companies were
to move away from the long-term employment pattern to a
more British or American type of job mobility and specialization? Such a change might benefit individual managers in their
careers but would it benefit the organization? Would the impressive team achievement that has characterized the collective
orientation of Japanese company structure be able to function
so effectively? Above all, would such changes be to management's advantage in the long run? It is reported that in 1975
'some weaker Japanese firms were considering codetermination
as an alternative to labour's demands for 15%–20% wage increases. Most managers rejected this as an intolerable limitation
of their control' (Gladwin and Walter, 1980, p. 400). The decision for long-term control, at the cost of shorter-term wage
increases, appears to indicate where Japanese management's
priorities lie. Because the companies are managerially controlled
and need not worry much about the short-time horizons of
individual investors, who generally receive a fixed rate, Japanese
management is also in a good position to see that its policies are
carried out in the long term. In this respect it is in an enviable
position compared to British management.

Some Japanese managers fear tampering with the 'pillars
of Japanese management' and that almost any change is likely
to be the thin end of the wedge. This apocalyptic view is
expressed by Sasaki, who entitles his concluding chapter
'Present Drastic Changes Towards a Collapse?', and asserts that
'changes may weaken the dynamism of Japanese companies and
may lead to a total collapse. They are destroying themselves'
(Sasaki, 1981, pp. 133–6). This follows a more measured
discussion of the internal and external pressures on Japanese
management, including an alleged shortage of management

resources (ibid., p. 123), based on Penrose's 'Theory of the Growth of the Firm'.

It is true that the oil crisis of 1973 caused a panic, including inflationary price rises. Some goods temporarily disappeared from the shops and trading companies and others were accused of profiting from land and commodity speculation, but the increase in exports, the energetic promotion of such domestic policies as energy conservation, and the restoration of public confidence demonstrated that the panic was a temporary mood. The popularity of a 'disaster' novel, such as Komatsu's *Nippon Chimbotsu* (*Japan sinks*), in the late 1960s and early 1970s, cannot be measured against industrial strategy and long-range company planning.

The alleged shortage of management resources is not in evidence in the City, where local staff consider that the staffing policy is intended to provide posts for the large intakes recruited in Japan. It is seen as another instance of the centralized structure of local operations. Personnel managers at some companies commented on the tactics used to avoid change in the position of local staff.

Yoshino's more outward-looking view is that 'in order to undertake major expansion internationally [Japanese companies] must bring about changes in their management system —changes that will not be easy. . . . And in the process, they may well sacrifice those elements that have made the system so effective internally' (Yoshino, 1976, p. 178). The last point is consistent with Sasaki's fear, although the apparent implication of a wish to expand internationally may be questioned.

From the decision-making study at Tanaka Trading Co. and from interviews elsewhere it was clear that companies maintain centralized control over all strategic or crucial policy matters, such as staffing, marketing, and production—whatever may be delegated to local staff at the level of interviewing secretaries or operators, selling goods in the local market within the framework of the company's overall strategy etc. Some local staff appeared to believe that the general manager in London had the authority to change the position of local staff, but it was clear from the decision-making study that even the London general manager of Tanaka Trading Co. was unable to change the decision-making structure—assuming he had wanted to.

The perspective from the inside was given by N. Kagami,

formerly Director of the Nomura Research Institute in London, and a manager with overseas experience in several countries:

Japanese society is characterised by insularity and by remoteness from external issues. The overriding concern is with domestic issues. There is a tendency to retreat into isolationism, which is bad for Japan and for the outside world. . . . Japanese people feel they should adapt in a reactive manner to the international order but the external demands are that they should play a more active role. . . . Crises arise periodically, as in trade with the USA, but it is always symptoms and never causes that are tackled. This is necessarily superficial. [Japan Society, London, 13 March 1979.]

His view supports the contention of 'reluctance' to become involved overseas, yet the Japanese economy depends on imported raw materials and on overseas markets for its exports of manufactured goods and cannot maintain living standards and employment without the outside world.

It was asked earlier whether there was a universal 'logic of multinationalization' that applied as much to Japanese firms as to American or Dutch firms; and how the problem of the internationalization of Japanese companies at the level of managerial practices was likely to be resolved.

The data support the view that Japanese corporations operating internationally are 'reluctant multinationals'. On instrumental grounds, related to national economic interests and to the conscious managerial strategies planned in that context, as well as on more value-laden grounds, there is little evidence that Japanese corporations are likely to change the employment and decision-making systems in their overseas subsidiaries. Home country personnel remain the full members of the firm, over whom the companies enjoy the greatest control, and from whom they can expect the greatest achievement because their own interests are at stake. A universally applicable 'logic of multinationalization' is incompatible with the evidence from the subsidiaries.

Explanations of Japanese management and of the overseas operations of Japanese companies based on abstract models of business logic fail to take Japan's industrial structure, which is the context within which the firms operate, into consideration. Use of a power dominance model leads to misinterpretation of the overseas spread of Japanese economic activity. Unlike the United States, for example, Japan is poor in resources, except for human resources, upon which the companies and society as a whole lay such emphasis. The rationale of Japanese and American overseas economic expansion and of its development is not the same.

Longitudinal studies of the development of Japanese economic expansion overseas could be expected to show its dynamism, and to demonstrate how dynamism in economic activity goes hand in hand with the maintenance of basic managerial policies and practices, in spite of pragmatic adjustments. If this approach is correct, it suggests that the universalistic model of multinationals, based on American prototypes, needs to be supplemented by a plurality of models, which would eventually apply to leading Korean, Brazilian, or Middle-Eastern companies, and which would necessitate a reappraisal of British, French, or Italian multinationals. Each has emerged in the context of a particular industrial and social structure. As in Ardagh's example of superficially Americanized French management and in the light of Inohara's dictum on Japanese management 'looking at the formal structure does not provide many lessons'.

As the situation stands, Japanese managers do not see it in their interest to change their basic policies, and only external pressure (cf. Kagami, above) might gradually oblige them to do so, but it would be likely to be a process accompanied by many delays.

It may in any case be asked why Japanese management should want to change. Out of the post-war crisis it has evolved a rational and effective system—even a 'historic compromise'. Its methods (cf. Hirschmeier and Yui, 1981) have succeeded beyond expectation. In the United States, the mecca of management theorists, major industries such as steel and automobiles face hard Japanese competition in their own market, and call for protection. Respected authorities wonder whether Japanese corporate organization and the rationality of its pay bargaining systems are not a more advanced model, towards which British organizations are painfully creeping (Dore, 1973, Ch. 13, 'Britain Catching Up?'). Increasing numbers of writers leap onto the Japanese management bandwagon, wishing to show companies in Europe and America how they can profit by becoming more Japanese. The UK, economically successful at an earlier innovatory, or 'buccaneering' stage of industrial organization (cf. Mant, 1979), is far less able than the USA to offer Japanese managers a credible model of 'international' organization. Many Japanese, conscious of the Meiji heritage of Western technology, now regard Europe as a place 'where there is nothing more for us to learn'.

It would obviously be superficial to argue that the internationalization or otherwise of Japanese companies depends on nothing more than such ideas, although there is a strong insular and exclusive 'tradition' at the policy level, in contrast to the openness to the adoption of new *techniques* at the level of the means required to realize the policy ends. What is at stake are 'goods', such as power, economic interests, and prestige, and it therefore seems unlikely that a rapid major change will come about from within. The two periods of greatest change in Japanese society in a little over the last hundred years have both resulted from external stimuli—after 1868 and after 1945. The significant determinant for the companies is managerial control and the distribution of power.

In the early years of this century Max Weber asked why the first wave of industrialization and the first steps towards the rationalization of management had taken place in the societies of the 'Protestant' West. Why did this not happen in other societies that had developed science and technology earlier, and that had numbers of educated people and entrepreneurial merchants, such as China and India?

At the present time it has been possible to see a new wave of industrialization and industrial organization in Japan, a younger industrial society, rather than in the older industrial societies of Britain, France, or the USA. Japanese companies have become the pace-setters, with the New Industrial Countries in pursuit, as what has been predicted as the 'Pacific century' approaches. We need to ask the same kind of questions about the new wave of modernization that Weber was asking about the first wave; otherwise its mainsprings and process of development will not become clear. To understand one another is not easy, but the facts of economic interdependence dictate that we either 'hang together or hang separately'.

Notes

1. The enthusiasm of workers at Minami Chemical Co. for Japanese style management was documented above.
2. The government-established National Economic Development Office (NEDO) publishes a series of booklets with the explicit title, 'Indus-

trial Policy in more Successful Economies'. No. 7 (Gibbs, 1980) is on Japan.

3. A British firm with 'Japanese' managerial practices, but without any apparently direct Japanese inspiration, is Hotpoint under C. Schreiber, a known innovator.

4. Hazama's 1975 survey showed that 67 per cent of British workers questioned were against the seniority system.

5. Cf. Quality Circles above.

6. Successful in reducing rejection rates, improving the quality of locally made components, motivating local employees, and monitoring their performance.

7. British management is more subject to shareholder influence than Japanese. It cannot browbeat shareholders, or worse (Kawamoto and Monma, 1976, '*Sokaiya* in Japan').

8. Substantial investment incentives, plentiful supply of (frequently skilled) labour, companies that can be taken over at attractive prices, labour costs among the lowest in Western Europe (see OECD figures). The takeover by Sanyo of the Philips television plant at Lowestoft and by Mitsubishi of the bankrupt Tandberg company's Scottish plant are exceptional.

9. It is *not* argued that this possible assumption is anything like the sole cause of Japanization. In large companies there may be the pressure of staff due for promotion behind overseas postings. In small companies there may be a shortage of home country personnel, due to financial weakness. Such data are normally confidential, but the high cost of assigning expatriates overseas and moving them at frequent intervals should be taken into consideration.

10. Cf. Mant's Swedish example above, but British managers, except the personnel manager and training manager, were less enthusiastic about the new style than the shop floor.

11. See the rather negative results of an opinion survey carried out by an official organization among Japanese who had been abroad (*Bulletin of the Anglo-Japanese Economic Institute*, London, No. 219, October 1980).

12. Cf. the expression *shimaguni konjo* ('island country spirit', i.e. insularity), which some might seek to explain by the two and a half centuries of isolation under the Tokugawa (1600–1868).

13. Hill sees conscious managerial policy leading historically to the tightening of managerial control by e.g. constraining the labour market by the recruitment (and retention) of school leavers, etc. (Hill, 1981, p. 55).

14. Differences in attitude between internationalists and traditionalists at Tanaka Trading Co. etc. were already referred to. Older children pose severe educational problems for expatriates. In some cases they go on to study at universities in Europe and America, where they then obtain employment.

15. Unions are also said to have increasing worries about jobs being 'exported' from Japan because of overseas investment.

APPENDIX: JAPANESE MANAGEMENT IDEOLOGY

'The Cycle of Goodness'

I firmly believe in the spirit of social service. Wages alone are not sufficient to assure our employees of a stable life and a rising standard of living. For this reason, we return to them a large share of the fruits of their labour, so that they may also participate in capital accumulation and share in the profits of the firm. Each employee, depending upon his means, deposits with the company at least ten percent of his wages and monthly allowances, and fifty percent of his bonus; the company, in turn, pays interest on these savings. Moreover, as this increases capital, the employees benefit further as stockholders in the firm. It is said that 'the accumulation' of savings distinguishes man from animals. Yet, if the receipt of a day are spent within that day, there can be no such cycle of saving.

The savings of all our employees are used to improve production facilities, and contribute directly to the prosperity of the firm. Superior production facilities improve the quality of the goods produced. Lower prices increase demand. And both factors contribute to the prosperity of other industries that use our products.

As society prospers, the need for raw materials and machinery of all sorts increases, and the benefits of this cycle spread not just to this firm, but to all related industries. Thus the savings of our employees, by enhancing the prosperity of the firm, are returned to them as dividends that enrich their lives. This results in increased savings which further advance the firm. Higher income means higher tax payments, and higher tax payments enrich the lives of every citizen.

In this manner, business income directly affects the prosperity of society; for businesses are not mere seekers after profit, but vital instruments for the improvement of society.

This cycle enriches our free society and contributes to the happiness of those who work within it. The perpetual working of this cycle produces perpetual prosperity for all.

This is the cycle of goodness.

Engineering Company, 1980
(President's Introduction to brochure)

BIBLIOGRAPHY

Abegglen, J. C. (1958), *The Japanese Factory; Aspects of its Social Organization*, Free Press, Glencoe, Ill.

Abraham, J. H. (1977), *The Origins and Growth of Sociology*, Penguin, Harmondsworth.

Allen, G. C. (1981), 'The Economic Context of Japanese Trade and Investment in Western Europe' (unpublished synopsis of address at ICERD Conference, 1981).

Anderson, H., Burton, N., Tennison, J., and Winter, J. (1980), 'A Comparison of the Personnel Policies and Procedures of Companies in Peterlee, County Durham' (unpublished; London School of Economics and Political Science).

Anglo-Japanese Economic Institute (1980), *Bulletin* No. 217, July–August, London.

Ardagh, J. (1977), *The New France: A Society in Transition 1945–1977*, 3rd edition, Penguin, Harmondsworth.

Aron, R. (1970), *Main Currents in Sociological Thought: Vol. 2, Pareto, Weber, Durkheim*, Penguin, Harmondsworth.

Aso, M. and Amano, I. (1972), *Education and Japan's Modernisation*, Ministry of Foreign Affairs, Tokyo.

Azumi, K. (1969), *Higher Education and Business Recruitment in Japan*, Columbia University, New York.

Ballon, R. J. (1969), ed., *The Japanese Employee*, Sophia University, Tokyo.

— (1980), 'Management Style', in *Business in Japan*, eds. P. Norbury and G. Bownas, Macmillan, London.

Befu, H. (1971), *Japan: An Anthropological Introduction*, Chandler, San Francisco.

Behrman, J. N. (1969), *Some Patterns in the Rise of the Multinational Enterprise*, University of North Carolina, Chapel Hill.

Bell, D. Wallace (1981), *Report on Japan*, in *Industrial Participation*, No. 574, Summer 1981, Industrial Participation Association, London.

Bellah, R. N. (1957), *Tokugawa Religion: The Values of Pre-Industrial Japan*, Free Press, Glencoe, Ill.

Bendix, R. (1966), *Max Weber: An Intellectual Portrait*, Methuen, London.

— (1974), *Work and Authority in Industry. Ideologies of Management in the Course of Industrialization*, University of California, Berkeley.

Benedict, R. (1935), *Patterns of Culture*, Routledge and Kegan Paul, London.

— (1946), *The Chrysanthemum and the Sword*, Houghton, Mifflin, Boston, Mass.

Bennett, P., Davies, A., Da Zoysa, L., and Jenner, F. (1979). 'An Interim Report on a Comparative Study of four Multinational Companies', Typescript, London School of Economics.

Bennett, J. W. and Ishino, I. (1963), *Paternalism in the Japanese Economy: Anthropological Studies of Oyabun-Kobun Patterns*, University of Minnesota.

Beresford, M. D. (1981), 'Joining battle with Japan', in *Management Today*, October 1981, London.

Bergsten, C. F., Horst, T., and Moran, T. H. (1978). *American Multinationals and American Interests*, Brookings Institution, Washington.

Bernstein, B. (1973), *Class, Codes and Control*, Paladin, London.

Bettignies, H. C. de (1980), 'The transfer of management know-how in Asia: an unlearning process', in *Breaking Down Barriers: Practice and Priorities for International Management Education*, by B. Garratt and J. Stopford, London, Gower.

— (1981), 'Can Europeans learn from Japan? Can we transfer Japanese management technology?', unpublished synopsis of address to ICERD Conference, 1981.

Bieda, K. (1970), *The Structure and Operation of the Japanese Economy*, Wiley, Sydney.

Bisson, T. A. (1954), *Zaibatsu Dissolution in Japan*, University of California, Berkeley.

Boissevain, J. (1974), *Friends of Friends: Networks, Manipulation and Coalitions*, Blackwell, Oxford.

Braverman, H. (1974), *Labour and Monopoly Capital: The Degradation of Work in the Twentieth Century*, Monthly Review Press, New York and London.

British Journal of Industrial Relations (1974), Vol. 12, London School of Economics and Political Science.

Broadbridge, S. (1966), *Industrial Dualism in Japan: A Problem of Economic Growth*, Cass, London.

Brown, W. (1960), *Exploration in Management: A Description of the Glacier Metal Company's Concepts and Methods of Organisation and Management*, Penguin, Harmondsworth.

Business Location File (1980), July, Vol. IV, Urban Publishing Co., London.

Clark, R. C. (1972), 'Social Relations in a Japanese Company', University of London thesis.

— (1979), *The Japanese Company*, Yale University, New Haven, Conn.

Cohen, A. (1974), *Two-dimensional Man: An Essay on the Anthropology of Power and Symbolism in Complex Society*, Routledge and Kegan Paul, London.

Cole, R. E. (1971), *Japanese Blue Collar: The Changing Tradition*, University of California.

— (1979), *Work, Mobility and Participation: A Comparative Study of American and Japanese Industry*, University of California, Berkeley.

Connors, M. F. J. (1976), 'Wage structure "Rationalisation" and labour unions in Japan', *Proceedings of the British Association for Japanese Studies*, Vol. 1, University of Sheffield.

Connors, M. F.. J. (1977), 'The Wage System Rationalisation and Labour in Japan', University of Sheffield thesis.

Crane, R. (1967), *Korean Patterns*, Royal Asiatic Society, Korea Branch, Seoul.

Cunnison, S. (1966), *Wages and Work Allocation: A study of Social Relations in a Garment Workshop*, Tavistock, London.

Department of Employment (1977), 'Industry, Education and Management: A Discussion Paper', London.

— (1981), *Employment Gazette*, January, Vol. 89, No. 1, London.

De Vos, G. (1973). *Socialization for Achievement: Essays on the Cultural Psychology of the Japanese*, University of California.

Dimock, M. E. (1968), *The Japanese Technocracy: Management and Government*, Weatherhill, New York.

Dodwell Marketing Consultants (1978), *Industrial Groupings in Japan*, Dodwell, Tokyo.

Dore, R. P. ed. (1971), *Aspects of Social Change in Modern Japan*, Princeton University, New Jersey.

— (1973), *British Factory—Japanese Factory: The Origins of National Diversity in Industrial Relations*, Allen and Unwin, London.

Durkheim, E. (1966), *The Division of Labour in Society*, Free Press, New York.

Embree, J. F. (1939), *Suye Mura: A Japanese Village*, University of Chicago.

FIET (International Federation of Commercial, Clerical and Technical Employees) (1978), *Multinational Banking Corporations and International Regulations*, Geneva.

Financial Times, London

Financial Times Publications (1981), *Learning from the Japanese*. Reprint of articles on Quality Circles and production quality, together with other articles on Japanese management.

Florence, P. S. (1972), *The Logic of British and American Industry*, 3rd revised edition, Routledge and Kegan Paul, London.

Fukutake, T. (1974), *Japanese Society Today*, University of Tokyo.

Funaki, Y. (1981), 'Japanese Management and Management Training', in *B.A.C.I.E. Journal*, January 1981, London.

— (1982) (n.d.), 'Cross Culture Management', address to 'Japan in Britain' Conference, 21 January 1982, Technology Transfer International, London.

Galbraith, J. K. (1972), *The New Industrial State*, 2nd revised edition, Deutsch, London.

Gerth, H. H. and Mills, C. W. (1970), *From Max Weber*, Routledge and Kegan Paul, London.

Gibbs, R. (1980), 'Industrial Policy in More Successful Economies: Japan', NEDO Discussion Paper 7, National Economic Development Office, London.

Gladwin, T. N. and Walter, I. (1980), *Multinationals under Fire: Lessons in the Management of Conflict*, Wiley, New York.

Goldthorpe, J. H. *et al.* (1968), *The Affluent Worker: Industrial Attitudes and Behaviour*, Cambridge University Press, Cambridge.

Goodman, J. F. B. and Whittingham, T. G. (1973), *Shop Stewards*, Pan, London.

Gould, J. (1981), 'Edward Shils' Achievement', in *Encounter*, May 1981, London.

Gouldner, A. W. (1971), *The Coming Crisis of Western Sociology*, Heinemann, London.

Grunberger, R. (1977), *A Social History of the Third Reich*, Penguin, Harmondsworth.

Guest, D. and Horwood, R. (1980), *The Role and Effectiveness of Personnel Managers; a Preliminary Report*, London School of Economics and Political Science.

Hadley, E. M. (1970), *Antitrust in Japan*, Princeton University, New Jersey.

Halliday, J. and McCormack, G. (1973), *Japanese Imperialism Today: 'Co-Prosperity in Greater East Asia'*, Penguin, Harmondsworth.

Halmos, P. ed. (1966), *Japanese Sociological Studies*, Sociological Review Monograph No. 10, Keele University, Staffs.

Hanami, T. and Dumortier, J. (1979), 'Japanese Enterprises and Labour Relations in Belgium', *Bulletin of comparative labour relations, No. 10*, Kluver, Amsterdam.

Hazama, H. (n.d.), 'Japanese Industrialisation and Labour Management Relations (1860's through 1930's)', Typescript, Waseda University.

Hearn, L. (1955), *Japan, An Attempt at Interpretation*, Tuttle, Rutland, Vt.

Hill, S. (1981), *Competition and Control at Work. The New Industrial Sociology*, Heinemann, London.

Hirschmeier, J. and Yui, T. (1975), *The Development of Japanese Business, 1600-1975*, 2nd revised edition, Allen and Unwin, London (new edition 1981 covers period 1600-1980).

Horsley, W. (1981), 'Made in Japan', *The Listener*, 1 October, BBC, London.

Howard, N. and Teramoto, Y. (1981), 'The Really Important Difference between Japanese and Western Management', draft typescript, University of Aston Management Centre, Birmingham.

Hutchins, D. (1980), 'Quality Circles: An Introduction', *Industrial and Commercial Training*, January 1980, Vol. 12, No. 1, London.

Hyman, R. (1972), *Strikes*, Fontana, London.

Idemitsu Oil Co. (1977), House magazine, No. 293 (in Japanese), Tokyo.

Iida, T. (1981), 'What is Unique about the Japanese Economy?', *Oriental Economist*, July 1981, Tokyo.

Inagami, T. (1981), 'When Quality-Conscious Japan made Q.C. Circles a Way of Life', *Japan*, Review No. 75, Anglo-Japanese Economic Institute, London.

Industrial Development Authority (Ireland) (1979), *Overseas sponsored companies in Ireland*, IDA, Dublin.

Inohara, H. (1972), 'Importing Managerial Techniques. Case: The Zero Defects Movement', *Bulletin of Socio-Economic Institute*, No. 35, Sophia University, Tokyo.

— (1977), 'The Personnel Department in Japanese Companies', *Bulletin of Socio-Economic Institute*, No. 63, Sophia University, Tokyo.

Isherwood, M. J. (1982), 'British Managers in Japanese Firms', address to 'Japan in Britain' Conference, 21 January 1982, Technology Transfer International, London.

Ishida, H. (1977), 'Exportability of the Japanese Employment System', in *Proceedings of the 1977 Asian Regional Conference on Industrial Relations*, Japan Institute of Labour, Tokyo.

Ishida, T. (1971), *Japanese Society*, Random House, New York.

Japan Company Handbook, Toyo Keizai Shinposha. (The Oriental Economist), Tokyo, annual publication.

Japan Culture Institute (1977), *Guides to Japanese Culture*, ed. H. Murakami and E. Seidensticker, Tokyo.

Japan External Trade Organisation (JETRO) (1979), 'An Outline of the New Economic and Social Seven-Year Plan', *Now in Japan*, No. 29, Tokyo.

— (1980), *The Japanese Consumer*, JETRO Marketing Series No. 6, revised edition, Tokyo.

— (n.d.), *A Case Study of Foreign Investment in Japan*, Business Information Series No. 3, Tokyo.

— (1981), 'Productivity and Quality Control. The Japanese Experience', *Now in Japan*, No. 30, Tokyo.

— (1981–2) (n.d.), 'Promotion of Small and Medium Enterprises in Japan', *Now in Japan*, No. 31, Tokyo.

Japan Institute of Labour (1971), *Japan Labour Bulletin*, Tokyo.

Japanese Embassay, London (1977), *The Japanese Market: Myths and Realities*, for MITI, London.

Japanese Government (1976), *Statistical tables*, Tokyo.

— (1980), *Statistical Handbook of Japan*, Tokyo.

Journal of Asian Studies, Association for Asian Studies Inc., University of Michigan, Ann Arbor, Mich.

Kahn, H. (1970), *The Emerging Japanese Superstate*, Penguin, Harmondsworth.

Kawamoto, I. and Monma, I. (1976), 'Sokaiya in Japan', *Hong Kong Law Journal*, No. 6, Part 2.

Kawasaki, I. (1969), *Japan Unmasked*, Tuttle, Rutland, Vt.

Kelly, J. (1968), *Is Scientific Management possible? A Critical Examination of Glacier's Theory of Organisation*, Faber, London.

Kerr, C. *et al.* (1962), *Industrialism and Industrial Man: The Problem of Labour Management in Economic Growth*, Heinemann, London.

Kidd, J. B. and Teramoto, Y. (1981), 'Japanese Production Subsidiaries in the United Kingdom: a Study of Managerial Decision Making', University of Aston Management Centre, Working Paper No. 203.

Kobayashi, K. (1975), 'Japanese Management and Labour', 5th Business Seminar, 'To Understand Japan and Japanese Business Practices', Shimoda, Tokyo.

Kojima, K. (1978), *Direct Foreign Investment*, Croom Helm, London.

Kuper, A. (1975), *Anthropologists and Anthropology: The British School, 1922–1972*, Penguin, Harmondsworth.

Lamb, W. and Turner, D. (1969), *Management Behaviour*, Duckworth, London.

Large, S. (1976), 'Nishio Suehiro and the Japanese Social Democratic Movement, 1920–1940', *Journal of Asian Studies*, No. 36, University of Michigan.

Leach, E. R. (1970), *Levi-Strauss*, Fontana, London.

Lebra, W. P. and Lebra, T. S. (1974), *Japanese Culture and Behaviour*, University of Hawaii.

Leclair, E. E. and Schneider, H. K. (1968), *Economic Anthropology: Readings in Theory and Analysis*, Holt, Rinehart and Winston, New York.

Liu, W. (1955), *A Short History of Confucian Philosophy*, Penguin, Harmondsworth.

Livingston, J., Moore, J., and Oldfather, F. eds. (1976), *The Japan Reader, Vol. 1. Imperial Japan: 1800–1945, Vol. 2. Postwar Japan: 1945 to the present*, Penguin, Harmondsworth.

Lockwood, W. (1954), *The Economic Growth of Japan*, Princeton University Press, New Jersey.

Lukes, S. (1975), *Emile Durkheim, His Life and Work: a Historical and Critical Study*, Penguin, Harmondsworth.

Lupton, T. (1963), *On the Shop Floor: Two Studies of Workshop Organisation and Output*, Pergamon, Oxford.

— (1971), *Management and the Social Sciences*, 2nd edition, Penguin, Harmondsworth.

Lyons, N. (1976), *The Sony Vision*, Crown Publishers, New York.

Magaziner, I. C. and Hout, T. M. (1980), *Japanese Industrial Policy*, Policy Studies Institute, London.

Mannheim, K. (1936), *Ideology and Utopia: An Introduction to the Sociology of Knowledge*, Harcourt, Brace and World, Inc., New York.

Mant, A. (1979), *The Rise and Fall of the British Manager*, revised edition, Pan Business Management, London.

Marsh, R. M. and Mannari, H. (1976), *Modernisation and the Japanese Factory*, Princeton University, New Jersey.

Ministry of International Trade & Industry (MITI) (1981), *White Paper on the International Trade*, Foreign Press Center, Tokyo.

Mintzberg, H. (1973), *The Nature of Managerial Work*, Harper and Row, New York.

Mitsui & Co. (1976), 'An Introduction to Mitsui and Co. Ltd. and London Branch', typescript, London.

Murakami, T. (1981), 'The Oil Crises and the Japanese Economy', *Bulletin of the Japan Society of London*, No. 93, March, London.

McGivering, I. C., Matthews, D. G. J., and Scott, W. H. (1960), *Management in Britain: A General Characterisation*, Liverpool University Press.

McGregor, D. (1960), *The Human Side of Enterprise*, McGraw-Hill, New York.

McIntyre, W. (1978), 'Mr Right—from the Right University to the Right Job', *Japan*, Quarterly review of the Anglo-Japanese Economic Institute, No. 64, January 1978, London.

McKean, M. A. (1981), *Environmental Protest and Citizen Policies in Japan*, University of California, Berkeley.

Nakamura, H. (1971), *The Ways of Thinking of Eastern Peoples: India, China, Tibet, Japan*, East–West Centre, Honolulu.

Nakane, C. (1973), *Japanese Society*, Penguin, Harmondsworth.

Nakaoka, T. (1981), 'Production Management in Japan before the Period of High Economic Growth', *Osaka City University Economic Review*, No. 17, Osaka City University.

Nakase, T. (1977), 'The Introduction of Scientific Management into Japan and the Historical Process of the Establishment of Sumitomo Zaibatsu: A study on the characteristics of Japanese type Business', *Journal of Osaka Industrial University, Social Sciences*, No. 46, October 1977.

— (1980), 'The Postwar Overseas Expansion of Japanese Monopoly Capital and their Multinationalizing Development', *Journal of Osaka Industrial University, Social Sciences*, No. 53, July 1980.

— (1980a), 'Some Characteristics of Japanese-type Multinational Enterprises today', typescript, Osaka Industrial University.

Nishiguchi, T. (1981), 'Sociology of the Entrepreneur with Particular Reference to Japan', typescript, M.Sc. thesis, Imperial College, London.

Nishikawa, S. ed. (1980), *The Labour Market in Japan*, University of Tokyo.

Northcott, C. H. (1950), *Personnel Management: Its scope and practice*, 2nd edition, Pitman, London.

Odaka, K. (1975), *Toward Industrial Democracy. Management and Workers in Modern Japan*, Harvard University, Cambridge, Mass.

Oriental Economist (1979), Vol. 47, No. 830, Ministry of Finance, Tokyo.

Orwell, G. (1968), *The Collected Essays, Journalism and Letters of George Orwell, Vol. 4, James Burnham and the Managerial Revolution*, Penguin, Harmondsworth.

Ouchi, W. G. (1981), *Theory Z: How American Business Can Meet the Japanese Challenge*, Addison-Wesley, Reading, Mass.

Ozawa, T. (1979), *Multinationalism, Japanese Style: The Political Economy or Outward Dependency*, Princeton University Press, New Jersey.

Pascale, R. T. (1978), 'Zen and the Art of Management', *Harvard Business Review*, March–April.

Pascale, R. T. and Athos, A. G. (1981), *The Art of Japanese Management*, Simon and Schuster, New York.

Passin, H. (1965), *Society and Education in Japan*, Teachers College, New York.

Patrick, H. ed. (1976), *Japanese Industrialisation and its Social Consequences*, Columbia University, New York.

Patrick, H. and Rosovsky, H. (1976), *Asia's New Giant: How the Japanese Economy Works*, Brookings Institution, Washington.

Pelling, H. (1976), *A History of British Trade Unions*, 3rd revised edition, Penguin, Harmondsworth.

Plath, D. W. (1964), *The After Hours: Modern Japan and the Search for Enjoyment*, University of California, Berkeley.

Reischauer, E. O. (1977), *The Japanese*, Harvard University Press, Cambridge, Mass.

Reischauer, E. O., Fairbank, J. K., and Craig, A. M. (1962), *A History of East Asian Civilization, Vol. 1: The Great Tradition. Vol. 2: The Modern Transformation*, Houghton, Mifflin, New York.

Rohlen, T. P. (1973), 'Spiritual Training in a Japanese Bank', *American Anthropologist*, Vol. 75.

Rohlen, T. P. (1974), *For Harmony and Strength: Japanese White-Collar Organisation in Anthropological Perspective*, University of California, Berkeley.

Sahlins, M. (1974), *Stone Age Economics*, Tavistock, London.

Sampson, A. (1974), *The Sovereign State: The Secret History of I.T.T.*, Coronet, London.

Sasaki, N. (1981), *Management and Industrial Structure in Japan*, Pergamon, Oxford.

Sato, K. ed. (1980), *Industry and Business in Japan*, Croom Helm, London; Sharpe, White Plains, N.Y.

Sekiguchi, S. (1979), *Japan's Direct Foreign Investment*, Allanheld, Osmun, New Jersey.

Sethi, P. S. and Holton, R. H. (1974), *Management of the Multinationals: Policies, Operations and Research*, Free Press, Macmillan, New York.

Simon, H. A. (1960), *The New Science of Management Decision*, Harper and Row, New York.

Smith, T. C. (1967), 'Japan's Aristocratic Revolution', in *Class, Status and Power*, ed. Bendix and Lipset, Routledge and Kegan Paul, London.

Stopford, J. M. and Wells, L. T. (1972), *Managing the Multinational Enterprise*, Basic Books, New York.

Storry, G. R. (1960), *A History of Modern Japan*, Penguin, Harmondsworth.

Strauss, G. and Sayles, L. R. (1972), *Personnel: The Human Problems of Management*, 3rd edition, Prentice-Hall, Englewood Cliffs, N.J.

Taira, K. (1970), *Economic Development and the Labour Market in Japan*, Columbia University, New York.

Takamiya, M. (1979), *Degree of Organisational Centralisation in Multinational Corporations*, International Institute of Management, Berlin.

—— (1979a), *Japanese Multinationals in Europe: Internal Operations and their Policy Implications*, International Institute of Management, Berlin.

Takamiya, S. (1979), 'Japanese Management at the Crossroads', *Management Japan*, Vol. 12, No. 2, Autumn 1979, Tokyo.

Takeda, Y. (1981), ' "Jishu Kanri" as a Key to High Productivity: The Autonomous Self-management at Nippon Steel', *Speaking of Japan*, Feb. 1981, Vol. 1, No. 2, Keizai Koho Centre (Japan Institute of Social and Economic Affairs), Tokyo.

Tanaka, H. (1981), 'New Employee Education in Japan', *Personnel Journal* (USA), January 1981.

Technova Inc. (1980), *Japanese Direct Investment in the UK: Its Possibilities and Problems*, 4 Vols., Tokyo.

The Times, 'The Pressures of Japan's force-feed education system', 8 August 1978, London.

Thurley, K. E. (1975), 'The Treatment of Management in Industrial Relations Studies: a New Start?', SSRC Seminar Group on Management Attitudes and Behaviour in Industrial Relations, typescript, London School of Economics and Political Science.

—— (1981), 'The British Worker and the Japanese way of work', *New Society*, 9 July 1981, London.

Thurley, K. E., Nangaku, M., and Uragami, K. (1976), 'Employment

Relations of Japanese Companies in the UK: A Preliminary Report', in *Proceedings of the British Association for Japanese Studies*, Vol. 1, University of Sheffield.

Thurley, K. E., Reitsperger, W. D., Trevor, M. H., and Worm, P. (1980), *The Development of Personnel Management in Japanese Enterprises in Great Britain*, International Centre for Economics and Related Disciplines, London School of Economics.

Thurley, K. E., Trevor, M. H., and Worm, P. (1981), *Japanese Management in Western Europe*, International Centre for Economics and Related Disciplines, London School of Economics.

Times Higher Education Supplement, London.

Trevor, M. H. (1983), 'Quality—a Japanese Re-export', *Euro-Asia Business Review*, No. 2, Jan. 1983, Euro-Asia Centre, INSEAD. Norbury, Tenterden, Kent.

Vernon, R. (1977), *Storm over the Multinationals: The Real Issues*, Harvard University Press, Cambridge, Mass.

Vogel, E. F. (1971), *Japan's New Middle Class: The Salary Man and His Family in a Tokyo suburb*, 2nd edition, University of California, Berkeley.

— (1975) ed., *Modern Japanese Organisations and Decision Making*, University of California.

— (1980), *Japan as Number One: Lessons for America*, Harvard University Press, Cambridge, Mass.

Von Mehren, A. T., ed. (1963), *Law in Japan: the Legal Order in a Changing Society*, Harvard University Press, Cambridge, Mass.

Warner, M. ed. (1973), *The Sociology of the Workplace: An Interdisciplinary Approach*, Allen and Unwin, London.

Weber, M. (1947), *The Theory of Social and Economic Organisation*, Free Press, New York.

— (1971), *The Protestant Ethic and the Spirit of Capitalism*, Allen and Unwin, London.

Whitehill, A. M. and Takezawa, S. (1968), *The Other Worker*, East–West Centre, Honolulu.

Whyte, W. H. (1960), *The Organization Man*, Penguin, Harmondsworth.

Yashiro, N. (1981), 'The economic rationality of Japanese-style employment practices', *Economic Eye*, March 1981, Tokyo.

Yoshino, M. Y. (1968), *Japan's Managerial System: Tradition and Innovation*, Massachusetts Institute of Technology, Cambridge, Mass.

— (1976), *Japan's Multinational Enterprises*, Harvard University Press, Cambridge, Mass.

INDEX

Note: Japanese companies studied in the UK and referred to by pseudonyms for reasons of confidentiality appear in *italics*.